Perspectives in Sustainable Management Practices

Embracing sustainable management practices is important for businesses and commercial organizations wishing to responsibly contribute to the socio-economic development of societies and communities. This book provides insights into recent trends, issues, and challenges in embracing these practices, while promoting growth and innovation in business.

The COVID-19 pandemic has redefined the necessity of implementing sustainable practices. This book looks at the process, implementation, and evaluation of sustainable practices in the social and commercial sectors in recent years. With case studies from different industries, these chapters explore and document creative applications of effective measures to chart out financial growth for businesses while reducing carbon emissions, focusing on corporate social responsibility, and working toward socio-economic sustainability for workers and communities, among others. They also examine how these innovative strategies can be scaled up and applied across diverse industries, for small and large businesses, and in different economic environments.

Part of the Contemporary Management Practices series, this book will be useful to practising managers, researchers, and students who are interested in business strategy, financial strategy, and social inclusion. It will be especially of use to those working in the areas of corporate governance, corporate social responsibility, green marketing, corporate finance, and organizational performance.

Satyajit Chakrabarti is the Director of Institute of Engineering & Management, Kolkata, India. He obtained his PhD in Nanotechnology from the National Institute of Technology and a Master's in Computer Science from the University of British Columbia. He is an avid philanthropist and social entrepreneur. He has published extensively in the fields of artificial intelligence, IOT and data science and has over 20 patents files in various fields of technology. His special expertise includes management consulting, strategic management, technology applications, and problem- solving using innovation and innovative technologies.

Soumik Gangopadhyay is Professor of Marketing at the Institute of Engineering and Management, Kolkata, India. He has done Bachelor in Pharmacy, MBA (Mktg.), MBA (HHSM) from BITS-Pilani and Doctor of Philosophy. He has conducted extensive training sessions in the areas of marketing, strategy, and decision making for senior Indian defence personnel and corporate executives such as those of the Indian Oil Corporation, CESC, and Eli Lilly, among others. He has published extensively in several areas of research on management.

Isita Lahiri is Professor in the Department of Business Administration, University of Kalyani, West Bengal, India. She has extensive research experience in creating and expanding knowledge in the field of management practices. Her areas of interest are marketing, consumer behaviour, brand management, and marketing research.

Soma Sur is Professor and Former Dean of Xavier Business School in St. Xavier's University, Kolkata, India. She is presently the Honorary Director of the Father Lafont Centre for Excellence in Research and Innovation. She has published widely and has experience in training and consultancy. Her teaching and research interests are in the areas of strategic management, marketing management, service marketing, consumer behaviour, customer relationship management, online marketing, green marketing, sustainable development, behavioural finance, and health management.

Subrata Chattopadhyay is Professor at the University of Engineering and Management, Kolkata, India. He has published extensively on computation in estate management, transport management, and values and ethics for engineers and managers. He was conferred the prestigious MTC Global Top Thinkers award in 2015. In 2019 he was awarded Mentor of the Year by HRD India.

Rishi Raj Sharma is currently associated with the Department of Business Management, and is Associate Dean of, Guru Nanak Dev University RC, Gurdaspur, Punjab, India. His areas of interest are marketing, consumer behaviour, behavioural marketing, social marketing, and digital marketing. He has published books and papers in the areas of general management, marketing, and others. He has received the Gold Medal for the best empirical research paper at a conference hosted by the All India Commerce Association, at Bangalore University (2013), KIIT University (2014), Panjab University (2018) and LPU (2020).

Contemporary Management Practices

Series editors: Dipak Saha, Department of Management, Institute of Engineering and Management, Kolkata, India; Rabin Mazumder, Department of Management, Institute of Engineering and Management, Kolkata, India

This series explores the latest and most effective methods, techniques, and strategies used by modern managers to achieve organizational goals and objectives. These methods are influenced by business environment, technology, and globalization, and are constantly evolving to meet the changing needs of organizations. The strength of the books in the "Contemporary Management Practices" series rests in the diversity of their viewpoints, since they include essays on various conventional and unconventional management approaches, scholarly concepts, and exploratory and analytical-based studies. This series will encourage practising researchers to formulate and implement innovative ideas in the field of social sciences. The series discusses the most pertinent themes in management and systematically highlights different functional areas of management including finance and digital transformations in business; marketing, innovation and strategy; sustainable management practices; and human resource management. The series provides guidelines and case studies for academics, researchers and practitioners to explore and implement best practices in these fields as well as in developing new and sustainable solutions on top of existing methods.

Perspectives in Marketing, Innovation and Strategy
Edited by Philip Kotler, Subhadip Roy, Satyajit Chakrabarti, Dipak Saha and Rabin Mazumder

Perspectives in Sustainable Management Practices
Edited By Satyajit Chakrabarti, Soumik Gangopadhyay, Isita Lahiri, Soma Sur, Subrata Chattopadhyay and Rishi Raj Sharma

Perspectives in Human Resources
Edited By Satyajit Chakrabarti, Ashutosh Muduli, Saikat Chakrabarti, Anirban Sarkar, Mrinal Das and Avijit Brahmachary

For more information about this series, please visit: www.routledge.com/Contemporary-Management-Practices/book-series/CMP

Perspectives in Sustainable Management Practices

Edited by Satyajit Chakrabarti, Soumik Gangopadhyay, Isita Lahiri, Soma Sur, Subrata Chattopadhyay and Rishi Raj Sharma

LONDON AND NEW YORK

First published 2024
by Routledge
4 Park Square, Milton Park, Abingdon, Oxon OX14 4RN

and by Routledge
605 Third Avenue, New York, NY 10158

Routledge is an imprint of the Taylor & Francis Group, an informa business

© 2024 selection and editorial matter, Satyajit Chakrabarti, Soumik Gangopadhyay, Isita Lahiri, Soma Sur, Subrata Chattopadhyay and Rishi Raj Sharma; individual chapters, the contributors

The right of Satyajit Chakrabarti, Soumik Gangopadhyay, Isita Lahiri, Soma Sur, Subrata Chattopadhyay and Rishi Raj Sharma to be identified as the authors of the editorial material, and of the authors for their individual chapters, has been asserted in accordance with sections 77 and 78 of the Copyright, Designs and Patents Act 1988.

All rights reserved. No part of this book may be reprinted or reproduced or utilised in any form or by any electronic, mechanical, or other means, now known or hereafter invented, including photocopying and recording, or in any information storage or retrieval system, without permission in writing from the publishers.

Trademark notice: Product or corporate names may be trademarks or registered trademarks, and are used only for identification and explanation without intent to infringe.

British Library Cataloguing-in-Publication Data
A catalogue record for this book is available from the British Library

ISBN: 978-1-032-44002-6 (hbk)
ISBN: 978-1-032-64196-6 (pbk)
ISBN: 978-1-032-64048-8 (ebk)

DOI: 10.4324/9781032640488

Typeset in Sabon
by Deanta Global Publishing Services, Chennai, India

Contents

List of Figures   *xi*
List of Tables   *xiii*
List of Contributors   *xv*
Series Editors' Preface   *xxvii*
Acknowledgements   *xxviii*

Introduction   1

PART 1
Social Sustainability   9

1   Rethinking the Environmental Kuznets Curve: Quantity Growth vs. Quality Growth   11
AYHAN KULOĞLU AND MERT TOPCU

2   Model framework characterizing long term sustainable and successful social enterprises: A case of Greenway Appliances   19
SMITA MEHENDALEC AND LALITPRAKASH BARAIK

3   Employment versus Unemployment: A Study on Psychological Distress During COVID-19   27
SHREYA BHATTACHARJEE AND ROOPREKHA BAKSI

4   Corporate Social Responsibility Practices in Small and Medium Indian Enterprises   35
KALYANI GOHAIN

5   Green Finance – Integral Adaptation to Climate Change   42
AJANTA GHOSH AND SUJIT DUTTA

viii Contents

6 Impact of the MGNREGA on Women's Empowerment in the Light of Social Sustainability – A Study on Selective Areas of West Bengal in India 52
MOHUA DAS MAZUMDAR AND SAJAL MONDAL

7 Impact of the COVID-19 Pandemic on the Migratory Behaviour of the Workers of Rural India: An Empirical Analysis 62
SUBRATO ADHIKARI, ANIRBAN MANDAL, AND SAIKAT CHAKRABARTI

8 Forms of Online Lectures: A Key Factor in Making Online Education a Sustainable Future Option for Lifelong Learning 70
LALIMA MUKHERJEE, SMITA DATTA

9 Influencers of Online Education and Social Sustainability of Blended Learning 77
ARIJIT GHOSH, ANIRBAN SARKAR, AND SUCHITRA KUMARI

10 Two-Part Public Policy to Balance Technological External Diseconomies: A normative approach 85
RABIN MAZUMDER

PART 2
Economic Sustainability 95

11 Socio-economic Repercussions of COVID-19 and Economic Sustainability in the Aftermath: An Indian Perspective 97
AMITAVA BASU, SUGATO BANERJEE, AMALENDU SAMANTA, SUBHAMAY PANDA, AND RAKHI CHOWDHURY

12 Toward Sustainable Livelihood Promotion for Artisans – A Holistic Marketing Framework for Improving the Indian Handicraft Sector 111
ARUNAVA DALAL, SUBRATA CHATTOPADHYAY, AND SUBHAJIT BHATTACHARYA

13 Perceptions of Financial Literacy among Students in Higher Education 120
GARGI DAS BHATTACHARYA AND ANIRBAN SARKAR

14 Impact of COVID-19 on the Share Prices of Life Insurance
    Companies: A Case of Economic Sustainability in India   129
    SHALINI SINGH, BHAVNA SHARMA, AND GARIMA MADAAN DUA

15 Sustainable Agronomic Practices: India's Efforts Toward
    Booming Agricultural Growth   139
    SWATI MISHRA AND MANJULA UPADHYAY

16 Is Health Insurance a Sustainable Strategy for achieving
    Universal Health Coverage in India?   153
    ARCHANA BAKSHI

PART 3
Strategic Sustainability   **163**

17 Inorganic Modes – An Inevitable Choice for the Sustainable
    Growth of RIL During the COVID-19 Pandemic   165
    MANISH SHARMA, KOMAL MISHRA, DINESH SHARMA, AND AKRITI SRIVASTAVA

18 Is the Premier League Really Balanced? Evidence From
    Multiple Measures   176
    MITHUN KUMAR GUHA AND SOMROOP SIDDHANTA

19 Innovative Strategies in the Hospitality Industry: A Systematic
    Literature Review   185
    PRATIM CHATTERJEE AND SMITA DATTA

20 Strategic Handling of the COVID-19 Crisis in the Christian
    Medical College, Vellore – A Case Study   193
    SAMUEL NJ DAVID, R. RAGHUNATHAN, SONIA VALAS,
    JOY MAMMEN, ABIMANESH S, KRUPA GEORGE,
    ARUN BENNET SAMUEL, AND PRABAKARAN RAVINDRAN

21 Determinants of Brand Loyalty and Purchase Intention for
    FMCG Products in the Days of COVID-19   204
    MRINAL KANTI DAS, SOUMYA MUKHERJEE, AND
    DIPAK SAHA

22 Customers' Attitudes to Using Artificial Intelligence–Enabled
   Applications for Internet-Based Home Services in their
   Daily Lives   219
   PRITHA GHOSH AND RABIN MAZUMDER

Index   229

Figures

1.1	Aggregation Process of Quality Growth Index	13
2.1	A model framework for long-term sustainable success of an SE	23
3.1	Mean of employed and unemployed male and female sample	31
3.2	Standard Deviation of employed and unemployed male and female sample	32
5.1	A forecast of Green Bond issuance to reach 1 Trillion by 2023 (Amount in US$ Billion)	46
10.1	Isoquant of the firm	88
10.2	Iso-cost line	91
10.3	Contract curve	92
10.4	Equilibrium without Pareto optimal	93
10.5	Pareto optimal	93
11.1	Trend in annual GDP growth percentage and the percentage of annual change of GDP growth	98
11.2	GVA by Agriculture, Forestry Fishing	99
11.3	Rate of growth of GVA	99
11.4	Gross and sector-wise performance of the industrial sector of the Indian economy	100
11.5	Performance of the service sector of the Indian economy	101
11.6	Trends in private final consumption, gross fixed capital formation, and the export and import of goods	101
11.7	Holistic strategies and economic sustainability	106
12.1	Four Bs to five Rs model	115
12.2	The operational model	116
14.1	Percentage Growth in Premiums during April–May 2021	130
14.2	New Business Premiums 2019–2020 (Rs '000 crore)	131
15.1	Sustainable Agriculture gives equal weight to environmental, social, and economic concerns in agriculture	142
15.2	Agricultural waste management functions	145
16.1	Domestic Health Expenditure of India (%age of Current Health Expenditure), 2015	154

17.1	Stake Sale in RIL Jio in 2020	168
17.2	RIL retail segment growth in comparison with Avenue Supermarket	170
17.3	Market shares of key service providers	171
17.4	BPCL & RIL Comparative	171
17.5	Value Creation through Innovation and R&D	173
20.1	COVID 19 Management – The CMC Model	196
20.2	CMC Training Initiatives	200
21.1	Proposed Conceptual Model	206
21.2	Structural Model Assessments with Control Variables	211
21.3	Adjusted Importance Performance Matrix for Purchase Intention	214
22.1	Conceptual model	226

Tables

1.1	Quality Growth Index Components	14
1.2	Unit Root Results	15
1.3	Regression Results	15
3.1	Showing Level of Psychological Distress	30
3.2	Showing Nature of Employment	30
3.3	Showing Level of Psychological Distress in male sample	31
3.4	Showing Level of Psychological Distress in Female Population	31
4.1	Classification of MSMEs	37
4.2	Estimated Number of MSMEs in India (by activity) According to the MSME Annual Report FY 2019-20	37
4.3	Distribution of Enterprises by Category	37
4.4	Distribution of Estimated Number of MSMEs by State	38
5.1	Some of the Issuers who Have Issued Green Bonds with a Maturity Period of Ten Years or More	46
5.2	List of Indian Cities that have Issued Municipal Bonds	48
6.1	The Dimension of Economic Empowerment as Compared between Beneficiaries and Non- Beneficiaries	56
6.2	The Dimension of Financial Empowerment as Compared between Beneficiaries and Non- Beneficiaries	57
6.3	The Dimension of Social Empowerment as Compared between Beneficiaries and Non- Beneficiaries	58
7.1	Descriptive Statistics	66
7.2	Correlation Matrix of Independent Variables	66
7.3	Model Fit	66
7.4	Regression Model	67
8.1	Results of Tukey Honest Significance Difference Test	73
9.1	KMO and Bartlett's Test	80
9.2	Total Variance Explained	81
9.3	Rotated Component Matrix	82
9.4	Hosmer and Lemeshow Test	82
9.5	Classification	82
13.1	Reliability Statistics	123
13.2	KMO and Bartlett's Test	123

13.3	Total Variance Explained	124
13.4	Rotated Component Matrix Depicting Factor Loading	125
13.5	Omnibus Tests of Model Coefficients	126
13.6	Hosmer and Lemeshow Test	126
13.7	Classification Table	126
13.8	Variables in the Equation	127
14.1	Regression Result of SBI Life on a Constant (general buy and sell strategy) Dependent Variable: SBI Life	133
14.2	Regression of SBI Life Based on the Trading Rule	134
14.3	Regression Result of HDFC Life on a Constant (general buy and sell strategy) Dependent Variable: HDFC life	134
14.4	Regression of HDFC Life Based on the Trading Rule	134
14.5	Regression Result of ICICIPRU on a Constant (general buy and sell strategy) Dependent Variable: ICICIPRU	135
14.6	Regression of ICICIPRU Based on the Trading Rule	135
15.1	Trap Crops for Managing Insect and Pest Damage	144
15.2	Medicinal and Aromatic Plants Cultivated in Few Regions of Uttar Pradesh under Crop Cluster	148
16.1	Population Coverage under Health Insurance (in millions)	158
16.2	Population Coverage under Different Categories of Health Insurance Business (in lakh)	159
17.1	RIL Technological Advancements and their Applications	169
17.2	Reliance Retails Store and EBITDA (in Rs. crores)	170
17.3	Comparison of Cash Flow Yields	174
18.1	Rank Correlation Values Calculated S-O-S	179
18.2	Noll-Scully Ratio Value Calculated S-O-S	180
18.3	ANOVA Calculation	180
18.4	C5 Index Ratio	181
18.5	K5 Rating Calculation	182
20.1	PEST and SWOT Analyses of the COVID-19 Situation	195
20.2	Statistics of Training Conducted	198
20.3	Strategic Lessons Learnt during Pandemic	203
21.1	Demographic Profile of Respondents	207
21.2	Quality Criterion for Reflective Model Assessments and Composite Model	208
21.3	Discriminant Validity Assessments	209
21.4	HTMT Ratio of Correlations for Discriminant Validity Assessments	210
21.5	Structural Model Assessment	212
21.6	Importance – Performance Map (Construct Wise Unstandardized Effects)	213
21A.1	Measurement Scales Used	218
22.1	Demographic Profile of the Total Sample	223
22.2	Categorization of Themes and Subtheme	224

Contributors

Abi Manesh M. is Associate Professor of Infectious Diseases, working in the Department of Medical Oncology in Christian Medical College Vellore. He has been instrumental and actively involved in development and dissemination of training programmes for core care teams in the institution throughout the COVID pandemic period. He continues to serve as one of the members of the COVID Command Centre of the institution.

Ajanta Ghosh is an Assistant Professor of Finance and Assistant Head of the Department of Business Administration of the Institute of Engineering and Management, Kolkata, India. She is also a research scholar at St. Xavier's University, Kolkata, India. She has over nine years of corporate experience of working with a leading bank and in the management accounting team of a leading publishing house in Kolkata, India. Her areas of interest are finance, particularly green finance, credit rating, stock pricing, and management accounting. She has a postgraduate in Commerce from the University of Calcutta, India and also a postgraduate in Management from the University of Calcutta, India.

Akriti Srivastava is a research scholar in the domain of Finance at Dr. Harisingh Gour Vishwavidyalaya, Sagar, Madhya Pradesh. She has qualified with a UGC – NET (December 2022). She has qualified with an MBA with Honours in Finance from the Institute of Engineering and Technology, Lucknow. She has published five research articles including journal articles, edited book chapters and conference proceedings. She has won the Late B.H Agalgatti Memorial Best Research Paper Award at the IIMS, Pune and the Best Research Paper Award at Osmania University.

Amitava Basu became Assistant Professor at Banwarilal Bhalotia College in 2002 and completed his PhD in 2004. He has published many research papers in journals of national and international repute. He has also completed a UGC research project and has acted as research supervisor to PhD students who have successfully completed their research under his guidance. Amitava Basu is currently the Principal of the prestigious Banwarilal

Bhalotia College, Asansol with more than 7000 enrolled students per academic session. In a short span of time, he has taken the College to new heights with his exemplary leadership and administrative prowess. He is also involved in community service and different social projects.

Amalendu Samanta is Assistant Professor in the Department of Commerce in Banwarilal Bhalotia College, Asansol. He graduated from St. Xavier's College, Kolkata and obtained his master's degree from the University of Burdwan. He was awarded a PhD in Business Administration by the University of Burdwan in 2015. He has a vast experience of teaching at undergraduate level. He regularly presents his research papers in different seminars. His research articles have been published in different national and international journals and edited volumes. He has worked as an editor for edited volumes of research articles and also authored an accounting textbook.

Anirban Sarkar, MCom, MBA, MPhil, PhD, is Professor of Marketing in the Department of Management and Marketing at West Bengal State University. He completed his MPhil and PhD at the University of Calcutta. He is currently the Head of the Department of Management and Marketing. In addition, he is the Director of the Centre for Management Studies, the Chairperson of the Undergraduate and Postgraduate Board of Studies, and also the Convener of the Board of Research Studies of the Department of Management and Marketing. He has published several papers in national and international journals of repute. His area of interest is in social science research.

Anirban Mandal is currently working as a Faculty Member at ICFAI Business School, Kolkata. He has worked as an Associate Professor and Head of the Department in the School of Management and Commerce at Brainware University. He completed his PhD at KIIT University, Bhubaneswar, India. He has more than 16 years of teaching experience in different renowned colleges and institutions across West Bengal. He was a Visiting Faculty member at Pelita Harapan University, Jakarta, Indonesia. He has authored many research papers in national and international journals of repute. He has acted as a resource person in different national and international seminars.

Archana Bakshi is Assistant Professor at the PG Department of Economics, Mehr Chand Mahajan DAV College for Women, sector 36, Chandigarh. She has more than 20years of teaching experience. Her areas of interest are industrial economics and health economics. She has published 15 research papers in international journals and contributed seven chapters to edited books. She has also presented ten papers at national and international conferences. She is a Life Member of the Indian Economic

Association and was a Member of the PG Board of Studies in Economics, Panjab University, Chandigarh (2019-2021).

Arijit Ghosh, M.Sc.NET, MBA, Ph.D., is Assistant Professor of Mathematics at St. Xavier's College (Autonomous), Kolkata. He received his PhD (Science) from Jadavpur University, Kolkata for his contribution to the field of Optimization. His current research is focused on the application of optimization techniques in the field of finance. With an overall teaching experience spanning two decades in higher education, Dr Ghosh has been associated as an accomplished Professor of Applied Mathematics, Statistics, Research Methodology and Operation Research in St. Xavier's College (Autonomous), Kolkata and served as a resource person in other institutes of repute. He has published several research papers in various national and international peer-reviewed refereed journals of repute and has supervised PhD students.

Arunava Dalal holds a BE from NIT Durgapur and a PGDM from Symbiosis, Pune. Professor Dalal has over 16 years of industry experience in the marketing of products, new product development, and the leading and managing of channel sales. He has organized market studies, analysed competitive moves and developed counters, reformed product packaging based on market needs, campaigned and enhanced brand visibility, resulting in enhanced market shares, and handled product management. He is presently pursuing his PhD and has joined academics due to his passion for teaching. His interest areas are service marketing, consumer behaviour, and areas related to sustainable marketing.

Arun Bennet Samuel is a PhD and Fellowship in Hospital Administration graduate, currently working as the Course Coordinator in the Department of Hospital Management Studies and Staff Training and Development. He is involved in academic aspects of the department including preparation of reports and papers toward publication.

Ayhan Kuloğlu is an Assistant Professor of Economics at Nevşehir Hacı Bektaş Veli University, Turkey. He completed his master's and doctoral degrees in the field of Economic Theory at Erciyes University, Turkey. The subject of his master's thesis is the analysis of the dynamics of energy demand, while his PhD thesis is on sectoral competitiveness analysis within the scope of the Porter Diamond model. His main research interests are quality growth and renewable energy. He has published several articles in a range of high-quality journals including, Energy, Economic Research – Ekonomska Istraživanja, Economic Computation, and Economic Cybernetics Studies and Research, among others.

Bhavna Sharma has a BCom, MBA, UGC-NET, and a PhD in Finance with 12 years of teaching and research experience, with a specialization in Accounting and Finance. She is a Member of the Editorial Board of the Journal of Isabela State University, Philippines, and a reviewer with the Journal of Social Science, Economics and Management, Indonesia. She has to her credit 2 patents, 6 chapters, and 13 papers published in Scopus indexed, UGC Care and other reputed journals. She has presented 25 papers in various national and international conferences organized by reputed institutions like IIM-Ahmedabad, University of Mumbai, University of Delhi, etc. She has also reviewed various papers, taken guest lectures, organized various workshops, done online courses, short-term training programs, and attended FDPs and workshops. She also developed 3 e-contents for the BCom course.

Dinesh Sharma is a Professor in the Department of Commerce, University of Lucknow. His qualifications include a Master's in Commerce and a PhD in HRD and Psychology. He was first elected as Mayor of Lucknow in 2006. Presently he is serving as Minister of Secondary and Higher Education and Deputy Chief Minister of the state of Uttar Pradesh, India, since March 2017. He has around two dozen PhD supervisions to his name. He has publications in national and international journals. He has authored books in the field of Commerce.

Dipak Saha is currently Professor in the Department of Management of the Institute of Engineering and Management, Kolkata, and has over 17 years of corporate and academic experience. He obtained his PhD from the University of North Bengal. He has published several articles in reputed and renowned scholarly journals, indexed in ABDC and Scopus, and UGC listed. He is the co-author of the textbook *Marketing: A Conceptual Framework*. He is a consultant and trainer in the fields of Critical Thinking in the Workplace and Strategic Management Decisions. He is the recipient of the AMP Academic Excellence Award 2020 from the Academy of Management Professionals, India. His areas of interest are marketing analytics, consumer behaviour and brand management.

Gargi Das, MCom, CA, is Lecturer in Finance at the Department of Commerce (Afternoon and Evening Section) of the Bhawanipur Education Society College. She completed her MCom with Accounts and Finance Specialization from Calcutta University in 2009. She is a member of the Institute of Chartered Accountants of India. She has a teaching experience of 10 years at the UG and PG levels. Her area of interest is in social science research.

Garima Madaan Dua was awarded a PhD in 2017 and holds a Master's degree in Management with a specialization in Finance. She has over 14 years' work experience, including three years of experience in the corporate sector. Dr. Garima has a keen interest in investment management, security analysis, management of financial services, financial reporting and analysis, financial accounting, and management accounting. She has previously worked with the School of Business Studies at Sharda University, as an Assistant Professor. Currently, she is working in an administrative role at Denmark Technical University, Denmark.

Joy Mammen is Professor of Transfusion Medicine in the Department of immunohaematology at the Christian Medical College Vellore. He is also a Post-Doctoral Fellow in Pathology and Laboratory Medicine. He has been instrumental and actively involved in the development and dissemination of training programmes for core care teams in the institution throughout the COVID-19 pandemic period. He continues to serve as one of the members of the institution's COVID Command Centre.

Kalyani Gohain is Research Scholar at the esteemed Royal School of Business, affiliated with the Assam Royal Global University in Guwahati. Her area of expertise lies in the field of corporate governance, reflecting her deep understanding and knowledge of the subject matter. She possesses a Master of Business Administration (MBA) degree, specializing in Finance and Human Resources, earned from the Assam Science and Technology University. Furthermore, she holds a Bachelor's degree in Mechanical Engineering from Gauhati University, Assam. Along with her academic achievements, she has accumulated 2 years of teaching experience and 1 year of industry experience, making her a well-rounded professional. Her dedication to research is evident in her publications, with one journal publication and three book publications to her credit.

Komal Mishra has a Company Secretaryship from the ICSI and an MBA Finance degree to her name. She has presented several papers in national and international forums. She has worked as Company Secretary in the corporate sphere.

Krupa George is Professor of Medicine in the Department of Medicine at the Christian Medical College, Vellore. She has been actively involved in the development and dissemination of training programmes for core care teams in the institution throughout the COVID-19 pandemic period. She continues to serve as one of the members of the COVID Command Centre of the institution.

Lalitprakash Baraik possesses a wealth of experience in managing projects, serving customers in the Information Technology services industry, and partnering in their growth and transformation journeys. His notable academic credentials include being a certified Project Management Professional (PMP), as recognized by the Project Management Institute (PMI), and having a Master's degree in business administration with specialization in Marketing. He keeps himself abreast of the latest trends in Branding, marketing, the retail industry, social entrepreneurship, and the

India growth story. His hobbies include travelling, exploring new places, and reading books across genres like fiction, self-help, personal development, business strategy, entrepreneurship, etc.

Manjula Upadhyay is currently the Principal of Navyug Kanya Mahavidyalay, Lucknow, Uttar Pradesh, and former Associate Professor with the Department of Economics, AP Sen Memorial Girls College, Lucknow. She completed her PhD in Economics from Dr. Ram Manohar Lohia Avadh University, Faizabad, Uttar Pradesh and has more than 23 years of teaching and administrative experience. Furthermore, Prof. Manjula has been felicitated with countless awards and scholarships due to her prominent contributions during her service. She is a member of the Uttar Pradesh State Higher Education Council, Uttar Pradesh Economic Association, Indian Economic Association, Uttar Pradesh and Uttarakhand Economic Association, Association of Socio-Economic Development Studies, and Centre for Scientific and Innovative Research, and has served these associations with her astounding knowledge, ideas, and thoughts.

Manish Sharma is Associate Professor in the Department of Management Studies, Siddharth University (State University) Kapilvastu, Siddharth Nagar, Uttar Pradesh. He earned a Master's in Commerce and a Master of Business Administration in the area of Finance in 2004 and 2011 respectively. He qualified with a UGC-NET in Commerce in December 2010, a UGC-NET Management in June 2011, and a UGC-NET in Commerce in December 2014. He was awarded a Doctorate in Commerce in 2018. He has international exposure as Senior Lecturer and Content Development Expert in Syscoms College, Lulu International Group, UAE. He has published several national and international research papers including in ARC ranked Journals. He has a national award to his credit for development of innovative pedagogy for Higher Education during the COVID pandemic.

Mert Topcu is an Associate Professor of Economics at Alanya Alaaddin Keykubat University, Turkey. His main research interests are development economics and panel data econometrics. He has published several articles in a range of high-quality journals in the areas of Renewable and Sustainable Energy Reviews, Finance Research Letters, Defence and Peace Economics, and European Review, among others. He also worked as visiting scholar at Georgia College and State University, and Valdosta State University in the US. As of April 2023, his h index, based on Web of Science, is 11, with 915 citations.

Mithun Kumar Guha is Assistant Professor in the Department of Business Management at the NSHM Business School, Durgapur. He has taken teaching assignments in Presidency University, Bengaluru and Lovely Professional University, Punjab in India. He has 15 years of experience in guiding and teaching MBA Students. He has an MBA in Marketing from the National

Institute of Technology, Durgapur and is currently pursuing a PhD from the Maulana Abul Kalam Azad University of Technology. His areas of interest are sports management and service quality in the financial sector.

Mohua Das Mazumdar, BCom, MCom. MPhil, PhD, has been serving Rampurhat College under the University of Burdwan since 2010. She has teaching experience of more than 17years and currently holds the position of Assistant Professor and HOD in the Department of Commerce, Rampurhat College. She served in different teaching posts, particularly teaching BBA and MBA students, and also served the Department of Business Administration under the University of Burdwan as a guest faculty member. Her areas of teaching and research interests include corporate finance, banking and sustainability.

Mrinal Kanti Das is Assistant Professor and Head of Commerce at Kanchrapara College, Kanchrapara, West Bengal. Before that, he was at the Centre for Management Studies, JISCE, Kalyani, West Bengal as a faculty member in Marketing Management. He has over 17 years of experience in academics. He earned his PhD from the University of Kalyani. One scholar has already been awarded a PhD in Marketing Management under his supervision. He has authored four books and has contributed research articles to various journals, indexed in ABDC, Scopus, and UGC listed, and also has edited volumes to his credit. He is associated with different management institutions and universities in the capacity of visiting faculty, paper setter, examiner, and moderator.

Prabakaran Ravindran is a mechanical engineer who worked in the Department of Hospital Management Studies and Staff Training and Development, CMC Vellore and is currently working in the Command Centre, CMC Vellore. He was involved in operations and manpower management of the COVID UDHAVI helpline initiative along with Mr. Azariah Pravinkumar during his time in the department.

Pratim Chatterjee is currently working as an Assistant Professor at Amity University, Kolkata and is a research scholar at the University of Engineering and Management, Kolkata. He is a graduate in hospitality management, has a postgraduate in business management and has a UGC-NET in management. His areas of research include hospitality innovation and hospitality and tourism marketing policy. He has published scholarly articles in internationally reputed journals (Scopus and ESCI Indexed) and nationally reputed journals (UGC Care). He has presented papers at national and international conferences. Altogether he has 14 years of working experience along with a great desire for research and contribution to society.

Pritha Ghosh has a BTech (Dr DY Patil, Pune, 2010), an MTech (Vellore Institute of Technology, Vellore, 2012), and an MBA (Alliance Business

Academy, Bengaluru, 2014). She is currently pursuing a PhD at the Institute of Engineering and Management (IEM), Kolkata, in Management. Her research interests lie in behavioural decision-making and brand management (mainly apparel). She has published in the ESCI-indexed Journal of Marketing Analytics. She has attended conferences in reputed colleges in Kolkata. She was the paper awardee at the IRPSS-2022 at IEM, Kolkata. She has an industrial experience of eight years. She is currently a senior manager in a private firm.

R. Raghunathan is Professor in the field of Strategy and Entrepreneurship. He has served for over 24 years as a faculty member at BITS Pilani. His research interests include Scholarship of Teaching and Learning (SoTL), business negotiations, managerial skills and competencies, strategy, entrepreneurship, international business, and channels of distribution. He is passionate about teaching and thus deliberately chose to teach several management courses. He has been identified as one of "The Top 50 Flipped Learning Leaders in Higher Education Worldwide" by Flipped Learning Global Initiative (FLGI), and has featured in their Annual List 2018 "100+ Global Flipped Leaders To Learn From".

Rabin Mazumder is Professor of Economics and Head of the Department of Management at the Institute of Engineering and Management, Kolkata, India. He has a PhD in business management from the University of Calcutta. He has around 17 years of academic experience. His research papers have appeared in reputed journals such as the Journal of Retailing and Consumer Services, International Journal of Organizational Analysis, International Journal of Online Marketing, Indian Journal of Marketing, and Indian Journal of Finance. His book chapters have been published in Springer Nature and Emerald publications. He also authored two books on economics at the secondary and undergraduate levels. His areas of interest are development economics, consumer behaviour and brand management.

Rakhi Chowdhury is Assistant Professor of Political Science at TDB College, Raniganj. She has served as an eminent Professor at the TDB College for the last 13 years. She is teaching political sociology, gender studies and human rights etc. Her current field of interest lies in the area of gender studies and human rights.

Rooprekha Baksi graduated from Gokhale Memorial Girls' College, University of Calcutta, with a degree in Psychology, and obtained a postgraduate degree in Applied Psychology from the University of Calcutta. She completed her PhD in HR at the University of Engineering and Management, Kolkata. She is currently working as an Assistant Professor at Amity University Kolkata in the Psychology and Allied Sciences department. Her teaching experience is more than ten years. She has published around 25 research papers; some are Scopus indexed, with one book chapter.

Samuel N.J. David is Professor of Hospital Management/Administration with commensurate academic qualifications in the areas of economics, human resources and industrial relations. He is presently the Head of the Department of Hospital Management Studies and Staff Training and Development, Christian Medical College, Vellore and also holds the post of Associate General Superintendent (Food and Beverages) in the organization. He has been instrumental in the coordination and delivery of training programmes for the entire organization toward COVID management, in both support and clinical verticals through various experts and staff. He has also been involved in the COVID Pulse lectures and COVID UDHAVI initiative.

Shalini Singh is Assistant Professor in the School of Commerce, Finance and Accountancy at Christ (Deemed to be University), Delhi NCR. She has a Doctorate in Finance from the Institute of Management Studies of Banaras Hindu University; she did her Master's in Commerce, and her PGDBM in Finance. She has contributed to educational management as an editor and as a member of IIC committee. She has contributed to more than 20 research papers, most of which have been published in peer-reviewed journals, UGC Care journals, and Scopus Indexed Journals, and some are also yet to be accepted for publication. Dr. Shalini Singh has written eight book chapters, which include work on the work–life balance of academics during the pandemic, financial planning as a road to life management, etc.

Saikat Chakrabarti is Associate Professor in the Institute of Engineering and Management, Salt Lake, Kolkata, West Bengal. He holds a PhD in Management. He has published articles in international and national level journals, held conferences/seminars on psychological contract, human resource planning, cross-cultural training and outbound training. He has also published chapters in the international case study book "ET-Cases" and in several books published by Emerald Publishing, Springer Publishing Company, Elsevier Publishing, etc. He is the editor of two books, and has more than 17 years of experience (both in industry and in educational institutions).

Sajal Mondal, BCom, MCom, MPhil, PhD, has been a State Aided College Teacher (SACT) in Commerce at the Dr. Gourmohan Roy College, Monteswar, under the affiliation of the University of Burdwan, since 2 November 1995. He has teaching experience of more than 27 years. He has been awarded the degrees of MPhil and PhD in Commerce from the University of Burdwan. He participates in various national and international conferences.

Shreya Bhattacharjee pursued her undergraduate degree at Amity University, Kolkata, in Applied Psychology, and her postgraduate at St. Xavier's University, Kolkata. Currently, she is a working professional in the government sector.

Smita Datta submitted her PhD thesis under the supervision of Dr. Anindita Chakraborty in February 2019. Prior to joining FMS, BHU, she gained an MBA from the Indian Institute of Social Welfare and Business Management, Kolkata. She qualified with a UGC-NET JRF in December 2013. Her areas of interest are capital markets and behavioural finance. She has published five research papers in national journals and one manuscript has been accepted for publication in an ABDC-B category journal. She has presented papers at various national and international conferences. She is a member of the Indian Finance Association.

Smita Mehendale is an Assistant Professor with the Symbiosis Institute of Management Studies, Symbiosis International (Deemed University), Pune. She has 18+ years of experience in diverse functions like finance, marketing and HR and across industries and educational institutions. She has worked in manufacturing, the service sector, and consultancy before stepping into academics. She has a PhD from SPPU, Pune, in online retailing. Her research interest is in retailing, consumer studies, social media, higher education, and sustainability. She has presented numerous papers at international conferences, won best paper awards, and published her research in high-ranking international journals.

Somroop Siddhanta has a PhD in Management from the National Institute of Technology and an MBA from the Indian Institute of Technology (ISM). At present, he is Professor and Head of the Faculty of Management Studies, Dr B C Roy Engineering College, Durgapur, with more than 17 years of academic experience. His research areas include marketing communications, marketing of services, consumer behaviour and mathematical modelling in sports. He has nine international journal publications to his credit including ABDC (A and C categories)and Scopus-listed journals.

Sonia Valas is an Assistant Manager and Deputy General Superintendent in the Office of the General Superintendent, Christian Medical College, Vellore. As a management professional who previously served in the Department of Hospital Management Studies and Staff Training and Development, Christian Medical College, Vellore, she is an expert in organizing and coordinating various training programmes and has served in the same capacity in the delivery of COVID related training programmes throughout the institution along with Dr. Samuel N.J. David. She continues to provide input toward the development and dissemination of training programmes, even in her current capacity.

Soumya Mukherjee is Associate Professor in Business Administration at Techno India (Hooghly Campus), Chinsurah, West Bengal, India. He is an accomplished educator with demonstrated ability and experience in teaching, motivating, and directing students while maintaining high interest and achievement. He has more than 15 years of experience in academics. He has authored two books and has several research articles in journals and conference proceedings to his name.

Suchitra Kumari, M.Com, NET, is Assistant Professor of Commerce at St. Xavier's College (Autonomous), Kolkata. Her current research is focused on the application of optimization techniques in the field of finance. She has published several research papers in various national and international peer-reviewed refereed journals of repute.

Subhajit Bhattacharya is Associate Professor, Marketing Area at XIM University Bhubaneswar (previously known as Xavier University Bhubaneswar). He has a PhD in Business Administration from the University of Burdwan. He has more than 14 years of experience in academics. Dr. Subhajit has published articles in several international journals mostly indexed in ABDC, Web of Science, and Scopus. He is are viewer with several leading international journals. Currently, he is researching the areas of brand chemistry, online consumer brand engagement, political marketing, value-based distribution equity, csr-led branding, consumer insight, and pedagogical issues in marketing education.

Subrata Chattopadhyay has an MSc, an MBA, and a PhD from IIT-ISM Dhanbad, and is currently Professor at the University Of Engineering and Management, Kolkata. He has contributed to more than 40 international journals and delivered more than 23 papers in conferences. Besides this, he has authored three books on computations in estate management, transport management and values and ethics for engineers and managers and was editor of the book published at the Sustainable Development Conference, MDI Murshidabad, 2018. He was conferred the prestigious MTC Global Top Thinkers award in 2015. In 2019 he was awarded Mentor of the Year by HRD India.

Sugato Banerjee is currently working as Associate Professor at NIPER Kolkata. He completed his PhD in Pharmacology and Experimental Neuroscience at the University of Nebraska Medical Centre, USA, and worked as a postdoctoral fellow at the University of California San Diego, USA. His current research interests include understanding the molecular pathways associated with metabolic disorder–associated CNS complications including depression and memory impairment. He has a vast experience in teaching and research. He has guided 3 PhD students and 30 Master's students. Besides this, he has more than 40 international publications and a number of book chapters. He has also successfully completed extramural projects.

Subhamay Panda is currently working as a faculty member at Banwarilal Bhalotia College, Asansol.Dr. Panda has an MSc in Zoology from the University of Burdwan and a PhD in Zoology from the University of Burdwan. Dr Panda received a Post Graduate Diploma degree in Bioinformatics from the Electronics Corporation of India (an enterprise under the Department of Atomic Energy, Govt. of India). He has 18 years of experience in teaching and research. Dr. Panda has more than 25 international publications and 5 book chapters. He is the recipient of several state and national-level awards in biological science research.

Subrato Adhikari is Deputy General Manager at HCL Technology with over 22 years of experience in delivery, presales and consulting, supporting all aspects of technical sales activities, technical delivery, managed service solutions, project management and consulting for the company, and is also a research scholar at Brainware University in the department of management. He possesses strong multi-tasking skills, with the ability to simultaneously manage several projects and schedules. He is an excellent public-facing point person for customers, vendors, and service providers. He has earned an MBA from IISWBM Kolkata, and a Master of Science degree in Information Technology from Sikkim Manipal University. He published research papers in national and international reputed journals.

Sujit Dutta is Professor and Head of the Dept. of Management, Institute of Engineering and Management, Kolkata. He has more than 12 years of professional experience serving in various public and private companies. His research areas include green environment, low carbon growth, green literacy, low carbon business opportunities, etc. He keenly advocates for green mindsets, which he considers to be a transforming factor in the present context of global climate change. He has a postgraduate degree in Commerce from the University of Calcutta and a is fellow of Institute of Cost Accountants of India (FCMA).

Swati Mishra is a Young Professional in the Ministry of New and Renewable Energy, New Delhi, India. She completed her BTech with honours in Electrical and Electronics Engineering and an MTech as a gold medallist in Energy Engineering. She is currently involved in the development of various solar PV schemes, namely, the Production Linked Incentive Scheme for High Efficiency Solar PV Modules, the Government Producer Scheme, and the Approved List of Models and Manufacturers, etc. She has more than five years of diverse experience in the field of renewable energy. Her past experiences have involved Energy Management Systems, Heating, Ventilation and Air Conditioning, Electric Vehicles, alternative energy resources (offshore energy and green hydrogen) and waste water treatment plants.

Series Editors' Preface

In this era of conscious consumerism, management innovation has often fetched the interest of practising managers due to its strategic contribution to competitive edging. The introduction of innovative techniques and/or the application of innovative practices have always helped to add value through problem solving or effective decision making. Sustainability is the buzzword of today's business world. It touches upon every industry in practice. It has both strategic and semiotic value. The ubiquitous value of the concept has macro-applicability with respect to the eco-friendly or commercial stability of an organization. Socio-economic, environmental factors have been observed to have a profound influence on the existence, stability, and growth of commercial organizations. This focus has gained more value due to its emerging customized value. The concept of sustainability has several dimensions and wide applicability. The theme of sustainable management practices is both people- and process-centric. Currently, it has flourished in the domains of social science, health management, and general management outside commerce. In the face of continuous flux, sustainable management techniques are a strategic escape route. Economic recessions and natural calamities have caused several financial or functional crises in commercial organizations, and the importance of sustainable techniques has gained new momentum in all such scenarios. The concept of sustainable practices has been felt even more in the crisis hour of the COVID-19 pandemic. In short, sustainable management practices are a necessity for survival. This book is a ray of hope for small, medium, and large business corporations.

Dipak Saha
Rabin Mazumder

Acknowledgements

First and foremost, we are thankful to the entire team at Taylor & Francis Routledge Publications, not only for their dedicated efforts, but also for their immense enthusiasm in shaping this creative and unique book. The hard work and constant partnering done by the editorial board are especially noteworthy.

Constructive criticism is always good, and is particularly very helpful when it is unbiased. We are thankful to all our reviewers, whose valuable inputs and comments have helped us to bring this book closer to perfection. Their belief and trust in the quality of our work gave us a much-needed impetus to introduce this unique book to the market. We have implemented as many suggestions as possible in this edition of the book.

We express our sincere gratitude to Prof. Satyajit Chakarbarti, President, IEM & UEM Group, Kolkata, and Mrs. Banani Chakarbarti, Registrar, IEM & UEM Group, Kolkata, for their constant motivation and support during the project.

This book has been planned with the support of many people to whom we are indebted. We gratefully acknowledge the contribution of the internal editorial team members who, through their learnt criticism, contributed substantially to improving the content, quality, and structure of the book.

We also extend our thanks to our well-wishers and friends for their constant support and encouragement to bring this book to life.

A unique feature of the book is the qualitative and quantitative research-based papers that are included in it. This book was the need of the hour, as we do not have any book to refer to as a handbook of marketing research practice.

We would also like to thank our families deeply and sincerely, who have been extremely supportive of this seemingly never-ending project.

This gesture of thanks would be incomplete without mentioning the contributions of our departmental colleagues, who played an important role in maintaining their trust and confidence in us.

Soumik Gangopadhyay

Introduction

Change is a function of compulsion. Sustainability has been engaged as an agent of change. Social, business, and environmental prosperity depends on both value creation and value addition. Sustainability is a theme of both social and economic debate in our market-driven economy, which justifies the exploration of its value with regard to both of these dimensions. In the business ecosystem, sustainable business models have been developed and applied to aid corporate stability and growth. Sustainable strategies were complemented as reactive instruments of need. For a business organization, sustainability is an exercise in building value. In the VUCA (volatile, uncertain, complex, ambiguous_) environment, sustainability is a means of survival. It flourishes through strategic planning. Scarcity of input, stagnation in operations/sales, inadequate growth, and unexpected competition are the driving forces of the adoption of sustainable growth. Corporations have considered sustainability to be a tool of business strategy in an economically fragile context, or as business software. Sustainability has been implemented as a supplementary reactive approach by businesses. But it is beyond strategic hangover. Without a constructive business philosophy, sustainability has only short-term strategic validity. Moreover, corporate crises are intricately interlinked with the environmental crisis. The success of a sustainable strategy depends on the choices and actions of the people who develop and use it. Sustainable strategies offer endless possibilities.

The battle between mankind and its environment has given rise to an existential crisis on the part of the human being. In this era of conscious consumerism, management innovation has often piqued the interest of practicing managers due to its strategic contributions to competitive edging. The introduction of innovative techniques and/or the application of innovative practices have always helped to add value through problem solving or effective decision making. The interventions of socio-economic and environmental factors have been observed to have a profound influence on the existence, stability, and growth of commercial organizations. This focus has gained momentum due to its increasing customized value. The concept

DOI: 10.4324/9781032640488-1

of sustainability has several dimensions and wide applicability. Sustainable management practice are both people and process-centric. In developing value-added ecological bases, organizational leaders need to establish a level of environmental commitment that is suitable and feasible given the conditions that the organization faces. The adoption of an ecological approach has proven beneficial to those companies that have adopted some kind of environmental accountability. But the relation of causality between an orientation toward the environment and a commitment to related practices is yet unclear.

Social sustainability is a progressive step that includes not only the management of inequality but also covers risk and productivity management. All stakeholders have the critical influence necessary to create and stabilize asocial value chain. Social sustainability encompasses issues that affect stakeholders, such as morale management, the design of welfare programmes, the empowerment of women, disability management, etc. Traditionally, policy makers have debated the effectiveness and efficiency of compensatory or transformative sustainable measures. All these areas proportionately relate corporate stability and growth. While it is the primary duty of governments to protect, respect, fulfil, and realize human rights, businesses cannot ignore or avoid their part in this task. At a minimum, corporations also have to perform due diligence to avoid harming, and to address any adverse impacts on human rights that have profound connection to their every-day activities. Problems inherent to corporations are also a matter of concern for corporate sustainability. Employee stress, labour problems, and capital-intensive operational hazards are a few examples of such problems. People-centred approaches can thus only provide oxygen to the social ecosystem. Existing academic texts have focused on each of these issues individually. On the contrary, this book considers all the aforementioned areas as sub-topics, each in a different chapter, to justify the broader dimensions of social sustainability.

Alternatively, social scientists have vouched for "going green", for the sake of civic society. The recent environmental crises also need to draw the attention of a larger audience. For extensive application of environmental protection methods by every stakeholders, a societal awareness is essential. Only an international interdisciplinary approach can make this viable. This is a mammoth task. Unfortunately, it has a low guarantee of success and is thus not immune to failure. Due to their increased conceptual value in such periods, sustainable business models are developed only during crises, and are only nurtured for a short time. Most of these models have been developed locally and on a case-to-case basis as an alternative method of support or as a means of escaping a crisis. Often such models have short gestation periods due to their time specificity, financial liability, and poor understandings of them. Thus, isolated case studies have a high reference value. It seems that, the strategic values of the sustainability models were none other than contextual obligatory behaviour. Therefore, the term "sustainability" shouldn't be confined to its current trend of being discussed in the narrow sense of being either a corporate or a social concept. Historically, academics have indulged this debatable term from either a conceptual or a geopolitical perspective. Therefore, an academic discussion that will cover the geopolitical, conceptual, and contextual dimensions of sustainability is essential.

The perceived value of sustainable practices increased as they were used to help navigate the financial crisis. Economists, as national policy makers, have often prescribed sustainability as a measure to improve inclusive growth. Several revenue-led reform initiatives also have sustainability as a fundamental theme. This was policy-centric rather than outcome-centric. Many national administrations have adopted the concept as a way to help them escape from a financial burden. Few conceptual models were derived and practiced as an exception. Further, sustainable practices have faced criticism due to poor understandings of their operational hazards. Due to such shortcomings, the transformations in business growth that were expected were unachievable in many cases.

As we continue to combat sporadic attacks from a few more strains of COVID-19, sustainability is becoming increasingly practical for both society and for corporations. The COVID-19 pandemic has brought new meanings to business sustainability, with respect to both health and safety and economic constraints. Moreover, in the era of the COVID-19 pandemic, the prime objective of human beings has become survival, rather than growth. During the COVID-19 pandemic, a surge in consumption fueled the inorganic growth of select products and services, which is an outcome of measures to avoid catching COVID-19. Therefore, new purchase behaviours are emerging. Online education is one such example. Consistency in such purchases will be a function of value differences. Moreover, similar crises may arrive in future that need to be prepared for proactively. The strategic value to commercial organizations of "going green" also addresses environmental stability. This academic content covers diverse sectors such as commerce and e-commerce, healthcare, fintech, and infrastructure. The content of this book focuses on specific emerging economies across India and the US.

This book, *Perspectives in Sustainable Management Practices*, provides an insight into the creation, communication, comprehension, confrontation, and collaboration aspects of sustainable approaches. Recent trends, issues and challenges in business practices have been explored by focusing on Corporate Governance, Corporate Social Responsibility, Information Technology, Psychological Stability, Green Marketing, Sustainability Pre- and Post-Pandemic, Organizational Performance. These explorations are intended to help readers understand the sustainable management practices of businesses. Unlike existing academic texts, this book takes a *gestalt* approach which is oriented toward the future. Its diagnostic and therapeutic content ranges over social, natural, and business dimensions. Sustainable issues in the context of both subjective and objective dimensions have been analyzed by the authors of the chapters. The fundamental theme of this book is invent-innovate-ideate.

This book has incorporated all the aforementioned dimensions associated with sustainability. It covers social, environmental and business-oriented issues directly or indirectly concerned with this discipline. Some chapters in the book explore creative applications of sustainable issues and trends in different fields of management. The thoughtfully-designed, game-changing sustainable business strategies narrated in this book will be an eye-opener for budding management practitioners and researchers. The 22 chapters in this book are focused on 3 specific sub-domains of sustainability: Social Sustainability, Economic Sustainability, and Future Sustainability. Each of the book's three parts are focused on one specific sub-domain of sustainability. In the first part, Social Sustainability, Chapter 1 explores the significance of the social dimension, alongside the growth fundamentals of reducing carbon emissions and contributing to environmental quality. This study uses a recently developed quality growth index to revisit the EKC hypothesis. To this end, it focuses on the USA from 1991–2018. Regression results have indicated the validity of the EKC hypothesis, regardless of whether growth is represented by economic growth *per se* or by the quality growth index. Finally, it concluded that environmental degradation reacts to quality growth index. Chapter 2 analyzes empathy as the key factor in strengthening the new sustainable business concept of People-Planet-Profit, with the help of a case study that also highlights empathy as a foundation for innovative design which can comparatively enhance the value of a business. The Greenway case exemplifies how people, the planet, and profit can be successfully amalgamated, how social problems that are taken for granted can be easily solved through low-cost innovative solutions, and how technology can play a crucial role in solving social issues. Chapter 3 concentrates on the fear-mongering state of current employees in the information technology sector who lost their jobs due to the COVID-19 pandemic and its reinforcing effect on their behaviour. Chapter 4 critically argues for the significance of the transition of corporate social responsibility from silent social responsibility to mandatory social responsibility with respect to Indian business enterprises operating on small, medium and large scales. It analyzes the complex connections between the silent social responsibility performed by SMEs and their sustainable growth. Chapter 5 substantiates the need to reinforce confidence in the green bond market, to help us gain a better understanding of this asset. A continuous effort is required to standardize its issuance through the development of a common green bond framework which will attract a larger number of issuers and investors to scale up the green bond market. In the context of social sustainability, Chapter 6 tries to highlight the empowerment of rural women through the MGNREGA (Mahatma Gandhi National Rural Employment Guarantee Act) scheme. It has revisited the impact of the government of India's MGNREGA scheme for the empowerment of women in a selective geography. It has been observed that in the three dimensions of the empowerment of women –economic, financial, and social – the beneficiaries of the scheme produce higher mean scores than those of the non-beneficiaries in most of the blocks of the district of Purba Burdwan. Chapter 7 explores reverse migration during the COVID-19 pandemic lockdown in the state of West Bengal, India, based on alternative estimations. It explores the impact of government-initiated reactive direct support for the migrants. Chapter 8 delves deep into the impact of socio-economic injustice among students affected by COVID-19in the context of a huge digital divide between the different states of India. The difficulty of the transition from physical to digital learning has been documented, with the future in mind. Chapter 9 notes3 critical dimensions –"E- Comfort", "E-stress", and "E-malpractice"– that have influenced online learning during the COVID-19 pandemic. The result of a binary logistic regression shows that most respondents did not favour blended learning. "E-stress" and "E-malpractice" have negatively influenced outlooks on sustainable blended learning. Chapter 10 attempts to justify the imposition of a Pigouvian production tax to help deal with negative externalities and improve social welfare. The imposition of Pigouvian taxes is often linked to political difficulties. Attempts by the government to impose such taxes are often met with opposition from lobbyists who support parties that might be impacted by the taxes (e.g., tobacco producers). As a result, certain taxes are not always the best option from a political standpoint. Part 2, Economic Sustainability, begins with Chapter 11, a multidimensional assessment of the impact of the COVID-19 pandemic on several sectors. A critical analysis of the problems discussed will reveal more productive combat strategies for the future. Chapter 12 is a conceptualized model-based discussion around a value chain analysis of Indian handicraft items. This model will be beneficial for stakeholders in developing and underdeveloped countries involved in the handicraft sector, and particularly for the sustainable improvement of the socio-economic status of all the artisans involved. The model will also ensure the preservation of the originating country's culture and heritage, which is integrally linked with handicrafts. The foundation of Chapter 13 is an established association between financial literacy and the subjective economic progress of a selective geography. The study concludes that acquiring financial knowledge from a young age will help individuals to be more financially active as adults, as young adults form an important part of the development of the overall economy of a nation. The chapter suggests that financial literacy levels should be raised among students, as it would help them to make sound financial decisions in the future and improve their economic well-being. Moreover, factors like financial knowledge, financial security, and financial risk-bearing capability are the factors that influence students' perceptions of financial literacy. The emergence of the COVID-19 pandemic has impacted the share price of life insurance companies in India, which is illustrated in Chapter 14. With the entry of COVID-19, which was a disaster, swiping away all the businesses and earnings in the country, leaving the nation helpless to cope with the losses arising in different sectors, assets under management declined, which led to an increased redemption of claims by investors to fulfil their urgent needs, and also due to a rise in deaths. Chapter 15 explores the provision of sustainable agriculture, balancing the environment, society, and the economy. It also explains an effective, sustainable, long-term agroecosystem model, with the support of knowledge, technical competence, and skilled labour.

In India a large informal sector, coupled with a large population base, limits the public health financing system from realizing the dream of universal health coverage. Chapter 16 reveals the continuation of the momentum of private health insurance, which is working to make health access more equitable and realize the dream of universal health coverage.

Discrete innovations have poor acceptance rates. Even product adoption and diffusion needs a solid base, a reasonable approach built on customer expectation. Thus, product adoption and diffusion analysis have immense value. Product diffusion is based on ideas, beliefs, attitudes, and values, whereas product adoption is subjective. The theme of Part 3 of the book is Innovative Strategies for Sustainability. Chapter 17 is a critical analysis of the impact of globalization, the fourth industrial revolution, and COVID-19 on the valuation of Reliance Industries Limited and their stocks, which would assist mergers with and the acquisition of various corporations, in order to gain synergy. Chapter 18 examines the long-term sustainability of the English Premier League with regard to Competitive Balance, which measures the uncertainty in the outcome of the results of any sporting league. Apart from financial constraints, the difference in the use of technology-based analytical tools in preparation for an encounter (including the lack of use of analysts), the quality of training infrastructure, and lean fan followings can be considered as reasons that need to be objectively looked at before narrowing down actionable means of improving the competitive balance. Chapter 19 is a systematic literature survey of innovative practices within the hospitality industry with respect to products, processes, marketing, and organizational innovation. During the COVID-19 pandemic, commercial value stabilization gained in importance. With partial preparedness, radical changes were adopted by the Indian healthcare giant CMC, Vellore. These strategic modifications have been summarized in Chapter 20. Chapter 21 is a research-based analysis, shedding light on the efforts of FMCG marketers to frame marketing strategies diligently, so as to stand out in the competitive market of the days of the COVID-19 pandemic. This study significantly demonstrates that all the factors play a decisive role in increasing purchase intention among prospects for FMCG products. To be more precise, this research emphasizes the fact that Advertisement and Celebrity Endorsement, as well as Retail and Shop Displays, majorly contribute to swaying potential customers toward FMCG products. This study also reveals that Pack

Size and Availability do not have such a strong effect on brand loyalty. The degree of impact is, thus, truly reflected by IMPA. Marketers have to diligently give emphasis to Advertisement and Celebrity Endorsement and Retail and Shop Displays and frame their strategies accordingly, so as to excel in the competitive market. Chapter 22 is entitled "Customers' Attitudes to the Use of Artificial Intelligence–Enabled Applications for Internet-Based Home Services in their Daily Lives". Its qualitative research analysis demonstrates the perceived value of customized technology, which can be applied as a competitive strategy to sustain businesses in the future.

AI has helped industries find innovative and smart ways to do business which can help them attain and leverage enormous amounts of information, to help them anticipate the user's next move. Owing to the fact that customers can access internet-based home services at any time and from anywhere, including on holidays, is very useful. Chatbots within the applications assist customers with customization and efficiency. To enrich the experience, customers are given benefits like online or offline transactions for bill payments to ensure privacy and security. The survey suggests that the customers believe that these internet-based home services make life easy, by offering solutions to the day-to-day problems of the maintenance of their homes, offices, and vehicles. Many participants expressed that they preferred AI-enabled personal assistants over humans and were ready to pay more for AI-enabled services. Through their experience, participants pointed out that AI has advantages such as high efficiency and low cost compared to traditional human services, but also, on the flip side, some expressed concern about inflexibility, rigidness, a lack of care or emotion, and the privacy of their data. Participants also believe that the government must encourage the AI industry to improvize its applications in the health and education sectors, among others, and overall people are ready to accept AI technology, with huge growth potential.

Thus, this book is a guide to policy makers, producers, service providers, regulators, and the designers of welfare.

Part 1

Social Sustainability

Chapter 1

Rethinking the Environmental Kuznets Curve

Quantity Growth vs. Quality Growth

Ayhan Kuloğlu and Mert Topcu

Introduction

Given their efforts to accelerate economic activity, countries have neglected the detrimental environmental impacts of production, and, as a consequence, carbon emissions have grown over time at the global level (Gyamfi et al., 2021). In order to measure how production levels are associated with environmental quality, the Environmental Kuznets Curve (EKC) hypothesis has been used widely among economists since its introduction by Grossman and Krueger (1991). The EKC hypothesizes that the relationship between pollution emissions and economic growth follows an inverted U-shaped pattern, indicating that environmental degradation initially increases and decreases as economic activity expands (Stern, 2018).

Contrary to its massive production capacity and, as a result, the large quantity of carbon emissions it produces, the US is one of the most environmentally sustainable countries on the planet. Therefore, the number of studies looking into the validity of the EKC hypothesis in the US context has dramatically increased over the last three decades.[1] Rupasingha et al. (2004) examine the relationship between toxic waste and per capita income in the US and report an inverted U-shaped relationship. Soytas et al. (2007) discuss the fact that income per se does not have an impact on the environment. Tevie et al. (2011) investigate the validity of the EKC hypothesis in terms of biodiversity risks and report that the hypothesis is not confirmed. Ajmi et al. (2015) examine the validity of the hypothesis in the G7 countries and find that the EKC hypothesis is not valid in the US. Baek (2016) reports that the hypothesis is verified in the short run, whereas an increasing income level is associated with an increase in emissions in the long run. Congregado et al. (2016) confirm the existence of the EKC hypothesis, excluding the industry sector over the period 1973–2015. Atasoy (2017) tests the validity of the EKC hypothesis in 50 US states during the period 1960–2010 and reports the validity of the EKC hypothesis in 30 out of the 50 states. Aslan et al. (2018) also confirm an inverted U-shaped pattern between growth and environmental pollution over the period 1966–2013. The findings of Ongan et al. (2021)

DOI: 10.4324/9781032640488-3

indicate that the results obtained from disaggregated models confirm the existence of the EKC hypothesis, whereas the results obtained from undifferentiated models do not.

Because economic development requires a more inclusive concept than economic growth, recent studies have addressed the importance of growth quality (see, for example: Raheem et al., 2018; Sharafutdinov et al., 2019; among others). However, the only attempt to provide a link between quality growth and environmental quality is, to the best of our knowledge, the study by Long and Ji (2019). Our study differs from that of Long and Ji (2019) on two fronts. First, the existing study provides country-level evidence by focusing on one of the world's most environmentally sustainable countries. Second, this study uses a recently developed quality growth index combining growth fundamentals with a set of social outcomes. Therefore, the objective of this study is to revisit the validity of the EKC hypothesis in the US using a quality growth index.

Section 2 describes the model, data, and methods. Section 3 provides empirical findings and discussions. Section 4 gives concluding remarks.

Methods

The empirical model is specified as a time series model of environmental degradation (*ed*) and described as a function of energy consumption (*ec*), economic growth (*eg*), and squared term of economic growth (*egsq*) as given in equation (1):

$$ed_t = \beta_0 + \beta_1 ec_t + \beta_2 eg_t + \beta_3 egsq_t + \varepsilon_t. \tag{1}$$

where *t* indicates the time period (t =1,.....,T) and εt is the random error term. Annual data on environmental degradation, energy consumption, and economic growth were obtained for the period 1991 to 2018 for the US.

Environmental degradation is measured in carbon emissions per capita while energy consumption is proxied by energy use per capita. Economic growth is represented by the annual change in the real GDP per capita.

Mlachila et al. (2017) state that many countries suffer from significant losses in unemployment, poverty, and inequality, although there is a serious path to macroeconomic stability and strong growth. In this respect, researchers and policymakers are faced with the question of what the quality of growth should be. Therefore, Mlachila et al. (2017)[2] define the concept of quality growth as sustainable, productivity-enhancing, strong growth, which also contributes to the reduction of poverty. The main purpose of establishing the quality growth (*qg*) index is to evaluate the development of economic growth quality across countries and over time. This index includes both the social dimension of growth and the basic growth dynamics, so that it models the concept of growth across multiple dimensions. Given this broad definition, it can help researchers describe quality growth as a phenomenon that creates employment, increases welfare and quality of life, and reduces poverty.

Rethinking the Environmental Kuznets Curve 13

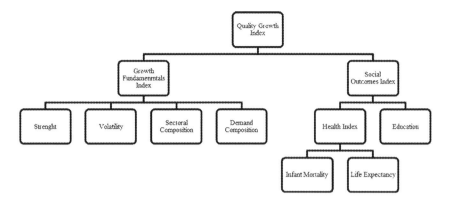

Figure 1.1 Aggregation Process of Quality Growth Index

The components of quality growth as proposed by Mlachila et al. (2017) can be summarized as follows: the index is composed of the aggregation of the fundamentals of, and the desired social outcomes from, growth. The four sub-dimensions of the fundamental variable of growth are (i) strength, (ii) stability, (iii) diversification of sources, and (iv) its outward orientation, whereas social outcomes come from (i) health and (ii) education.

Figure 1.1 shows the components of quality growth, resulting from the aggregation of the growth fundamentals and the desired social outcomes from growth. The four sub-dimensions of the fundamental variable of growth are (i) strength, (ii) stability, (iii) diversification of sources, and (iv) its outward orientation whereas social outcomes come from (i) health and (ii) education.

In this study, quality growth is derived from the proposal of Mlachila et al. (2017). Table 1.1 defines the variables that represent each component.

To construct the quality growth index, we follow a two-step procedure: first, we standardize the variable into indices of the same scale, and then we aggregate the indices into a single index. Following Mlachila et al. (2017), we also use "the Min-Max approach" for the standardization of the components. Unlike Mlachila et al. (2017), for whom aggregation depends on equal weighting, we use "Principle Component Analysis" to construct the quality growth index[4,5]. Figure 1 describes the aggregation procedure for the construction of each sub-index, as well as the quality growth index.

With the inclusion of the quality growth index, we can augment economic growth as shown in eq. (1) with the quality growth index, to test the validity of the EKC curve with regard to the quality growth index. The augmented econometric version can be given as follows:

$$ed_t = \beta_0 + \beta_1 ec_t + \beta_2 qg_t + \beta_3 qgsq_t + \varepsilon_t \qquad (2)$$

Table 1.1 Quality Growth Index Components

Component	Variable	Definition
Strength	per capita GDP growth	annual change in real GDP (2010 constant prices) per capita
Volatility	coefficient of variation (CV) on the real GDP per capita growth	the inverse of CV on the real GDP per capita growth CV: the ratio of the standard deviation over the mean. A 5-year rolling window is used to derive the time-varying coefficient of variation
Sectoral Composition	Herfindahl–Hirschman index (HHI)	One minus Herfindahl–Hirschman index (1-HHI)
Demand Composition	net exports	the difference between exports and imports, both as a share of GDP
Health	infant mortality	the reverse of the infant mortality rate
	life expectancy	life expectancy at birth
Education	schooling	mean years of schooling[3]

Source: Mlachila et al. (2017).

Data for all the variables used in the construction of the quality growth index were extracted from the World Bank World Development Indicators (2020) database, with the exception of education. Data on mean years of schooling were gathered from the United Nations Human Development Indices (2020). In addition, data on energy consumption and GDP growth were also gathered from the World Bank World Development Indicators (2020) database. Finally, data regarding carbon emissions were extracted from the Statistical Review of World Energy Report released by British Petroleum (2020).

In order to validate the accuracy of our new index, we tested the correlations between a currently used development index and the quality growth index. The quality growth index is positively correlated[6] with the well-established United Nations Human Development Index, indicating that the quality growth index could be another legitimate part of the toolkit available for gauging the United States' progress toward inclusive growth.[7]

Results & Discussions

As a preliminary step, this study uses the Dickey Fuller Generalized Least Squares (DF-GLS) unit root procedure proposed by Elliott et al. (1996). The empirical results reported in Table 1.2 reveal that each variable contains a unit root, with the exception of economic growth.

After the unit root investigation, we estimate slope coefficients using the pooled Ordinary Least Squares (OLS) technique[8]. The regression results

Table 1.2 Unit Root Results

Variable	DF-GLS	DF-GLS in first difference
ed	0.140	-4.771***
ec	-0.744	-5.289***
eg	-2.914**	
qg	-0.348	-1.900*

The lag length in the DF-GLS test is chosen using the modified AIC, considering the correction by Perron and Qu (2007), and the maximum number of lags is 1.
Significance at the 1%, 5%, and 10% levels are denoted by "***", "**" and "*", respectively.
Source: Our estimations.

Table 1.3 Regression Results

Variable	Eq (1)	Eq (2)
ec	2.279***	2.688***
eg	0.066***	
egsq	-0.003*	
qg		0.102***
qgsq		-0.007**

Significance at the 1%, 5%, and 10% levels are denoted by "***", "**" and "*", respectively.
Source: Our estimations.

reported in Table 1.3 reveal that energy consumption has a positive and statistically significant impact on carbon dioxide emissions in each specification, ranging between 2.279 and 2.688. The estimated coefficients of either the economic growth variable in Eq. (1) or the quality growth index variable in Eq. (2) confirm the validity of the EKC hypothesis, indicating an inverted U-shaped relationship. Given these coefficients, the inflection points for economic growth and for the quality growth index are calculated as 11 and 7.28, respectively.

The difference resulting from these inflection points has several important policy implications. First, this study strengthens the "growth-mania" concept argued by Long and Ji (2019). Policymakers that consider income growth as the sole indicator of economic development have a biased perception of social welfare and sustainability, so income growth should not be regarded as a convenient indicator of social welfare and sustainability. Given these shortcomings, policymakers should take a broad developmental indicator into account in any decision-making process in order to avoid possible mistakes. Notice that a broader development index considering the value of human capital, the social dimension, and growth fundamentals is expected to yield effectual outcomes. In this sense, the quality growth index could be a good complement, offering further insights into social welfare with its promising improvements in accounting for environmental costs (Long and Ji, 2019).

Furthermore, the modelling projections regarding the EKC hypothesis would probably misestimate the level of environmental degradation and, as a result, energy conservation policies aimed at mitigating greenhouse gas emissions would fall short of their intended targets (Emirmahmutoglu et al., 2021).

Finally, inclusive development leads to an improvement in economic structure, technology, and human intelligence, each of which no longer puts extra pressure on the expansion of the macroeconomic scale as economic growth does. Instead, it prompts an increase in social welfare, which, in turn, eventually halts the conflict between humans and nature. Underlining the quality rather than the quantity of growth should be a rational approach to protect the environment from the disease of "growth-mania" (Daly, 2014; Long and Ji, 2019).

Conclusion

This study utilizes a recently developed quality growth index to revisit the EKC hypothesis. To this end, we focus on the US over the period 1991–2018. Regression results indicate the validity of the EKC hypothesis, regardless of whether growth is represented by economic growth per se or by the quality growth index. Once the inflection points are calculated, however, we find that environmental degradation reacts to the quality growth index even before economic growth.

There are also potential research agendas on this issue. For instance, a future study including a panel group of countries with different development levels would be worthwhile, in order to find out which countries tend to pass the pooled inflection point.

Notes

1 There is also a parallel literature investigating the convergence of emissions in the US (see, for example: Apergis and Payne, 2017; Apergis et al., 2017; among others).
2 This study was built on Martinez and Mlachila (2013)'s work exploring the quality of the high-growth episode in sub-Saharan Africa.
3 Unlike in Mlachila et al. (2017), the proxy of education in this study is mean years of schooling due to data availability.
4 See Mlachila et al. (2017) for a detailed discussion regarding the data description and construction processes.
5 The PCA outcomes are available upon request.
6 The correlation coefficient is 0.8351.
7 Mlachila et al. (2017) argue that the concept of the quality growth index (QGI) is a more comprehensive variable than the recognized Human Development Index (HDI) developed by the United Nations and takes not only income level but also growth into account. They state that the QGI index is also different from the

Social progress index developed by Scott et al. (2014), in which growth fundamentals are mostly ignored.

8 We also utilized the ARDL (Autoregressive Distributed Lag) framework. Due to the relatively limited number of observations, however, the model failed in terms of diagnostic checks. Therefore, the results of the ARDL approach are not reported.

References

Ajmi, A. N., Hammoudeh, S., Nguyen, D. K., & Sato, J. R. (2015). On the relationships between CO2 emissions, energy consumption and income: The importance of time variation. *Energy Economics*, 49, 629–638. https://doi.org/10.1016/j.eneco.2015.02.007

Apergis, N., & Payne, J. E. (2017). Per capita carbon dioxide emissions across US states by sector and fossil fuel source: Evidence from club convergence tests. *Energy Economics*, 63, 365–372. https://doi.org/10.1016/j.eneco.2016.11.027

Apergis, N., Payne, J. E., & Topcu, M. (2017). Some empirics on the convergence of carbon dioxide emissions intensity across US states. *Energy Sources, Part B: Economics, Planning, and Policy*, 12(9), 831–837. https://doi.org/10.1080/15567249.2017.1310956

Aslan, A., Destek, M. A., & Okumus, I. (2018). Bootstrap rolling window estimation approach to analysis of the environment Kuznets curve hypothesis: Evidence from the USA. *Environmental Science and Pollution Research*, 25(3), 2402–2408.

Atasoy, B. S. (2017). Testing the environmental Kuznets curve hypothesis across the US: Evidence from panel mean group estimators. *Renewable and Sustainable Energy Reviews*, 77, 731–747. https://doi.org/10.1016/j.rser.2017.04.050

Baek, J. (2016). Do nuclear and renewable energy improve the environment? Empirical evidence from the United States. *Ecological Indicators*, 66, 352–356. https://doi.org/10.1016/j.ecolind.2016.01.059

British Petroleum. (2020). *Statistical review of World Energy Report*. https://www.bp.com/en/global/corporate/energy-economics/statistical-review-of-world-energy/downloads.html

Congregado, E., Feria-Gallardo, J., Golpe, A. A., & Iglesias, J. (2016). The environmental Kuznets curve and CO 2 emissions in the USA. *Environmental Science and Pollution Research*, 23(18), 18407–18420.

Daly, H. E. (2014). *From uneconomic growth to a steady-state economy*. Edward Elgar Publishing.

Elliott, G., Rothenberg, T. J., & Stock, J. H. (1996). Efficient tests for an autoregressive unit root. *Econometrica*, 64(4), 813–836. https://doi.org/10.3386/t0130

Emirmahmutoglu, F., Denaux, Z., & Topcu, M. (2021). Time-varying causality between renewable and non-renewable energy consumption and real output: Sectoral evidence from the United States. *Renewable and Sustainable Energy Reviews*, 149, 111326. https://doi.org/10.1016/j.rser.2021.111326

Grossman, G. M., & Krueger, A. B. (1991). Environmental impacts of a North American Free Trade Agreement. *National Bureau of Economic Research*, w3914. https://doi.org/10.3386/w3914

Gyamfi, B. A., Adebayo, T. S., Bekun, F. V., Agyekum, E. B., Kumar, N. M., Alhelou, H. H., & Al-Hinai, A. (2021). Beyond environmental Kuznets curve and policy implications to promote sustainable development in Mediterranean. *Energy Reports, 7*, 6119–6129. https://doi.org/10.1016/j.egyr.2021.09.056

Long, X., & Ji, X. (2019). Economic growth quality, environmental sustainability, and social welfare in China-provincial assessment based on genuine progress indicator (GPI). *Ecological Economics, 159*, 157–176.https://doi.org/10.1016/j.ecolecon.2019.01.002

Mlachila, M. M., & Martinez, M. M. (2013). *The quality of the recent high-growth episode in Sub-Saharan Africa* (No. 2013/053). International Monetary Fund.

Mlachila, M., Tapsoba, R., & Tapsoba, S. J. (2017). A quality of growth index for developing countries: A proposal. *Social Indicators Research, 134*(2), 675–710.

Ongan, S., Isik, C., & Ozdemir, D. (2021). Economic growth and environmental degradation: Evidence from the US case environmental Kuznets curve hypothesis with application of decomposition. *Journal of Environmental Economics and Policy, 10*(1), 14–21. https://doi.org/10.1080/21606544.2020.1756419

Perron, P., & Qu, Z. (2007). A simple modification to improve the finite sample properties of Ng and Perron's unit root tests. *Economics Letters, 94*(1), 12–19. https://doi.org/10.1016/j.econlet.2006.06.009

Raheem, I. D., Isah, K. O., & Adedeji, A. A. (2018). Inclusive growth, human capital development and natural resource rent in SSA. *Economic Change and Restructuring, 51*(1), 29–48.

Rupasingha, A., Goetz, S. J., Debertin, D. L., & Pagoulatos, A. (2004). The environmental Kuznets curve for US counties: A spatial econometric analysis with extensions. *Papers in Regional Science, 83*(2), 407–424. https://doi.org/10.1111/j.1435-5597.2004.tb01915.x

Scott, S., Wares, A., & Orzell, S. (2014). Social progress index 2014. In P. O'Sullivan (Ed.), *The social progress imperative*.

Sharafutdinov, R. I., Akhmetshin, E. M., Polyakova, A. G., Gerasimov, V. O., Shpakova, R. N., & Mikhailova, M. V. (2019). Inclusive growth: A dataset on key and institutional foundations for inclusive development of Russian regions. *Data in Brief, 23*, 103864. https://doi.org/10.1016/j.dib.2019.103864

Soytas, U., Sari, R., & Ewing, B. T. (2007). Energy consumption, income, and carbon emissions in the United States. *Ecological Economics, 62*(3–4), 482–489. https://doi.org/10.1016/j.ecolecon.2006.07.009

Stern, D. I. (2018). The environmental Kuznets curve. In N. Castree, M. Hulme, & J. D. Proctor (Eds.), *In Companion to environmental studies* (pp. 49–54). Routledge.

Tevie, J., Grimsrud, K. M., &Berrens, R. P. (2011). Testing the environmental Kuznets curve hypothesis for biodiversity risk in the US: A spatial econometric approach. *Sustainability, 3*(11), 2182–2199. https://doi.org/10.3390/su3112182

United Nations Human Development Indices. (2020). *Human Development Index*. http://hdr.undp.org/en/content/human-development-index-hdi

World Bank. (2020). *World Development Indicators* [Dataset]. https://databank.worldbank.org/source/world-development-indicators

Chapter 2

Model framework characterizing long term sustainable and successful social enterprises

A case of Greenway Appliances

Smita Mehendalec and Lalitprakash Baraik

Introduction

Entrepreneurship drives the progress of a nation. It contributes to economic growth and development, creates jobs, improves quality of life, and has a favourable impact on the masses.

Social entrepreneurship has gained importance in recent years. Its salience is further accentuated by the COVID-19 pandemic, which led to a significant negative impact on the bottom of the pyramid (BOP), with health and education systems found wanting, jobs lost overnight, and income streams withdrawn, resulting in widespread poverty and apathy. Social enterprises (SEs) positively impact society, as, beyond the generation of profits, their objective is to produce greater social good.

Local and national governments, especially in developing nations like India, may not be able to solve grassroots problems on their own. The inefficient use of grants for social causes or rural development, with scant accountability and frequent misallocation of funds and resources, further exacerbate the situation. Big corporations also have little interest in investing in the BOP, as the general perception of such investments is one of high investments and low returns.

Of late, however, both governments and corporations have started taking cognizance of investment in social causes. The Start Up India scheme launched by the Government of India (GOI) in 2016 has proved a fillip to entrepreneurship. Its sister scheme, Stand Up India, facilitates credit to Scheduled Caste, Scheduled Tribe, or women borrowers, through individual bank branches, for setting up a greenfield enterprise. Every year, the Ministry of Commerce and Industry organizes the National Start Up Awards, with a specific award category for SEs. Corporations, on the other hand, are now becoming conscious of their Environmental, Social, and Governance responsibilities, and a significant amount of money is being put towards Corporate Social Responsibility (CSR) activities.

These initiatives have provided a major thrust to and interest in entrepreneurship in general, and social entrepreneurship in particular. India needs

DOI: 10.4324/9781032640488-4

it like never before, to help solve the plethora of social problems still rampant in the country, like poverty, inequality, inadequate health and education infrastructure, a lack of job opportunities, and unemployment.

SEs invariably fall under the category of Micro, Small and Medium Enterprises (MSMEs). MSMEs contribute approx. 30% to India's GDP. India's national interest lies in nurturing SEs. Successful SEs like Jaipur Rugs, the Aravind Eye Hospital, Goonj, ITCs e-Choupal, Jaipur Foot, etc. in India, and a textbook example of a runaway SE success, that of Bangladesh's Grameen Bank, have shown the way, exemplifying the tremendous role SEs can play in producing a positive social impact.

This article uses a case method to examine the factors essential to the long-term success of a SE. It suggests a model framework for a sustainable and successful SE, based on secondary research on Greenway Appliances – India's largest manufacturer of clean stoves, which is bringing about a positive change by offering cleaner cooking methods in rural areas.

In their research, Satar and John (2016) determined 13 factors essential for the success of SEs. Their proposed conceptual model broadly classifies these success factors into 3 categories: Individual, Organizational and Governmental support. Individual factors include 1. business planning skills, 2. entrepreneurship orientation, 3. leadership, 4. Networking. organizational factors include 5. innovative financing, 6. triple bottom line planning, 7. social enterprise marketing, 8. community engagement, 9. human capital, 10. organizational culture, 11. social Impact Evaluation, 12. frugal innovation and 13. Government support.

Sengupta et al. (2021) explored the contingencies behind the acceptance or rejection of digitized business model innovation at the BOP. Using a case study method to evaluate eKutir, an SE in India that leverages digital technologies and platforms to deliver value to smallholder farmers, the research emphasised stakeholder stability and incentives as major aspects determining the acceptance of a given digitalized business model innovation. Besides this, accessibility, availability, affordability, awareness, and acceptability were determined to be crucial factors contributing to stakeholders' adoption of a given digitalized business model innovation.

Grameen Bank is a world renowned and successful SE. A micro finance institution (MFI) based out of Bangladesh, it provides collateral-free lending to the poor. In their research, Chowdhury et al. (2021) studied the relationship between CSR, SEs, and a developing economy, with regard to the case of Grameen Bank. The study illustrates an SE framework in the context of a developing economy like Bangladesh. It suggests that the model for an SE is a workflow with a hierarchy of 5 phases, namely: need identification, goal setting, solution-based business plans, business plan assessment, and business plan execution. The research underlines that an SE can augment social benefits in the most efficient and sustainable manner.

The role of IT and digital transformation has gained wider attention and acceptance in recent years, and has accelerated since the onset of the COVID-19 pandemic. In an era of widespread adoption of digital technologies, SEs also have to adopt such technologies, so as to stay relevant. Without using technology, any business, be it social or traditional, is bound to achieve little success.

Pankaj and Seetharaman (2021) studied the importance of IT in the context of a non-digital SE, and its impact on long term sustainability of a SE. The study stated that through an innovative use of IT, an SE can establish and maintain shared value, resulting in business stability and efficiency, financial viability, and also the ensured effectiveness and scalability of their social impact.

Methods

Secondary research has been employed to gather information from media sources which include: the Economic Times, a business-focused media platform owned by the Times Group, and Crunchbase, a platform for finding business information about private and public companies. Further, a case study is used to elaborate on the success factors of an SE, Greenway Appliances. Sources include the digital platforms of Greenway Appliances, Ashden, a UK-based organization that supports innovative solutions to combat the harmful effects of climate change, and Clean Cooking Alliance, a not-for-profit organization promoting clean cooking technologies in lower and middle-income countries, among other publicly available sources.

Case of Greenway Appliances

Many households in rural India depend on traditional fuels like firewood and dung to light their *chulhas* – their traditional mud stoves. Used by rural women for cooking, they have damaging effects on both health and on the environment. Using a *chulha* for an hour is as harmful as smoking 20 cigarettes. Continued usage can result in eye and skin irritation. Smoke and harmful emissions from *chulhas* contribute to climate change, with damaging environmental effects. Traditional cooking methods contribute around 2% of the worlds Greenhouse Gas (GHG) emissions, and thus to climate change. They are also responsible for four million global deaths yearly, and a quarter of these occur in India.

In rural areas, traditional firewood has to be gathered by cutting trees, harming green vegetation. Rural communities spend more than the required amount of time and income on gathering firewood, instead of investing the same time, effort, and energy on more productive activities. Cooking based on traditional methods and fuel collection robs women and young girls of adequate opportunities for poverty alleviation and investments in other productive efforts. Frost (2017) mentions women and girls bear a disproportionate burden of the lack of clean energy access, travelling to collect fuel and water, affecting their security and their opportunities to escape poverty.

Mumbai-based Greenway Appliances, founded in 2011, offers an eco-friendly stove as a replacement for traditional *chulhas,* with 65% fuel savings and 70% smoke reduction. Greenway stoves work seamlessly on all solid biomass fuels (like wood, dry dung, crop waste, coconut waste, bamboo etc), enabling clean cooking for rural households, and eliminating inconvenience to rural women. These stoves, built using patented air regulation technology, minimize Carbon Monoxide and particulate matter and GHG emissions, leading to better health, savings, climate change mitigation, and everyday convenience. The single-burner stove, with a simple and ergonomic front loading design, is portable and convenient to carry from one place to another.

In terms of social impact, Greenway stoves are used in over 700,000 homes in India, have helped mitigate up to 2.5 million tonnes of carbon emissions, and have reduced total cooking times by 30 minutes per day. To ensure affordability to the rural poor, Greenway has enabled purchases on credit to over 250,000 customers.

Greenway has been recognized for its social impact efforts in many forums, winning the Ashden Award for climate innovation in 2014, the Intel Award for Green innovation in 2012, and its co-founder Neha Juneja was recognized as the woman entrepreneur of the year by the Clean Cooking Alliance in 2019.

The Greenway factory in Vadodara, Gujarat has the capacity to produce 800,000 stoves per year. It is India's largest clean stove company. The market in India is still very underserved. Even today, the vast majority of people still use traditional cooking fuels. With a 70% rural population in India, there is a significant opportunity for market development, scalability, and reach for Greenway.

With the Greenway case in mind, we can now present a model framework to assess the long-term success for a SE.

Empathy is the prime mover of any successful SE. The single, mission-driven question of "Why?", and the deep desire to make a change in people's lives by understanding their problems and tailoring solutions to their needs, enables an SE to join a long-term success path. Neha Juneja and Ankit Mathur, the co-founders of Greenway, made painstaking efforts to travel across India to understand the problems of rural women working with traditional mud *chulhas.* With their pilot study, they found that even though existing cooking practices were a regular part of rural life, their consequences were highly underrated, and the issues associated with them were largely ignored. This set the co-founders on the path of a cause-driven SE.

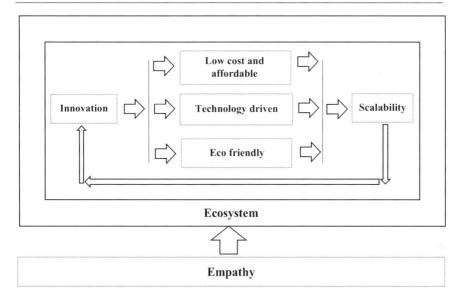

Figure 2.1 A model framework for long-term sustainable success of an SE.

Source: Authors' creation

A favourable and healthy ecosystem helps SEs to flourish. Ecosystems include governments, NGOs, investors, national and international organizations, other SEs, the BOP market, etc. Greenway's mission aligns with that of the government. The Ujjwala Yojana programme provides free LPG cylinders to women of Below Poverty Line (BPL) families, so that they can transition to clean cooking fuels. Greenway's partner network includes more than 2,000 entrepreneurs as part of their ecosystem. Further, its huge BOP market is present not only in the Indian sub-continent, but also overseas. The Clean Cooking Alliance (2020) mentions Greenway having started operations in Zambia with their first carbon revenues project, involving 100,000 stoves.

Funding is crucial for the survival of enterprises. Today, investors are looking to put their money in good businesses, and venture capital firms are investing in for-profit SEs. In 2016, Greenway secured Series A funding of $2.5 Million from Acumen, a non-profit impact investment fund, which invests in social businesses in developing countries.

Innovation-led, low cost, technology-driven, and eco-friendly solutions are imperative for long-term success. It requires the meticulous study of local issues, an understanding of consumer behaviour, and innovative pricing and distribution models, etc. Technology is indispensable for SEs if they wish to remain competitive and sustainable. With the increased adoption of the internet by the BOP market segment, an extensive geographical reach is possible. Technology-enabled solutions ensure efficiency and productivity in product/service usage. The low purchasing power of the target segment necessitates low cost solutions, and, to remain profitable, enterprises must invest in economies of scale, to create reductions in production costs that can be passed on to their customers. Offering credit facilities is important, as the BOP invariably earns on a daily basis, and they do not wish to spend large chunks of their savings instantly. Greenway stoves are price-data competitive at Rs 1799, with its jumbo version priced at an affordable Rs 2999. Even here, when affordability and insufficient money comes in the way of owning these stoves, Greenway offers finance options to the rural poor. Greenway's appliances has collaborations with MFIs and banks who facilitate part payments with EMI options to people aspiring to purchase their stoves.

Low cost, eco-friendly, and technology-led solutions are the ingredients which allow an SE to scale up. Technology enables SEs to scale up quickly and efficiently in newer markets, due to production and manufacturing efficiencies. Digital platforms are imperative, as they enable a global reach. Greenway has scaled up its product reach beyond India. In India itself, the market is largely untapped, and the opportunity is enormous. With many rural women continuing to use traditional cooking methods, Greenway stoves have further scalability potential.Pandit (2018) mentions that Greenway operates India's largest biomass stove factory, with a production capacity of more than 800,000 units per year.

Once a certain scale is achieved, the model framework envisages Continuous Innovation (CI) for further scalability and sustainability. CI helps an enterprise stay competitive and relevant, as, due to intense competition, a business model or a product may be easily replicated by peers, resulting in a stagnant business and a loss of market share.

Results and Discussions

The case and the proposed framework envisage the core essential factors for an SE's success.

Empathy is non-negotiable for an SE to succeed. It starts with the founders' purpose and vision, intended to make a social impact. SEs mostly serve the BOP market segment, which is often ignored by mainstream enterprises and considered unworthy of quality products and services. Due to decades of neglect, this segment is low on self-respect and dignity. Every act of an SE must reflect empathy -- clean facilities, courteous and respectful staff, ethical promotional and marketing practices, easy credit and payment solutions, prompt action on customer complaints, etc.

An SE offering eco-friendly and sustainable solutions is more likely to survive in the long run. Its practices may take the form of a minimal use of plastic pollutants, the use of renewable energy for daily operations, organic farming practices, offering products that have a positive impact on nature (as studied in the Greenway case) and a smarter and cleaner alternative to traditional cooking methods.

Creating and being part of an ecosystem helps SEs achieve a wider social impact. Partnering with like-minded organizations – NGOs, MSMEs, local government bodies, self-help groups, etc., enables a widespread impact. Today, the SE ecosystem is seeing a plethora of investment opportunities, as angel investors and venture capitalists are willing to invest in socially good businesses. The Start Up India and Stand Up India programmes run by the GOI are playing their part in encouraging entrepreneurship.

The BOP segment has invariably been denied the fruits of innovation – improved products or services – owing to a lack of investments by for-profit organizations, government apathy, or the inefficient use of funds. Most of the segment is still using age-old practices, resulting in poor quality of life, low yields, low income, and poverty. Innovative products, services, and practices promise a much better yield and return on investment. Low cost innovations like the Greenway stoves are the need of the hour.

Contrary to general perceptions, studies show that the BOP is as receptive to technology as their well-off counterparts. Technology-driven solutions enable better efficiency and productivity. They also enable scalability and reach, be it through investments in CRM, technology-enabled manufacturing, digital stores, mobile applications, data dashboards enabling data-driven decision making, digital marketing and promotions, social media presences, etc. Investments in manufacturing enable economies of scale, which are crucial for SEs to keep their production costs low. Their presence in digital stores enables a worldwide reach, as social problems are not restricted to a particular region but can be seen worldwide.

People on the lower rungs have low purchasing power, thus the creation of low cost solutions is imperative. However, *low cost* should not be construed as meaning *low* or *inferior quality* products or services.

Invariably, SEs have innate scalability potential, as they cater to the huge underserved market of the BOP. Approx. 65% of the population in India lives in rural areas. Globally, this number is approx. 43 %, based on World Bank (WB) estimates. Likewise, poverty estimates suggest that approx. 22% of people in India are living below the poverty line according to the World Bank's definition of poverty, living on less than $1.90 a day. There is no dearth of markets for SEs.

Conclusion

The Greenway case exemplifies how people, the planet, and profits can be successfully amalgamated, how social problems which are taken for granted can easily be solved using low cost, innovative solutions, and how technology can play a crucial role in solving social issues.

The proposed framework provides an effective gauge for assessing the potential growth and continued success of an SE. Existing SEs may use existing assessments to foresee long-term success, and aspiring SEs may take into consideration the factors in this framework, to be incorporated at early stages of their development.

With empathy as a chief consideration, facilitated by favourable ecosystems, innovation-led solutions for scalability, along with a mindset of Continuous Innovation, can help an SE prime for long-term sustainable success.

References

Chowdhury, F. N., Mustafa, J., Islam, K. M. A., Hasan, K. B. M. R., Zayed, N. M., & Raisa, T. S. (2021). Social business in an emerging economy: An empirical study in Bangladesh. *The Journal of Asian Finance, Economics and Business, 8*(3), 931–941. https://doi.org/10.13106/jafeb.2021.vol8.no3.0931

Clean Cooking Alliance. (2020, May 6). *Scaling to new markets: An interview with the leadership team of greenway appliances*. Clean Cooking Alliance. https://cleancookingalliance.org/news/05-06-2020-scaling-to-new-markets-an-interview-with-the-leadership-team-of-greenway-appliances/

Frost, E. (2017, August 29). An interview with AnkitMathur, Co-founder of 2014 winner greenway appliance. Ashden. https://ashden.org/news/an-interview-with-ankit-mathur-co-founder-of-2014-winner-greenway-appliances-1/

Pandit, V. (2018, January 24). Start-up sets up India's largest biomass cook-stove factory in Gujarat. *The Hindu Business Line*. https://www.thehindubusinessline.com/news/national/startup-sets-upindias-largest-biomass-cookstove-factory-ingujarat/article6936959.ece

Pankaj, L., & Seetharaman, P. (2021). The balancing act of social enterprise: An IT emergence perspective. *International Journal of Information Management, 57*, 102302, ISSN 0268-4012. https://doi.org/10.1016/j.ijinfomgt.2020.102302

Satar, M. S., & John, S. (2016). A conceptual model of critical success factors for Indian social enterprises. World Journal of Entrepreneurship, Management and Sustainable Development, *12*(2). https://doi.org/10.1108/WJEMSD-09-2015-0042

Sengupta, T., Narayanamurthy, G., Hota, P., Sarker, T., & Dey, S. (2021). Conditional acceptance of digitized business model innovation at the BoP: A stakeholder analysis of eKutir in India. *Technological Forecasting and Social Change, 170*, 120857, ISSN 0040-1625. https://doi.org/10.1016/j.techfore.2021.120857

Chapter 3

Employment versus Unemployment

A Study on Psychological Distress During COVID-19

Shreya Bhattacharjee and Rooprekha Baksi

Introduction

The Novel Coronavirus outbreak, which first appeared in late 2019, poses a threat to millions of people's health and well-being. It is highly infectious and can cause serious respiratory illness, which has had an immediate effect on governments and public health. Governments have responded by declaring a national and international health emergency, and by taking immediate steps to restrain the spread of the virus. Because of its high degree of communicability and higher fatality rate than many other flu-causing viruses, the COVID-19 pandemic has caused concern among a large number of people around the world. There have only been a few selected vaccines developed to date, which are also not highly available. The World Health Organization (WHO) has issued recommendations or guidelines for dealing with the pandemic, both bio-medically and psychologically.

The pandemic has led to a massive drop in the economic condition of the world, and as a result, many employees have lost their jobs and are under constant threat. The relationship between employer and employee is regarded as a contract between the two parties, employees being reimbursed for their labour with a token of remuneration. Although employees may negotiate certain aspects of an employment agreement, the employer manages most of the terms and conditions. But the ongoing pandemic has strongly affected employment all over the world. Companies are facing huge losses and so many people are losing jobs, which is leading to a high rate of unemployment. Some employees are attached to certain organizations, but their job role is not at par with their skills, and so they are also recognized as unemployed. The American Psychological Association (APA) explains psychological distress as an arduous mental and physical manifestation associated with normal mood swings in most of the population. Many presumed measures of self-reporting, including depression and symptoms of anxiety, are thought to assess it. Due to this rise in unemployment, feelings of helplessness, unworthiness, anxiety, and loneliness are being developed, especially in the minds of young working adults who are freshly in need of employment. It has been

DOI: 10.4324/9781032640488-5

seen that long-term unemployed people have a significantly higher chance of suffering from mental illness than employed people, as well as people who are unemployed for a very short amount of time, and the burden of illness increases with the length of unemployment.

This paper will assess the levels of psychological distress in employed and unemployed people and will discover the difference between them. Relevant statistics will be used in this study. This study will also highlight the persisting COVID-19 unemployment situation, as people try to adjust to the new normal.

Unemployment among young working adults can lead to greater levels of psychological distress. The consequences of unemployment are exacerbated by feelings of powerlessness, and the attribution of the responsibility for job losses to structural or political causes. The evidence in favour of "culture of poverty" theories in relation to job participation is inconclusive. The unemployed young population mostly comprises "poor people" rather than "problem people" (Hannan et al., 1997). Mediators and moderators contributed to a link between unemployment and psychological distress mainly caused by poor economic conditions and low self-esteem (Kokko & Pulkkinen, 1998).

Studies of previous disease outbreaks, as well as of the latest COVID-19 outbreak, have shown increased psychological distress and negative effects on people's mental health and psychological well-being. After the COVID-19 outbreak, research found psychological distress to be highly pervasive among Nepalese respondents (Gautam et al., 2020). The findings of another study showed that lockdowns had a significant effect on people's psychological well-being, but had a lesser impact on their physical activity (Joshi, 2020). Sinha (2018) attempted to investigate the reaction of the psychological manifestation of unemployment and to gain a better understanding of the experiences of unemployed Indian graduates. It aimed to explore three potential consequences of unemployment (psychological, financial, and social), as well as how these unemployed graduates cope with their joblessness. According to the results, unemployed graduates were mentally affected, with feelings of worthlessness, social humiliation, and high levels of stress. Some people explained that they lacked inspiration and purpose in their lives (Sinha, 2018).

A new study looked at whether losing one's job during the COVID-19 pandemic is linked to mental and physical health. The findings revealed that losing a job during the pandemic was linked to both mental and physical health, with social relationships and financial resources acting as moderators (Griffiths et al., 2021). Saito et al. (2021) performed a study in Japan aiming to discover the psychological effects of the state of emergency. Job statuses and socioeconomic variables were among the questions on the questionnaire. Non-permanent employees were not a victim of mental health issues during the COVID-19–related state of emergency in Japan. But one crucial component that affects the mental well-being of staff in general is unemployment.

Methods

The steps of our study are as follows: firstly, we will discover the traits of our sample, i.e., of the employed and unemployed people suffering from psychological distress; secondly, we will measure the psychological distress levels of all the employed and unemployed male and female respondents; and lastly, we will search for the difference between the employed male and female and unemployed male and female populations in terms of psychological distress levels.

Hypothesis 1: there exists no major observable difference between the employed and unemployed population.

Hypothesis 2: No significant difference is there between female employed and unemployed respondents.

Description of sample: the target population of the research consisted of employed young adults working in the IT sector, and unemployed young adults who lost their jobs in several IT sectors due to the pandemic, who were in search of jobs for themselves. This was a cross-sectional study which was carried out among young adults, using a purposive sampling technique. The study's final sample comprised 80 respondents and the participants' ages ranged between 25 years to 40 years. Both male and female members volunteered to participate.

Data Collection Technique: data collection was performed using the survey method. Using Google Forms, an online semi-structured questionnaire was created, with an appended consent form. Demographic details were included in the questionnaire. In the end, 80 responses were recorded.

Design: only participants over 25 years of age, who were able to understand English, and were ready to give their well-informed consent were included in the study. We were able to collect data from participants across Kolkata's IT hubs. Socio-demographic variables which were included were age, gender, employment status, salary range and education. The self-reported online questionnaire produced by the investigators included sections about psychological distress during the novel Coronavirus pandemic.

Measures: to measure psychological distress, an online questionnaire was produced. The scale included a K10 (Kessler Psychological Distress) scale, and the respondents were asked to provide their demographic details. Every respondent agreed and signed the consent forms.

Kessler Psychological Distress Scale (K10): this scale is implemented to determine the levels of distress among the respondents. It is a 5 point Likert scale, with one being "none of the time" and five being "all of the time". The lowest score or minimum value would have been 10, with the highest value being 50. Here lower scores indicate minimal psychological distress, higher scores revealing severe psychological distress. Serraglio (2003) listed a collection of cut-off scores that can be used to test for psychological distress. They include the following: a score of 10-19 means that the person is "likely to be well"; 20-24 means to "likely have a mild disorder"; 25-29 means the person is "likely to have an average disorder"; and 30-50 indicates that the person is "likely to have a severe disorder".

Data Analysis: in this study, the collected data was studied using Google Sheets, a spreadsheet software offered by Google, and Microsoft Excel. In this study, the aim of the researchers was to interpret the result through descriptive statistics and to discover the characteristics of the sample. A mean, a Standard Deviation and a t-value have been used to estimate the findings of the study.

Ethical Considerations: the participants of the study were briefed about the research and the method of conducting it. Their informed consent was acknowledged, and they were told that they could withdraw without any difficulties at any time. They were also told to keep their details confidential and to maintain anonymity. The safety of the participants was made clear.

Results and Discussions

The target sample of our study consisted of employed and unemployed young adults in the IT sector, and the ages of the sample group ranged between 25 and 40. The purposive sampling method was used, and the psychological distress scale (K10) was employed. The tables given below have been methodologically structured, and the following bar graphs highlight the range of differences in "n" values, along with the mean, followed by standard deviation, with reference to Tables 3.3 and 3.4. Psychological distress was studied separately based on gender (male and female), and is depicted in Table 3.1.

Table 3.2 displays the mean difference between the employed and unemployed respondents in this study.

Table 3.1 Showing Level of Psychological Distress

Variable	Sample	N	Mean	Std. Deviation	t-value	df	Level of Sig
Psychological Distress	Male	47	21.8	5.44	0.413	78	Not Sig
	Female	33	21.33	4.46			

Source: Author's analysis

Table 3.2 Showing Nature of Employment

Variable	Sample	N	Mean	Std. Deviation	t-value	df	Level of Sig
Psychological Distress	Employed	35	17.94	2.73	7.477	78	Sig at 0.01 level
	Unemployed	45	24.46	4.56			

Source: Author's analysis

Table 3.3 Showing Level of Psychological Distress in male sample

Variable	Sample	N	Mean	Std. Deviation	t-value	df	Level of Sig
Psychological Distress	Male Employed	19	16.94	2.75	7.459	78	Sig at 0.01 level
	Male Unemployed	28	25.1	4.18			

Source: Author's analysis

Table 3.4 Showing Level of Psychological Distress in Female Population

Variable	Sample	N	Mean	Std. Deviation	t-value	df	Level of Sig
Psychological Distress	Female Employed	16	19.12	2.24	3.856	78	Sig at 0.01 level
	Female Unemployed	31	23.29	3.99			

Source: Author's analysis

Table 3.3 shows the difference in psychological distress levels between male employed and male unemployed respondents.

Lastly, Table 3.4 shows the difference in psychological distress levels observed between female employed and female unemployed respondents.

The entire world is affected by this pandemic, and it affected the young employees of India as well. Ahad et al. (2020) in the study on an analysis of the effects of the crisis states that the recent emergence of significant job losses and the increasing economic insecurity of employment is having an especially painful impact on young generation around the world. So, taking

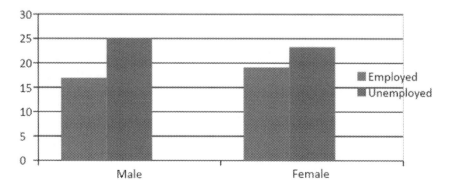

Figure 3.1 Mean of employed and unemployed male and female sample.

Source: Author's analysis

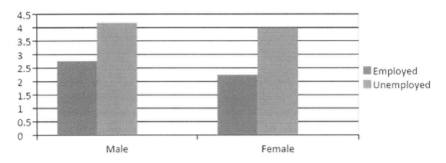

Figure 3.2 Standard Deviation of employed and unemployed male and female sample.

Source: Author's analysis

this situation into consideration, our study was conducted to look upon the matter of unemployment and psychological distress in young adults.

This study mainly focused on the rising levels of unemployment and the increasing levels of psychological distress in unemployed young adults. In this study, levels of psychological distress seemed to be high among unemployed people, but, besides that, we could not ignore the fact that psychological distress also existed in employed people as well. Due to COVID-19, many people have lost their jobs, and it is quite natural to think about the stress levels they are experiencing.

The mental health of the people observed by the researchers throughout this study has been devastated. The data consisted of those unemployed people who were being fired, or whose companies were totally shut, and who were thus in search of jobs, and their responses highlighted an increased level of psychological distress. From each response it was noted that the young adults in our sample group face certain difficulties in their daily life. Some people find difficulty in sitting still for some time due to stress, and others are drowning in waves of depression. It was very sad to see such differences between the levels of psychological distress in unemployed people, compared to those who are employed. In the present context we cannot hide the fact that those who are still currently working are also under a lot of pressure. Managing families as well as working from home is very difficult. Their fear of losing their employment is very high. The struggle of survival is real and cannot be denied when people are working day and night to save their jobs.

Arora and Vyas (2020) conducted a detailed diagnosis of work satisfaction indices in the Indian IT Sector during the COVID-19 period. According to the results, working conditions and coworker cohesion seemed to be the major factors leading to job satisfaction during COVID-19. Consistent employment has been a source of concern and discontent. This study shows that some level of distress exists among young adults who are also currently working under a lot of pressure.

Conclusion

The COVID-19 pandemic, as well as the current economic crisis, poses a serious threat to mental health. According to present economic estimates, India's and other countries' markets will take a considerable amount of time to recover and to regain stability. Furthermore, we may assume that other situational stress factors linked to the Coronavirus outbreak, such as risk of infection, concerns about elderly family members, and social constraints, could reinforce the correlation between unemployment and psychological distress. Most trained people and health professionals are aware of the risk of infection during the Coronavirus pandemic, the potential prevention steps one can take to avoid it, and the importance of social distancing and of the policy initiatives which have been taken to limit the spread of infection.

Limitations

This study is limited only to the IT sector and to the unemployed young working adults who lost their jobs in the IT sector during the pandemic. The study's sample size was small, and so there may be some difficulty in generalizing the results. Face to face interactions or interviews were not possible due to lockdowns, so the data collection was done only through Google Forms. Despite this, the researchers took a lot of care during the sampling and during the data collection procedure.

The present study involved only employed and unemployed young adults. Similar studies in the future may wish to include other sectors including a more vulnerable population. Similarly, subsequent studies may incorporate a larger sample group to increase accuracy and generalizability. In later studies, individuals belonging to states and cities from different parts of India may be included. Future research may also be conducted with the use of other variables such as depression, stigma, financial worry, job satisfaction, or being affected or having someone closely affected by COVID-19.

Reference

Ahad, M., Parry, Y. K., & Willis, E. (2020). Spillover trends of child labor during the coronavirus crisis-An unnoticed wake-up call. *Frontiers in Public Health*, 8, 488.

Arora, S., & Vyas, S. (2020). Job satisfaction at the time of COVID-19: An investigation of information technology sector in India. *Mukt Shabd Journal*, 9(9), 251–263.

Gautam, K., Adhikari, R. P., Gupta, A. S., Shrestha, R. K., Koirala, P., & Koirala, S. (2020). Self-reported psychological distress during the COVID-19 outbreak in Nepal: Findings from an online survey. *BMC Psychology*, *8*(1), 1–10.

Griffiths, D., Sheehan, L., van Vreden, C., Petrie, D., Grant, G., Whiteford, P., & Collie, A. (2021). The impact of work loss on mental and physical health during the COVID-19 pandemic: Baseline findings from a prospective cohort study. *Journal of Occupational\Rehabilitation*, *31*, 455–462.

Hannan, D. F., Riain, S. Ó., & Whelan, C. T. (1997). Youth unemployment and psychological distress in the Republic of Ireland. *Journal of Adolescence*, *20*(3), 307–320.

Joshi, S. (2020). Assessing the impact of COVID-19 lockdown on physical activity and psychological status in individuals of various age groups using Google forms. *International Journal of Health Sciences and Research*, *10*(10), 130–136.

Kokko, K., & Pulkkinen, L. (1998). Unemployment and psychological distress: Mediator effects. *Journal of Adult Development*, *5*(4), 205–217.

Saito, S., Tran, H. T. T., Qi, R., Suzuki, K., Takiguchi, T., Ishigami, K., & Takahashi, O. (2021). Psychological impact of the state of emergency over COVID-19 for non-permanent workers: A Nationwide follow-up study in Japan. *BMC Public Health*, *21*(1), 1–12.

Serraglio, A., Carson, N., & Ansari, Z. (2003). Comparison of health estimates between Victorian Population Health surveys and National Health surveys. *Australian and New Zealand Journal of Public Health*, *27*(6), 645–648.

Sinha, N. (2018). Understanding the effects of unemployment in Indian graduates: Psychological, financial and social perspectives. *Psychological Studies*, *63*(3), 315–324.

Chapter 4

Corporate Social Responsibility Practices in Small and Medium Indian Enterprises

Kalyani Gohain

Introduction

Corporate social responsibility and sustainability are two terms that are strong trends in the corporate world. A business cannot survive for very long if it pursues only its economic objectives. Businesses are an important part of society, and thus they must fulfill their social responsibilities to ensure their smooth functioning. A company needs to be accountable for its performance, for the effectiveness of its products, the performance of its supply chain, and the well-being of its employees. SMEs play a dynamic role in settling India's strategically important global position because of their contributions to its economic structure, contributions such as export, import, output, and employment. MSMEs contribute around 6.11% of India's manufacturing GDP and 24.63% of its GDP from service activities, as well as 33.4% of India's manufacturing output in FY 2019. MSMEs have become the second largest sector in India after the agricultural sector.

According to the United Nations Industrial Development Organization (UNIDO), corporate social responsibility (CSR) is a "management concept whereby companies integrate social and environmental concerns in their business operations and interactions with their stakeholders". This concept is clearly understood within the Triple Bottom Line Approach, which holds CSR as the means by which a company can achieve a balance between its economic, environmental and social imperatives.

Based on "Triple Bottom Line" perspectives, the three Ps of CSR are *People, Planet* and *Profit*.

1. People, or employee safety and commitment: employees are companies' ultimate assets. They should be committed to the company.
2. Planet, or environmental protection: companies should insist that each of their activities be eco-friendly, from imports to production and exports, as part of shouldering their responsibilities.
3. Sustainable profit: companies are focusing more on long-term profits than short-term profits, as they consider it to be more sustainable.

DOI: 10.4324/9781032640488-6

Approaches to CSR

CSR approaches vary from company to company based on their available resources, size, and corporate culture. Different approaches to CSR include:

1. Corporate Philanthropy: this approach involves companies gifting to charitable organizations. Gifting can involve donating money, products, or services to any social cause.
2. Cause-Related Marketing (CRM): this approach involves corporations associating sales of their product with donations or support to charitable organizations.
3. Environmental Sustainability: businesses are engaged in their environmental activities These activities include recycling, water management, waste management etc.
4. Social Entrepreneurship: this refers to a positive impact built into the mission of the company.
5. Community Involvement: this approach involves engaging people and contributing to their well-being.
6. Ethical Marketing: this approach suggests that companies that have marketed their products/services ethically have higher value to their customers.
7. Social Marketing: this approach involves using marketing techniques to pursue social goals.

SMEs in India

SMEs play a very important role in contributing to economic growth in terms of industrial employment, output, and exports (Vadera, 2013). SMEs are less capital-intensive and more labour-intensive. In accordance with the provisions of the Micro, Small and Medium Enterprises Development (MSMED) Act, 2006, Micro, Small and Medium Enterprises are classified in Table 4.1:

Drivers of CSR in SMEs

1. First, the Institutional environment influences the SME's environmental behavior in Dutch and British (Spence et al., 2000).
2. Second, SMEs are stakeholder-driven, focusing on how they can meet the expectations of their stakeholders (Massoud, 2010).
3. Third, the strongest external influences on SMEs are their institutional environments and pressure from their stakeholders. However, the most frequently cited factor regarding CSR and SMEs is the owners themselves. Owners possess more control over SMEs, and more autonomy regarding how they will operate their business (Besser, 2001; Fernandez, 2007; Jenkins, 2006).

Table 4.1 Classification of MSMEs

[SECTOR	Manufacturing
Enterprise category	**Investment in Plant and Machinery**
Micro Enterprises	Does not have 2.5 million rupees
Small Enterprises	Has more than 2.5 million but not more than 50 million rupees
Medium Enterprises	Has more than 50 million rupees but not more than 100 million rupees
SECTOR	**Service**
Enterprise category	**Investment in equipment**
Micro Enterprises	Does not have a million rupees
Small Enterprises	Has more than a million rupees but does not have more than 20 million rupees
Medium Enterprises	Has more than 20 million rupees but does not have more than 50 million rupees

Source: (MSME Annual Report, 2019–20)

Table 4.2 Estimated Number of MSMEs in India (by activity) According to the MSME Annual Report FY 2019-20

Activity category	Estimated number of enterprises (in lakhs)		
	Rural	Urban	Total
Manufacturing	114.14	82.50	196.65
Electricity	0.03	0.01	0.03
Trade	108.71	121.64	230.35
Other services	102	104.85	206.85
All	324.88	309	633.88

Source: (MSME Annual Report, 2019-20)

Table 4.3 Distribution of Enterprises by Category

Sector	Micro	Small	Medium	Total	Share
Rural	324.09	0.78	0.01	324.88	51
Urban	306.43	2.53	0.04	309.00	49
All	630.52	3.31	0.05	633.88	100

Source: (MSME Annual Report, 2019–20)

SMEs play a crucial role in triggering economic growth and development in India. The business activities of SMEs are generally performed closer to their stakeholders, thus allowing them to be first-hand witnesses to the needs expressed by them. Therefore, SMEs are continuously confronted by the need to participate actively in the development of their environments and to act ethically (UNIDO, 2008).

Table 4.4 Distribution of Estimated Number of MSMEs by State

Sl.no	State/UT	Estimated no. of MSME (No. in Lakhs)			
		Micro	Small	Medium	MSME
1	Andhra Pradesh	33.74	0.13	0.00	33.87
2	Arunachal Pradesh	0.22	0.00	0.00	0.23
	Assam	12.10	0.04	0.00	12.14
3	Bihar	34.41	0.04	0.00	34.46
4	Chhattisgarh	8.45	0.03	0.00	8.48
5	Delhi	9.25	0.11	0.00	9.36
6	Goa	0.70	0.00	0.00	0.70
7	Gujarat	32.67	0.50	0.00	33.1
8	Haryana	9.53	0.17	0.00	9.70
9	Himachal Pradesh	3.86	0.06	0.00	3.92
10	Jammu & Kashmir	7.06	0.03	0.00	7.09
11	Jharkhand	15.78	0.10	0.00	15.88
12	Karnataka	23.58	0.21	0.00	23.79
13	Kerala	23.58	0.21	0.00	23.79
14	Madhya Pradesh	26.42	0.31	0.01	26.74
15	Maharashtra	47.60	0.17	0.00	47.78
16	Manipur	1.80	0.00	0.00	1.80
17	Meghalaya	1.12	0.00	0.00	1.12
18	Mizoram	0.35	0.00	0.00	0.35
19	Nagaland	0.91	0.00	0.00	0.91
20	Odisha	19.80	0.04	0.00	19.84
21	Punjab	14.56	0.09	0.00	14.65
22	Rajasthan	26.66	0.20	0.01	26.87
23	Sikkim	0.26	0.00	0.00	0.26
24	Tamil Nadu	49.27	0.21	0.00	49.48
25	Telangana	25.94	0.10	0.01	26.05
26	Tripura	2.10	0.01	0.00	2.11
27	Uttar Pradesh	89.64	0.36	0.00	89.99
28	Uttarakhand	4.14	0.02	0.00	4.17
29	West Bengal	88.41	0.26	0.01	88.67
30	A & N Islands	0.19	0.00	0.00	0.19
31	Chandigarh	0.56	0.00	0.00	0.56
32	Dadra & Nagar Haveli	0.15	0.01	0.00	0.16
33	Daman & Diu	0.08	0.00	0.00	0.08
34	Lakshadweep	0.02	0.00	0.00	0.02
35	Puducherry	0.96	0.00	0.00	0.96
	TOTAL	630.52	3.31	0.05	633.88

Source: (MSME Annual Report, 2019–20)

SMEs contribute a very large proportion of the country's output, employment, and revenue generation. According to the latest data, SMEs account for 90% of the business worldwide and in total 50% to 60% of employment generation. It has a positive impact on social welfare. It is necessary to understand the role CSR plays in SMEs with regard to stakeholders and society (Parameshwara and Raghurama, 2013).

According to a study conducted by the European Commission in 2007 ("Corporate Social Responsibility in SMEs – SMEs Good Practice"), CSR can directly influence the competitiveness of SMEs, in various ways, such as by improving products, producing high customer loyalty and fully-motivated, innovative, and creative employees, reducing costs, increasing profitability through the optimal use of resources, enhancing business networking, and improving brand images. Thus, it is always advisable for the government to look into policies and legislations for the benefits of SMEs, thus adapting CSR and taking up initiatives aimed at encouraging SME involvement in CSR in ways that are easily accessible and relevant (Parameshwara and Raghurama, 2013).

In recent years, CSR in Indian SMEs has gained increased attention from practitioners, NGOs, and international agencies. In one comparative study, conducted on CSR practices in Dutch Multinationals and SMEs operating in India, it was discovered that large multinationals had already formulated CSR policies that were approachable to the public. CSR is not at all institutionalized in SMEs. The reasons for this failure to institutionalize CSR in SMEs include resource constraints, a lack of mandatory pressure from customers and NGOs, and the inability to see any benefit in doing CSR (Bains, 2013).

It has been discovered that SMEs in compliance with CSR have faced challenges in maintaining a balance between their environmental and social obligations. SMEs have limited resources and, with a view to lowering their financial burden and reducing operational costs, they have bridged the gap by conducting CSR activities collectively, pooling their available resources in the same geographical area.

Promoting CSR in SMEs

1. **Understanding CSR:** CSR approaches cannot be transferred to SMEs. SMEs practice "silent social responsibilities". They have a great understanding of their local cultural and political contexts. They have more links with civil society and a greater commitment to operating in a specific area. Ethically strong and philanthropic approaches are mostly exhibited by family-owned businesses.
2. **Benefits to SMEs:** some of the benefits include a closer alignment with consumer concerns, partnership opportunities with transnational companies, improvements in productivity, and an improved capacity for learning and innovation. Some of the benefits for SMEs in developing countries include upgrades to better technological quality, and the fact that management and marketing are more likely to be aligned with social and environmental impacts.
3. **Integration of a core business strategy:** the integration of CSR with core business strategies has proved to be a strong approach. Philanthropic approaches to CSR are more vulnerable to cost-cutting.

4. **Requirement of the global economy:** the global economy emphasizes the importance of CSR practices among global firms and their suppliers, including SMEs that form part of the supply/value chain. There are risks for enterprises that do not adhere to socially responsible ways of doing business, including practices related to managing environmental impacts, compliance with labour standards, and the like. Global firms are encouraged to mandate the adoption of CSR practices among their suppliers, mostly in developing economies. There are many benefits offered by global firms in terms of access to business opportunities.
5. **Meeting the needs of large firms:** SMEs have problems meeting the standards of large firms in terms of quality, quantity, and reliability. These problems are due to the constraints faced by SMEs in terms of improving their competitiveness: little access to capital, technology, markets, and cheaper inputs; inadequate infrastructure; regulatory barriers; governance gaps; and burdensome taxation.
6. **Sustainability and competitiveness of large firms:** SMEs are the only potential solution providers to large firms. Many firms believe that improving the competitiveness of SMEs would lead to improvements in the competitiveness of large firms. CSR initiatives in SMEs are still modest and advocates for the construction of such initiatives are likely necessary to increase involvement. (Parameshwara and Raghurama, 2013)

Conclusion

The adoption of CSR is a must for SMEs; it will benefit them in terms of improved products and services, greater customer loyalty and satisfaction, and more satisfied and loyal employees, resulting in improved creativity and innovation. CSR is turning out to be a competitive tool, and we are seeing a shift toward its being made mandatory. The involvement of SMEs in societal development activities through CSR will help them to build their public image, networking opportunities, and profitability. CSR activities can help increase the survival rates of SMEs and offer great opportunities for competitive business. Involvement in CSR activities will help in developing an entrepreneurial foundation across the whole nation by supporting enterprises through the supplychain and production. Voluntary CSR could be an opportunity for SMEs if it were to lead toward a re-channelling of corporate power and thus address the systematic problems of the overall economy. More opportunities are open to SMEs involved in societal developmental activities. The government need to look after the policies and legislations which help SMEs adopt CSR, and incorporate initiatives that are aimed at encouraging SMEs to get involved in CSR activities.

According to the Companies Act 2013, Section 135, which says CSR is mandatory in all companies with a net worth over 20 million, there is no specific CSR policy for SMEs in India, and their contribution toward CSR is not clearly visible. It is the duty of all SMEs to make CSR practices mandatory, both for the sustainability of their businesses, and for the general development of society. CSR in SMEs is an issue to pay attention to as there is no legal requirement for CSR practices.

References

Besser, T. (2001). Is the good corporation dead? The community social responsibility of small. *The Journal of Socio-Economics, 30*, 221–241.

Dr. Anupama Bains, A. T. (2013, October). A study of Indian CSR Practices in Small and Medium enterprises. *Indian Journal of Advanced Research in Management and Social Sciences, 2*, 92–103.

Fernandez, J. D. (2007). The collaborative creation of a strategic stakeholder. *Corporate Governance, 7*, 524–533.

Jenkins, H. (2006). Small business champions for corporate social responsibility. *Journal of Business Ethics*, 241–256.

Massoud, J. (2010). *Exploring small and medium enterprise social responsibility in Argentina*. New Mexico State University.

Parameshwara, & Raghurama, D. A. (2013, July). CSR and SME's in India. *Indian Journal of Research, 2*, 22–25.

Report, U. S. (2008). UNIDO. Retrieved from UNIDO: http://www.unido.org /fileadmin /user_media/Services/PSD

Spence et al. (2000). Communication about ethics with small firms: Experience from the U.K. *Business Ethics Quarterly, 27*, 945–965.

Vadera, S. K. (2013). Role of SMEs sector in the emerging Indian. *International Journal of Advanced Research in Management and Social Sciences*, 92–102.

Chapter 5

Green Finance – Integral Adaptation to Climate Change

Ajanta Ghosh and Sujit Dutta

Introduction

Climate change is not a new phenomenon. The earth's temperature and climate have been changing significantly over the past millions of years. Climate change not only impacts the environment, but is also detrimental to the economic and social aspects of sustainable development (OECD, 2009). According to the latest research from the Intergovernmental Panel on Climate Change (IPCC), time is running out to make the transformations necessary to avoid the worst impacts of climate change. According to the estimates of the World Bank in 2018, three regions (Latin America, sub-Saharan Africa, and Southeast Asia) will generate 143 million more climate migrants by 2050[1]. Deepa and Parvin (2011) note that the impact of GHG emissions on climate change will severely affect the tropical areas, which mainly consist of developing countries, including India. Therefore, addressing climate change is possibly one of the most demanding issues facing our planet and its inhabitants – hence the relevance of sustainable practices, which have become essential from both an economic and a social perspective. The ongoing COVID-19 pandemic has forced the human race to switch to sustainable practices all the more in order to conserve mother nature.

Our literature review on green finance includes some reports from international organizations and academic publications that played an important role in giving shape and promotion of the green finance agenda. Green finance, which is also known as "sustainable finance", "environmental finance", "climate finance", or "green investment" (Frimpong et al., 2020), refers to an increase in the level of financial flows (from banking and other financial institutions) moving from profitable "business as usual" (BAU) investments to sustainable development priorities. Zhang et al. (2019) consider green finance in the general context. World Bank assistance may be discontinued for all corporations and nations not making the protection of the environment an equal priority (Urban & Wójcik, 2019; Zhang et al., 2019). The Chinese Central Bank has developed and implemented regulations to guide green finance transactions in the banking sector (Liu et al., 2019). In many

DOI: 10.4324/9781032640488-7

nations, national banking regulatory bodies and central banks have accepted the need for developing and implementing green finance policies (Durrani et al., 2020). Many Central banks now require banks to attain green certifications, green credit scores, and scores for environmental innovation and social inclusion (Chen et al., 2019; Dikau and Volz., 2021). Though a large number of banks in different parts of the world realize the importance of green finance to support green growth, this being the need of the hour, they have been quite lackadaisical with regard to the development of financial products on green finance. Consequently, green finance is yet to be implemented in many regions across the globe to foster sustainable and green financing projects. (Frimpong et al., 2020).

Green finance – Growing international interest

Changes in the global environment caused by climate change increasingly challenge business around the world. Companies around the world are increasingly realizing that a proactive and diverse strategy is needed to address this global change, and that the promotion of sustainability has become a key focus for businesses (Dutta, 2017). The environment can be notably protected by changing business as usual (BAU) practices to sustainable business practices. Dutta (2016) suggests that business houses across the world are gradually becoming aware of their stakes in society and are engaging in various social and environmental activities, and green growth is therefore becoming crucial in the current climate change scenario.

Along with a shift from the BAU model of brown investment to sustainable investment aimed at ensuring climate change mitigation and sustainable growth, all actors across the financial system including global financial institutions, banks, institutional investors, market-makers such as rating agencies and stock exchanges, as well as central banks and financial regulatory authorities, need to be aligned, and should come up with favourable policies.

Usually financial institutions prefer fossil fuel projects over green projects, mainly because there are still several risks associated with these new technologies and their rate of return is relatively low. In order to achieve sustainable growth, it is of the utmost importance that new green projects are encouraged and that all financial institutions come up with new financial instruments and new policies, such as green bonds, green banks, carbon market instruments, fiscal policies, municipal-based green funds, etc., which can be called "green finance".

Green finance can be described as structured financial arrangements that are specifically used for projects that are environmentally sustainable or projects that tackle aspects of climate change. Sharif and Vijay (2018) emphasize that all nations, irrespective of development, should make endeavours toward green, and state that worldwide green financing will reach $40 trillion between 2012 and 2030. These financial investments will involve the reduction of greenhouse gas (GHG) emissions, industrial pollution control, or biodiversity protection. The green finance market includes market-oriented mechanisms and financial products that can support environmentally sustainable projects, such as the production of energy from renewable sources like solar power, wind power, biogas, etc.; clean transportation with lower greenhouse gas emissions; energy-efficient projects like green buildings; waste management practices including recycling, efficient disposal, and conversion to energy, etc.

The government of India had an ambitious target of producing 175 GW of renewable energy by 2022, 100 GW of which was to come from solar energy, 10 GW from bio-power, 60 GW from wind energy, and 5 GW from small hydropower projects (UN, Sustainable Development Goals).

Methods

The Paris Agreement is a legally binding international treaty on climate change. The Paris Agreement's central aim is to strengthen the global response to global warming, so as to limit it to well below 2, preferably to 1.5 degrees Celsius, as compared to pre-industrial levels. If the Paris Agreement is to be implemented, it requires a social transformation in the financial market also. Green bonds allow investors to invest in sustainable projects and this paper attempts to improve general knowledge of green finance opportunities and of their potential contribution to reaching the Paris target.

With the above objectives in view, this study has been conducted on the basis of available conceptual and empirical studies on green finance and how companies are following it in the field of green business opportunities. Regarding the sources of these data, the study has used secondary data, e.g., literature surveys as included in journals, magazines, books, newspapers, and various websites.

Results and Discussions

Green Bond – A definition with some degree of elasticity

One common green finance instrument is the green bond. To qualify for this title, a bond must adhere to criteria on the use of proceeds, have a process for project evaluation and selection, ensure proper management of any proceeds, and offer detailed reporting. The development of green stocks and bonds is conducive to the function of optimizing the allocation of resources in the capital market and serving the real economy (Yuan & Gallagher, 2018). Stock markets emphasize the development of green bonds, an acceleration of the innovation of green index products, and a deepening of international cooperation in green finance (Frimpong et al., 2020).

The term "green bond" refers to a type of fixed-income financial instrument for raising capital through debt capital market where the issuer publicly states that the purpose of raising capital is to fund green projects, assets, or business activities with an environmental benefit like the generation of energy from renewable sources, energy efficiency, clean transportation, the reduction of carbon emissions, sustainable water projects, etc.

In order to qualify as a green bond, the International Capital Market Association (ICMA) has recommended four core components under its Green Bond Principles:

a) The proceeds from the bond must be used for green projects.
b) They must maintain transparency in managing the proceeds.
c) A detailed description must be given of the process adopted for project evaluation and selection.
d) They must enable the reporting of information pertaining to the use of the proceeds.

The Securities and Exchange Board of India (SEBI) notified a circular on 30th May 2017, providing the disclosure requirements for the issuance and listing of green bonds in India. According to the circular, a green bond is defined as a debt security that is to be used for projects or assets fulfilling any of the following criteria:

a) For generating renewable and sustainable energy including solar, wind, bioenergy, and other sources of energy which use clean technology, etc.
b) For climate change adaptation.
c) For clean public transportation.
d) For sustainable water management which includes clean and/or drinking water, water recycling, etc.
e) For energy efficiency, which includes efficient and green buildings, etc.
f) For sustainable waste management including recycling, reuse, and the efficient disposal of waste, etc.
g) For sustainable land use, including sustainable forestry, afforestation, and sustainable agriculture, etc.
h) For biodiversity conservation.
i) For any other category as may be notified by SEBI.

Lately, green bonds have gained huge popularity globally and are seen as an attractive opportunity to both investors and corporations looking at funding through debt capital.

A Growing Market

The global issuance of green bonds crossed $250 billion in 2019 – about 3.5% of total global bond issuance ($7.15 trillion). It is estimated that sustainable

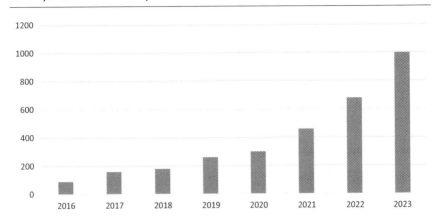

Figure 5.1 A forecast of Green Bond issuance to reach 1 Trillion by 2023 (Amount in US$ Billion).

Source: Author's creation

bond issuance globally will hit a record high of $450 billion this year, and there is a forecast of issuance surpassing $1 trillion in 2023.

Globally, the developed economies have contributed largely to the issuance of green bonds. Among the emerging economies, India stands at second position, next to China, in the cumulative emerging market of Green Bond Issuance, 2012-2020.

Since its first issuance of a green bond by Yes Bank in 2015, India has emerged as the second largest green bond market, with $7.2 billion in issuance. The majority of the green bonds issued since 2015 had maturities of five years or above, but of less than 10 years.

Again ReNew Power Pvt. Ltd. issued green bonds with a maturity period of less than 5 years in 2019. About 76% of the green bonds issued in India since 2015 were denominated in US$. India has, however, witnessed a mixed response to green bonds. In order to develop the green bond

Table 5.1 Some of the Issuers who Have Issued Green Bonds with a Maturity Period of Ten Years or More

Year of issue	Name of issuer
2017, 2019	Indian Renewable Energy Development Agency Ltd.
2017	Rural Electrification Corporation Limited or REC Ltd.
2017	Power Finance Corporation Ltd.
2017	Indian Railway Finance Corporation Ltd.
2019	Adani Renewable Energy Ltd.

Source: Author's creation

market significantly, India needs to take steps to incentivize it at the earliest opportunity.

While Indian corporations raised close to $4.96 billion through sustainable bonds, including green bonds, in the first half of 2021, the major issuers of green bonds in India have primarily been public banks, private banks, public sector power companies, and some clean energy companies. But the green bond market holds tremendous opportunities for other sets of users, specifically municipal bodies, which is evident in the global context as well. Municipal bonds, or "Muni", as they are called, have been a key source of urban financing in countries like the United States, Germany, Sweden, and other European countries. The US municipal green bond market stood at $4.1 billion in 2015 and $2.4 billion in 2014. US municipal green-labelled debt will continue to grab a larger share of the municipal market in 2021, increasing from 3.4% of total municipal issuance in 2020 to 4.1% in 2021 (S&P Global Ratings). On average, sustainable debt's share of total municipal market issuances increased by 51% per year from 2014 through 2020.

As India moves toward urbanisation, with more than 590 million people expected to be living in cities by 2030, urban infrastructure financing is of significant importance. It is estimated that between 2012 and 2031, India will need to invest INR 39,187 billion ($653 billion), to meet its urban infrastructure requirements. In spite of this estimate, India's municipal expenditure has remained low, while it should be growing. The issue of municipal bonds could be the answer to this municipal fund crunch (Chaturvedi, 2017 March)

A Municipal Corporation in India is the urban local government that works for the development of any city with a population of more than one million (World Green Building Council). The metropolitan cities – Delhi, Mumbai, Kolkata, Chennai, Bangalore, Hyderabad, Pune, Jaipur and Ahmedabad – have the largest municipal corporations (Chaturvedi, 2017)

Municipal bonds were first issued in India in the year 1997. The first urban local body to issue municipal bonds was the Bangalore Municipal Corporation. Ahmedabad followed Bangalore in the following years. Since municipal bonds lost ground after the initial investors' attraction, and failed to raise the amount of funds necessary to revive it, SEBI came up with guidelines for the issue of municipal bonds in 2015 (Municipal bonds: Definition, how they work & taxability, 2021, August 02)

A municipality should meet the following criteria to issue municipal bonds in India:

a) The municipality must not have had a negative net worth in each of the three previous years.
b) The municipality must have no default in the repayment of debt securities and loans availed from banks or non-banking financial companies in the last year.

Table 5.2 List of Indian Cities that have Issued Municipal Bonds

City	Amount (In crores)
Amravati	Rs. 2000
Vishakhapatnam	Rs. 80
Ahmedabad	Rs. 200
Surat	Rs. 200
Bhopal	Rs. 175
Indore	Rs. 140
Pune	Rs. 495
Hyderabad	Rs. 200
Lucknow	Rs. 200

Source: Author's creation

c) The municipality, promoter, and directors must not be listed among the wilful defaulters published by the Reserve Bank of India (RBI). The municipality should have no record of default in the payment of interest and repayment of principal with respect to debt instruments.

Nine Indian cities have issued Municipal Bonds so far, as mentioned in Table 5.2.

With the launch of national missions such as the Smart Cities Mission, the Swachh Bharat Mission, and the National Solar Mission, the prevalence of projects that would be eligible for municipal green bonds is increasing. Though the municipal bond market in India is still at a nascent stage, there are several advantages for municipal corporations in issuing green bonds. Some of these are that green bonds expand the quantum of clean energy finance and broaden investor base; green bonds are cost competitive and thus provide access to low cost, long-term capital; green bonds increase liquidity and propagate green investment by enabling refinancing; and that green bonds create investment opportunities to meet climate commitments (NRDC: Green India's Financial Market, 2016 April)

Case Study
Ghaziabad Nagar Nigam

In India, Ghaziabad Nagar Nigam became the first to issue Green Municipal Bonds and list them on BSE in April, 2021. Ghaziabad Municipal Corporation is a civic body in Uttar Pradesh, that has raised Rs 1.5 billion by issuing green bonds, the proceeds going toward a tertiary sewage and water treatment plant, which in turn will benefit industries in Ghaziabad. Moreover, in order to achieve various goals related to the water supply, the Ghaziabad Municipal Corporation has entered into an understanding with Sahibabad

Industries Association. An incentive of Rs 195 million from the Union government was received by the municipal corporation for raising funds through municipal bonds. According to the corporation, the bonds got oversubscribed, with bids worth over Rs 4.01 billion. According to Mahender Singh Tawar, the Municipal Commissioner of the GMC, the oversubscription happened within minutes on the bid date at the competitive coupon rate of 8.10%, which is one of the lowest of any municipal bonds in India. He also added that the capital raised would enforce financial discipline and give a path-breaking lead to the corporation for bigger fundraising in the future. Even foreign institutional investors are looking at this new means of funding Indian municipalities. AK Capital Services Ltd and HDFC Bank Ltd were the merchant bankers to the bond issue (Financial Express, 8 April 2021; Economic Times report, 8 April 2021). Ashish Chauhan, MD and CEO of the BSE, said that this listing would develop the green bond market for urban local bodies. He also said that the Bombay Stock Exchange could now be used as a platform by urban local bodies to raise funds (The Economic Times E-Paper, 8 April 2021).

Lucknow Municipal Corporation

Even in the context of COVID-19, the Lucknow Municipal Corporation issued INR 2 billion in municipal bonds and got it listed at the BSE on 2nd December 2020. Lucknow became the 9th city to raise municipal bonds, incentivized by the Ministry of Housing and Urban Affairs (MOHUA) under the auspices of the AMRUT (Atal Mission for Rejuvenation and Urban Transformation). The total issue of INR 1 billion attracted considerable investor interest and received bids totalling INR 450 crores from 21 investors. It closed at a coupon rate of 8.5% for a ten-year bond, which might be observed as a record during the COVID-19 pandemic. The investor demand for good quality and well-structured municipal bonds is here made evident. India Ratings has rated this bond issue from Lucknow Municipal Corporation as "AA", and it was rated "AA (CE)" by Brickwork Ratings. It was proposed that the proceeds of this issue should be invested in a water supply project being implemented under the Government of India's AMRUT scheme, and in a housing project. Lucknow Municipal Corporation was to get 260 million to subsidize its interest burden. The clear support shown by the government of Uttar Pradesh for this issue will show the way for other local bodies in India to raise funds through the issue of municipal bonds (PIB Delhi, 2020).

Conclusion

A continuous effort is required to standardize the issuance of green bonds through the development of a common green bond framework which will attract more issuers and investors, thus scaling up the green bond market. Despite the growth of the green bond market, there is a serious need to reinforce confidence in it, and to gain a better understanding of this asset. In order to strengthen confidence among potential investors, clear standards are needed, especially in taxonomy, certification, and regulation.

Note

1 Kumari Rigaud, Kanta, Alex de Sherbinin, Bryan Jones, Jonas Bergmann, Viviane Clement, Kayly Ober, Jacob Schewe, Susana Adamo, Brent McCusker, Silke Heuser, and Amelia Midgley. 2018. Groundswell: Preparing for Internal Climate Migration. The World Bank Pg 2. https://openknowledge.worldbank.org/handle/10986/29461

References

Chen, S., Huang, Z., Drakeford, B. M., & Failler, P. (2019). Lending interest rate, loaning scale, and government subsidy scale in green innovation. *Energies*, *12*(23), 4431.
https://www.scopus.com/inward/record.uri?eid=2-s2.0-85076112301&doi=10.3390%2Fen12234431&partnerID =40&md5=22d0e368b008d47164941e060e2ed4b5

Chaturvedi, A. (2017). *GIZ_Green_Municipal_Bond_eReport*. https://www.niua.org/csc/assets/pdf/RepositoryData/UP_Green_Cover/GIZ_Green_Municipal_Bonds_eReport.pdf

Deepa, L. R., & Parvin, N. (2011). *Impact of Climate change and adaptation to green technology in India*. IEEE Xplore.

Dikau , & Volz. (2021). Central bank mandates, sustainability objectives and the promotion of green finance

Durrani, A., Rosmin, M., & Volz, U. (2020). The role of central banks in scaling up sustainable finance–what do monetary authorities in the Asia-Pacific region think? *Journal of Sustainable Finance and Investment*, *10*(2), 92–112.

Dutta, S. (2016). Green Growth Initiatives: A pathway to Corporate Social Responsibility. *ICTAT Journal of Management Studies*, *2*(3), 342–348.

Dutta, S. (2017). A pathway to green growth and green business – Some evidences of Indian companies. *Siddhant- A Journal of Decision Making*, *17*(4), 263–270.

Frimpong,I. , Adeabahb, D. , Ofosuc, D. , & Tenakwaha, T. (2020). A review of studies on green finance of banks, research gaps and future directions. *Journal of Sustainable Finance and Investment*. https://doi.org/10.1080/20430795.2020.1870202

Liu, R., Wang, D., Zhang, L., & Zhang, L. (2019). Can green financial development promote regional ecological efficiency? A case study of China. *Natural Hazards*, *95*(1–2), 325–341.

Municipal bonds: Definition, How they Work & taxability. (2021, August 02). https://cleartax.in/s/municipal-bonds-all-you-need-to-know

https://www.nrdc.org/sites/default/files/india-financial-market-green-bonds-report.pdf

OECD. (2009). *Integrating climate change adaptation into development cooperation: Policy guidance*. OECD.

Press Information Bureau (2020, December 02). https://pib.gov.in/PressReleseDetail.aspx?PRID=1677604

Sharif, M., & Vijay, K. (2018). Green finance: A step towards sustainable development. https://www.spglobal.com/ratings/en/products-benefits/products/sustainable-financing-opinions.

The Economic Times E-Paper (2021, April 8). Ghaziabad Municipal Corp. Lists First Green Bonds. https://m.economictimes.com/markets/stocks/news/ghaziabad-municipal-corp-lists-first-green-bonds/articleshow/81974055.cms

UN, Sustainable Development Goals. https://sustainabledevelopment.un.org/partnership/?p=34566

Urban, M. A., & Wójcik, D. (2019). Dirty banking: Probing the gap in sustainable finance. *Sustainability*, *11*(6), 1745. https://www.scopus.com/inward/record.uri?eid=2-s2.0-85063488316&doi=10.3390%2fsu11061745&partnerID=40&md5=8b1fad1175a8609ebf922291a107529c

Yuan, F., & Gallagher, K. P. (2018). Greening development lending in the Americas: Trends and determinants. *Ecological Economics*, *154*, 189–200. https://www.scopus.com/inward/record.uri?eid=2-s2.0-85051392760&doi=10.1016%2fj.ecolecon.2018.07.009&partnerID=40&md5=2a857d76168179e4237e7ad539fa9292

Zhang, D., Zhang, Z., & Managi, S. (2019). A bibliometric analysis on green finance: Current status, development, and future directions. *Finance Research Letters*, *29*, 425–430.

Chapter 6

Impact of the MGNREGA on Women's Empowerment in the Light of Social Sustainability – A Study on Selective Areas of West Bengal in India

Mohua Das Mazumdar and Sajal Mondal

Introduction

In 2015, the United Nations identified seventeen sustainable development goals (SDGs). One aspect of these is social sustainability, which aims to do away with problems like poverty, hunger, gender inequality, social injustice, and poor public health, to name a few. It is of real importance, as it makes a positive contribution to society. Social sustainability provides better opportunities for all people and, when it is practised alongside economic and environmental sustainability, it can demolish social inequality and lead to a reduction in poverty. Social sustainability is mostly defined as the systems and structures that support current and future generations in creating healthy, prospering communities by considering the principles of equity, human rights, diversity, security, quality of life, and citizen engagement (Boström, 2012; Ajmal et al., 2018). The concept of social sustainability is associated with the needs, rights, and well-being of the local community, and it is instrumental in achieving different aspects of empowerment, decision making, and governance (Boström, 2012).

To ensure a fair means of livelihood and generate employment for people in need, the Government of India adopted the Mahatma Gandhi National Rural Employment Guarantee Act (MGNREGA). The MGNREGA aimed to provide wages for 100 days to members of the rural population who wanted to earn by means of unskilled manual work, irrespective of their caste, creed or sex. The MGNREGA is actually a scheme taken up as part of the Eleventh Five-Year Plan in all the states of India. Under this scheme, women have unveiled themselves and, apart from managing their households, have started participating in the scheme. Since its inception, the scheme has proved to be well and widely accepted. Interdependent with these thoughts, the concept of empowerment refers to the improvement of one's ability to make strategic life choices in a context where this ability was previously denied (Perry, 2020). The concept of the empowerment of women is multidimensional, and includes economic, financial, social, political, legal, sociological,

DOI: 10.4324/9781032640488-8

and psychological factors (Hirway and Mahadevia, 1996; Mehta, 1996). In conformity with the United Nations' approach to social sustainability, women's empowerment aims to change a society that confines women's power, and allow them access to one that enriches their power in terms of (i) women's awareness, competence and self-confidence in transforming their lives; (ii) their decision making authority within their households, communities, and local economies; (iii) their access to and control over assets, including health care, education, and money; and (iv) their capability to promote their own interests (Cornwall, 2016; Taylor & Pereznieto, 2014; Rocheleau et al., 2013). In the context of social sustainability, an attempt has been made in this study to examine the impact of the MGNREGA on women's empowerment in the district of Purba Bardhaman, in West Bengal. Kumar et al. (2021) have studied the impact of the MGNREGA among its beneficiaries in the district of Hardoi, in Uttar Pradesh. The authors concluded that the MGNREGA provides a source of income for village people. SS (2020) conducted a study in Anad Grama Panchayat to understand the social life of women workers associated with the MGNREGA. According to the author, the MGNREGA changed the socio-economic dynamics of Anad Grama Panchayat, and the scheme contributed to the empowerment of women workers in rural areas. Chaturvedi et al. (2019) examined the impact of MNREGA on women's empowerment in the Faizabad district of Uttar Pradesh. According to the authors, the constraints on women's empowerment are the non-issue of job cards within 15 days of application, non-assurance of the 100 days' wage employment, and a lack of facilities such as water, shade, and medicine at worksites, etc. In her study, Rajalakshmi (2017) examined women's empowerment, its issues and challenges, and the impact of the MGNREGA scheme in India from 2005 to 2015. The author opines that the MGNREGA scheme has economically empowered women, as well as rendering them more independent and improving their lifestyles. Ravinder (2016) tried to study the relationship between women's empowerment and the MGNREGA in the state of Telangana. The study highlighted the social and economic aspects of women job seekers in the context of the MGNREGA. The study showed that there was a 30% increase in the incomes of the respondents due to employment provided by the MGNREGAS. Xavier and Mari (2014) conclude that the income and expenditure of the households of women residing in the Sivaganga area of the state of Tamil Nadu, and who were beneficiaries of the scheme, were higher in comparison to that of the households of women not working under the MGNREGA scheme. The study also revealed that the women working under the scheme enjoyed greater independence with regard to decision making than their counterparts. Avanya and Mahima (2013) concluded that the MGNREGA economically empowered women and laid the basis for greater independence and self-esteem. The enactment of the scheme improved the living conditions of the women featured in the study, which laid the path for their empowerment as well.

Methods

The Purba Bardhaman district of the state of West Bengal has been chosen for the purposes of our study, as this district is considered the best performing according to the State Employment Guarantee Council. Accordingly, the impact of this programme has been studied in the district of Purba Bardhaman over the time period 2018–2019 to 2019–2020. There are twenty-three blocks in Purba Bardhaman. There are a total of 215 gram panchayats operating under these twenty-three blocks. 30% of the gram panchayats have been selected randomly from each block, and from each gram panchayat a list of job card holders has been prepared by classifying them into beneficiaries with working job cards and non-beneficiaries with non-working job cards. Ten beneficiaries and ten non-beneficiaries have been chosen from each of the selected gram panchayats, making up a random sample of 460 respondents to be considered in this study. Primary data have been collected from these 460 respondents through personal interviews. Our secondary data on different aspects of women's empowerment have also been collected from the official website of the MGNREGA.

In order to assess the impact of the MGNREGA on women's empowerment, our study follows the impact evaluation methodology of the World Bank (2011). The difference between the mean outcome of the randomly assigned beneficiary group and the mean outcome of the randomly assigned non-beneficiary group constitutes the true impact of the MGNREGA on women's empowerment.

Following the study by Laha and Kuri (2014), we consider only three dimensions of the empowerment of women – economic, financial, and social – and the following proportional measures are used in our study:

Proportional Measure of the Economic Empowerment of Women (EEW) = ((Women beneficiaries (or non-beneficiary) members of the panchayats)/(Total women beneficiary (or non-beneficiary) members of the blocks))/((Number of women households of the panchayats)/(Total women households of the block))

Proportional Measure of the Economic Empowerment of Women (EEW)

$$= \frac{\text{women beneficiaries members of the panchayats to total women beneficiary(or non-beneficiary) members of the blocks}}{\text{Number of women households of the panchayats to total women households of the block}}$$

Proportional Measure of the Financial Empowerment of Women (FEW) = ((Number of bank accounts of women beneficiary (or non-beneficiary) members of the panchayats)/(Total women beneficiary (or non-beneficiary) members of the blocks))/((Number of women households of the panchayats)/(Total women households of the block))

$$= \frac{\text{number of bank accounts of women beneficiary (or non-beneficiary) members of the panchayats to total women beneficiary (or non-beneficiary) members of the blocks}}{\text{Number of women households of the panchayats to total women households of the block}}$$

Proportional Measure of Social Empowerment of Women (SEW) = ((Number of literate women beneficiary (or non-beneficiary) members of the panchayats)/(Total women beneficiary (or non-beneficiary) members of the blocks))/((Number of women households of the panchayats)/(Total women households of the block))

$$= \frac{\text{Number of literate women beneficiary (or non-beneficiary) members of the panchayats to total women beneficiary (or non-beneficiary) members of the blocks}}{\text{Number of women households of the panchayats to total women households of the block}}$$

Results and discussions

After computing the three dimensions of women's empowerment in the selected gram panchayats, the computed figures have been averaged to find the three dimensions of women's empowerment in each of the twenty-three blocks of the district of Purba Bardhaman, and the computed results regarding the economic empowerment of women, the financial empowerment of women, and the social empowerment of women are presented in Table 6.1, Table 6.2 and Table 6.3 respectively.

From Table 6.1, it can be observed that the F-test values are significant, reaching either 1% or 5% in sixteen blocks, and for seven blocks the F-test values are not statistically significant. Accordingly, a t-test has been applied under the conditions of equality of variances and inequality of variances to test the mean differences between beneficiaries and non-beneficiaries in terms of the economic empowerment of women. With regard to the economic empowerment of women, it is observed that the mean average ratio for the beneficiaries is greater than that of the non-beneficiaries in all the twenty-three blocks of the district of Purba Bardhaman, but the mean difference between these two groups is statistically significant either at 1% or 5% in sixteen blocks, and the t-test values are not significant for seven blocks. This implies that the women are economically empowered in most of the

Table 6.1 The Dimension of Economic Empowerment as Compared between Beneficiaries and Non- Beneficiaries

Dimension of Women's Empowerment	Blocks in the Purba Bardhaman District	Beneficiaries	Non- Beneficiaries	t-test for mean difference	F-test for equality of variance
Economic Empowerment of Women	Ausgram-1	0.75	0.45	-3.219***	-4.329***
	Ausgram-2	0.60	0.19	-3.324***	5.215***
	Bhatar	0.10	0.03	-2.858**	4.832**
	Burdwan-1	0.78	0.77	-1.32	1.326
	Burdwan-2	0.86	0.79	-1.76	1.765
	Galsi-1	0.08	0.03	-2.941**	4.965***
	Galsi-2	0.35	0.04	-2.873**	4.542**
	Jamalpur	0.27	0.15	-3.941***	5.125***
	Kalna-1	0.35	0.27	-2.231**	-4.291***
	Kalna--2	0.54	0.42	-2.361***	-4.421***
	Katwa-1	0.41	0.39	-3.218***	-3.248***
	Katwa--2	0.56	0.45	-1.62	-1.02
	Ketugram-1 ketugram-2	0.61	0.57	-1.39	-1.86
	Khandaghosh	0.31	0.34	-2.293**	-3.242***
	Monteswar	0.24	0.25	-2.165**	-2.381**
	Memari-1	0.54	0.51	-2.582***	-3.461***
	Memari-2 Mongolkote	0.82	0.78	2.741**	-2.371**
	Purbasthali-1	0.76	0.64	-3.265***	-2.113**
	Purbasthali-2	0.51	0.43	-3.412***	-3.179***
	Raina-1	0.42	0.35	-2.438***	-2.325***
	Raina-2	0.45	0.39	-0.82	-1.567
		0.59	0.52	-0.98	-1.983
		0.51	0.48	-1.91	-1.942

Note: *** indicates significance at 1% and ** indicates significance at 5%.
Source: Author's calculations

Impact of MGNREGA on Women's Empowerment 57

Table 6.2 The Dimension of Financial Empowerment as Compared between Beneficiaries and Non- Beneficiaries

Dimension of Women's Empowerment	Blocks in the Purba Bardhaman District	Beneficiaries	Non- Beneficiaries	t-test for mean difference	F-test for equality of variance
Financial Empowerment of Women	Ausgram-1	0.45	0.44	1.323	1.387
	Ausgram-2	0.65	0.20	-3.231**	4.975**
	Bhatar	0.15	0.07	-2.821**	4.164**
	Burdwan-1	0.87	0.89	1.321	1.549
	Burdwan-2	0.28	0.16	-3.121***	5.216***
	Galsi-1	0.22	0.12	-2.987**	4.328**
	Galsi-2	0.29	0.14	-2.881**	4.850**
	Jamalpur	0.25	0.17	-3.112***	5.438***
	Kalna-1	0.43	0.47	1,650	1.098
	Kalna--2	0.49	0.42	1.541	1.437
	Katwa-1	0.75	0.63	-4.254***	3.541**
	Katwa--2	0.35	0.27	-3.761***	3.298**
	Ketugram-1 ketugram-2	0.76	0.69	1.675	1.327
	Khandaghosh	0.45	0.36	-2.561**	3.642**
	Monteswar	0.41	0.32	-3.247**	3.671**
	Memari-1	0.39	0.24	-3.677**	3.881**
	Memari-2 Mongolkote	0.55	0.47	-2.341**	3.463**
	Purbasthali-1	0.39	0.27	1,341	1.348
	Purbasthali-2	0.45	0.41	-2.452***	2.296**
	Raina-1	0.72	0.69	-3.457***	3.328**
	Raina-2	0.58	0.62	-3.481***	3.250**
		0.72	0.75	-1.639	1.438
		0.69	0.73	-1.517	1.238

Note: Author's calculations
Source: Own calculations

58 Mohua Das Mazumdar and Sajal Mondal

Table 6.3 The Dimension of Social Empowerment as Compared between Beneficiaries and Non-Beneficiaries

Dimension of Women's Empowerment	Blocks in the Purba Bardhaman District	Beneficiaries	Non-Beneficiaries	t-test for mean difference	F-test for equality of variance
Social Empowerment of Women	Ausgram-1	0.45	0.34	-2.541**	3.367***
	Ausgram-2	0.59	0.23	-2.987**	5.841**
	Bhatar	0.20	0.09	-2.769**	4.539**
	Burdwan-1	0.47	0.45	2.976**	3.676***
	Burdwan-2	0.55	0.49	-2.742**	5.532***
	Galsi-1	0.13	0.05	-2.779**	4.972**
	Galsi-2	0.22	0.06	-2.801**	4.439**
	Jamalpur	0.19	0.07	-3.429***	5.981***
	Kalna-1	0.55	0.51	-3.231***	3.253**
	Kalna--2	0.64	0.53	-3.570***	3.456***
	Katwa-1	0.54	0.43	-2.259***	3.146***
	Katwa--2	0.37	0.23	2.455**	2.367**
	Ketugram-1 ketugram-2	0.45	0.34	-3.368***	2.457**
	Khandaghosh	0.53	0.45	-2.336**	3.256***
	Monteswar	0.42	0.29	-4.670***	3.367***
	Memari-1	0.39	0.13	-4.669***	2.368**
	Memari-2 Mongolkote	0.13	0.10	-3.141***	2.477**
	Purbasthali-1	0.22	0.21	-2.497**	3.471***
	Purbasthali-2	0.19	0.-9	-3.546***	2.367**
	Raina-1	0.55	0.35	-2.345**	4.864***
	Raina-2	0.64	0.51	-3.469***	-4.568***
		0.54	0.39	-4.567***	-4.654***
		0.36	0.29	-4.457***	-3.567***

Note: Same as Table 6.1
Source: Author's calculations

blocks in the district of Purba Bardhaman due to the implementation of the MGNREGA scheme.

Table 6.2 shows that the F-test values are significant either at 1% or 5% in fifteen blocks, and the F-test values are not statistically significant for eight blocks. This means the variances between beneficiaries and non-beneficiaries, in terms of the financial empowerment of women, are not equal for sixteen blocks and are equal for eight blocks. Accordingly, a t-test has been applied under the conditions of equality of variances for eight blocks, and a t-test has been applied under inequality of variances for fifteen blocks in the district of Purba Bardhaman. With regard to the financial empowerment of women, it is observed that the mean average ratio for the beneficiaries is greater than that of the non-beneficiaries in eighteen blocks, and the mean average ratio for the non-beneficiaries is more than that of the beneficiaries in five blocks of the district, namely Burdwan-1, Kalna-1, Purbasthali-2, Raina-1, and Raina-2. The t-test values are also statistically significant, reaching either 1% or 5% in fifteen blocks, and the t-test values are not significant for eight blocks. This implies that women are more financially empowered in most of the blocks in the district of Purba Bardhaman due to the implementation of the MGNREGA scheme.

In terms of social empowerment, the results have also been more favourable for beneficiaries than for non-beneficiaries, and the t-test values are also significant, at 1% over all the twenty-three blocks. The computed results regarding social empowerment, shown in Table 6.3, show that women are more socially empowered in all the blocks in the district of Purba Bardhaman due to the implementation of the MGNREGA scheme.

Conclusion

The concept of social sustainability is linked with the needs, rights, and well-being of the local community, and it is instrumental in achieving empowerment, increased roles in decision making, increases in information access, and democratic governance (Boström, 2012). India is a country characterized by over-population and an abundance of labour. Moreover, unskilled labour is ample in a country like India. So, to ensure a fair means of making a livelihood and to generate employment for people in need, the Government of India adopted the MGNREGA scheme. The MGNREGA aimed to provide wages for 100 days to members of the rural population who wanted to earn by means of unskilled manual work, irrespective of their caste, creed, or sex. For the purposes of the MGNREGA, the bottom level in the three-tier executive system is involved, the Gram Panchayats. The Gram Panchayats actually plan and implement the scheme for the development of rural areas. In the context of social sustainability, the present study tries to highlight the empowerment of rural women through the MGNREGA scheme.

From the major findings of the study, it can be observed that in the three dimensions of women's empowerment – economic, financial, and social – the beneficiary group produces higher mean scores than that of the non-beneficiary group in most of the blocks in the district of Purba Bardhaman due to the implementation of the MGNREGA. It may thus be concluded that the MGNREGA scheme is instrumental to the empowerment of women in the district of Purba Bardhaman in West Bengal, India, something that may be considered one of the most important aspects of social sustainability.

Reference

Ajmal, M. M., Khan, M., Hussain, M., & Helo, P. (2018). Conceptualizing and incorporating social sustainability in the business world. *International Journal of Sustainable Development and World Ecology*, 25(4), 327–339. https://doi.org/10.1080/13504509.2017.1408714

Boström, M. (2012). A missing pillar? Challenges in theorizing and practicing social sustainability: Introduction to the special issue. *Sustainability: Science, Practice, and Policy*, 8(1), 3–14. https://doi.org/10.1080/15487733.2012.11908080

Chaturvedi, S., Singh, D., Choudhary, H. S., Singh, V. B., & Kumari, S. (2019). MNREGA: Constraints of women empowerment in Pura Bazar block of Faizabad district, Uttar Pradesh. *Journal of Pharmacognosy and Phytochemistry*, 8(2), 400–402.

Cornwall, A. (2016). Women's empowerment: What works? *Journal of International Development*, 28(3), 342–359.

Hirway, I., & Mahadevia, D. (1996). Critique of gender development index-towards an alternative. *Economic and Political Weekly*, WS87–WS96.

Kumar, J., & Kumar, U. (2021). Impact study of MNREGA among the beneficiaries and working system of MNREGA. *Medical Care*, 89(11), 11–00.

Laha, A., & Kuri, P. K. (2014). Measuring the impact of microfinance on women empowerment: A cross country analysis with special reference to India. *International Journal of Public Administration*, 37(7), 397–408.

Lavanya, V. L., & Mahima, S. (2013). Empowerment of rural women through MGNREGA with special references to Palakkad. *ZENITH International Journal of Multidisciplinary Research*, 3(7), 271–276.

Mehta, A. K. (1996). Recasting indices for developing countries—A gender empowerment measure. *Economic and Political Weekly*, 31(43), WS80–WS86.

Perry, W. (2020). Social sustainability and the argan boom as green development in Morocco. *World Development Perspectives*, 20, 100238.

Rajalakshmi, V., & Selvam, V. (2017). Impact of MGNREGA on women empowerment and their issues and challenges: A review of literature from 2005 to 2015. *Journal of Internet Banking and Commerce*, 22(Suppl.7), 1.

Ravindar, M. (2016). Empowerment of women through Mgnregs: A study in Warangal District of Telangana State. *International Journal of Multidisciplinary Research and Modern Education (IJMRME)*, II(I). ISSN [Online]. 2454–6119. www.rdmodernresearch.org

Rocheleau, D., Thomas-Slayter, B., &Wangari, E. (2013). *Feminist political ecology: Global issues and local experience*. Routledge.

Taylor, G., & Pereznieto, P. (2014). *Review of evaluation approaches and methods used by interventions on women and girl's economic empowerment.* Overseas Development Institute. https://goo.gl/YS8E5t

Xavier, G., & Mari, G. (2014). Impact of MGNREGA on women empowerment with special reference to KalakkanmoiPanchayat in Sivgangai District, Tamil Nadu. *International Journal of Economics and Management Studies, 1*(1), 1–5.

Chapter 7

Impact of the COVID-19 Pandemic on the Migratory Behaviour of the Workers of Rural India

An Empirical Analysis

Subrato Adhikari, Anirban Mandal, and Saikat Chakrabarti

Introduction

A permanent or semi-permanent movement of people from one location to another is referred to as migration. Migration from one location to another has rarely been one-way, and it is frequently followed by some reverse movement toward the place of origin (Dhar & Bhagat, 2021). Ravenstein (1885) posits that each migration produces a return migration stream, which may or may not be equal. As a result, return migration can be considered the movement of migrants back to their place of origin (Gmelch, 1980). Numerous economists agree that labour migration can be seen as one of the most important factors affecting the economy's structural development (Thakur, 2020).

India declared a statewide lockdown on 24 March 2020 to combat COVID-19, which resulted in the closing of factories, shops, malls, and other companies, costing millions of jobs and livelihoods. Because of the lockdown, the informal sector saw a significant drop in economic activity. As it turned out, the pandemic was far worse for the migrants (Kumar & Anand, 2020). Migrant workers, who make up a substantial portion of these informal workers, face an even more dire scenario. When the COVID-19 pandemic hit, most of the people who had left the state in pursuit of work and better living conditions had returned after the announcement of the lockdown (Sengupta & Jha, 2020; Adhikari et al., 2021). When they returned to the village, they were greeted with hostility by the villagers. The villagers' terror of COVID-19 was evident in their behaviour (Kumar & Anand, 2020). With the return of the migrants, the loads on restricted landholdings increased, causing family strife. The plight of the migrants' was exacerbated immediately upon their return, as they were thought to be carriers of the virus. After some time, the family members of migrant workers began to experience hardship due to loss of income. An attempt is made in this article to describe reverse migration, and it tries to outline a perspective on reverse migration in the state of West Bengal, India. No official data is available to determine the exact magnitude of this migratory behaviour, so this study will rely on alternative estimations.

DOI: 10.4324/9781032640488-9

In the wake of the COVID-19 worldwide pandemic, migrant workers have been forced to return to their homes. The crisis has made the situation in developing countries, notably in India, precarious (Panwar & Mishra, 2020; Sengupta & Jha, 2020). It is estimated that India's internal migrants number 453.6 million, which is equivalent to 37% of the country's total population (Census of India, 2011). Uttar Pradesh, Bihar, Madhya Pradesh (MP), Odisha, Punjab, Rajasthan, Uttarakhand, Jammu and Kashmir, and West Bengal are the key source areas (Panwar & Mishra, 2020). This sudden influx of return migration created substantial pressure in the place of origin (Kumar & Anand, 2020). There is a surplus of wage employees as a result of return migration, which has affected wages and increased intra-worker competition over the limited local jobs available. As a result of the lockdown, the government's claims of offering sufficient livelihood opportunities for returning migrants were overblown and far from adequate (Kumar & Anand, 2020). As a result, more research is needed to help policymakers and planners understand the complementarities between urban informal and formal economies, rural and urban economies, and the role of rural–urban migration in benefiting both rural and urban communities (Panwar & Mishra, 2020; Barhate et al., 2021).

Wage Discrimination: the pay gap has been the subject of substantial research in the social sciences and economics. In addition to variations in productivity and gender discrimination (Blau & Kahn, 2000; Goldin, 2014), the skill level of the labour force plays a role in this discrepancy. Wage differentials have been recognized as the primary driving mechanism behind movement of the people, and are considered to be an important element of migration. During the Green Revolution in India, the wage gap was one of the motivating factors for migration. Migrant workers' working conditions appear to be deteriorating due to factors such as an increase in the commissions charged by middlemen who facilitate migration, longer working hours, piece-rate payments becoming predominant in their pay schedules, an increase in the proportions of children among migrants, and various indications of an increase in exploitation (Deshingkar & Akter, 2009). Nevertheless, the implicit assumption is that better production technology in cities leads to increased worker productivity and higher wages, as supplied by urban sector enterprises. This produces a wide gulf between urban and rural living standards, which in turn drives rural–urban migrants to the city to make a better life there (Panwar & Mishra, 2020). Wage inequality could lead to a crisis around people's health and well-being, as well as around education, civic life, and human development (Lakshmanasamy & Maya, 2020).

Hypothesis 1: There is a significant relation between wage discrimination and migratory behaviour.

Discontinuation of Income: migrant workers have been compelled to return home as a result of losing their jobs and money (Adhikari et al., 2021). An ongoing statewide lockdown has exacerbated the migrant workers' plight, characterized by homelessness, hunger, and unanticipated human sufferings (SWAN, 2020; Sumalatha et al., 2021). As a result of the announcement of the lockdown, millions of migrants and informal sector employees were left jobless, with only funds sufficient to feed them for a week or two at most. When it came to food handouts, many of them did not possess ration cards. People fled cities on foot, covering hundreds of kilometres, while many more are still stranded in cities (Guha et al., 2021; Khanna, 2020). On returning to their villages, they continued to face problems. Villagers rely on the money sent home by their migrants. The money those migrant workers send home to their families in villages is spent on essential things (Kumar & Anand, 2020). For some households, daily expenses are exclusively funded by migratory family members. Because of the statewide lockdown, migrant workers were forced to return to their villages, so this regular influx of money ceased. Financial as well as psychological effects were felt by both migrants and their families (Kumar & Anand, 2020).

Hypothesis 2: Discontinuation of income has a significant impact on migratory behaviour.

Abundance of Labour: the majority of the returned workers are concerned about their ability to buy food and other necessities of life. An extra supply of labour appeared, due to many workers returning home. For the same kind of labour, there were more workers available. A sense of uneasiness about their livelihood set in as competition among the workers rose (Kumar & Anand, 2020; Khanna, 2020). Given that most workers are strapped for cash, this type of competitive environment could have resulted in confrontations between workers. There is a hidden competition between workers to be the first to receive a given job. As a result, there has been an increase in contractors bargaining with workers for cheaper wages. Pay cuts and other types of exploitation could lead to social unrest between landowners and workers, as well as conflicts within the labouring classes, over time (Kumar & Anand, 2020). Therefore, most of the workers decided to go back to their workplaces after lockdown was over.

Hypothesis 3: Abundance of labour has a significant impact on migratory behaviour.

Methods

This section examines the details of the instruments and procedures used in data collection. A structured questionnaire was developed following a reliability study carried out with the help of Cronbach's alpha. A reliability value of more than 0.70 indicates that the questionnaire is reliable. In this case, the alpha value was 0.85 which indicates that the questionnaire is reliable for collecting relevant information from the target respondents. A total of 131 respondents were surveyed using a convenience sampling technique. The survey was conducted during the month of February 2021 when the majority of the workforce returned, having decided or already having planned to go back to their original place of work. This was a crucial phase in which migratory movement started increasing in momentum. According to census statistics, almost 500,000 individuals migrated from West Bengal between 2001 and 2011, putting the state in fourth place in terms of the number of people who migrated during various census years. According to the 2011 census report, district-level data is still unavailable. The authors have grounded their findings on research by Debnath et al. (2018), who identified Burdwan (then undivided), Nadia, Hooghly, and Murshidabad as the key districts that saw the highest out-migration from West Bengal.

To discover the perceptions of the respondents from the perspectives of our three research variables, different measures were constructed with the help of past studies in the field. Perceptions related to the variable "wage discrimination" were revealed with the help of three measures (Deshingkar & Akter, 2009; Kumar & Anand, 2020); perceptions around the "discontinuation of income" were revealed with the help of four measures (Guha et al., 2021; Kumar & Anand, 2020); and perceptions around "abundant" were revealed with the help of four measures (Kumar & Anand, 2020; Khanna, 2020). Lastly, migratory decisions were analyzed from the perspective of the three variables (Deshingkar & Akter, 2009).

To analyze our three hypotheses, the following regression model was developed:

Y (Migratory Behaviour) = α + β_1 (Wage Discrimination) + β_2 (Discontinuation of Income) + β_3 (Abundant Labour) + e (errors)

Where,
Migratory Behaviour (Y) is the dependent variable and
Wage Discrimination (X1), Discontinuation of Income (X2) and Abundant Labour (X3) are all independent variables. β_1 to β_3 are all coefficients for X1, X2 and X3 respectively.

Results and Discussion

Out of the respondents, around 89% were male migrants, and the rest were female migrants who moved out as a part of a family. Thus, most of the migratory movements of the female group happened not because of income but because of family related movement. Around 67% of migrants completed their class 12 education, 13% completed class 10 education, and the rest of the 30% did not have formal education, nor had they completed primary education. Their monthly earnings at their places of destination were between Rs. 15,000 to Rs. 20,000, but this income is not fixed and their actual monthly income would vary during their stay. All the migrants are engaged in informal sectors, with no facilities other than their daily wage.

Table 7.1 Descriptive Statistics

Variable	Mean	Standard Deviation
Wage Discrimination	3.93	0.8837
Discontinuation of Income	4.08	0.6910
Abundant Labour	4.02	0.8082

Source: Author's analysis

Table 7.2 Correlation Matrix of Independent Variables

Variable	Wage Discrimination	Discontinuation of Income	Abundant Labour
Wage Discrimination	1.00		
Discontinuation of Income	0.511**	1.00	
Abundant Labour	0.388**	0.396**	1.00

** Significant at 0.01 level of significance
Source: Author's analysis

Table 7.3 Model Fit

ANOVA[a]

Model		Sum of Squares	df	Mean Square	F	Sig.
1	Regression	17.131	3	5.710	8.593	.000[b]
	Residual	84.396	127	.665		
	Total	101.527	130			

a. Dependent Variable: Migratory Behaviour

Source: Author's analysis

The data shows that the discontinuation of income is the factor with the strongest effect on migratory decisions. The result is a validation of the nation-wide lockdown and its after-effects on the informal economy.

The correlation matrix of the independent variables shows that all the variables are highly correlated with each other, and that significant result is produced for each of the variables. The result also shows a very strong correlation (0.511) between discontinuation of income and wage discrimination. It is a fact that migratory movements take place primarily because of wage discrimination. Wage discrimination is also associated positively with abundant labour. It justifies the outcome that if the labour supply is increased in a particular region, wage discrimination will also be high (Deshingkar & Akter, 2009).

Table 7.4 Regression Model

*Coefficients*ᵃ

Model		Unstandardized Coefficients		Standardized Coefficients	t	Sig.
		B	Std. Error	Beta		
1	(Constant)	1.945	.480		4.048	.000
	Wage Discrimination	.245	.096	.246	2.544	.012
	Discontinuation of Income	.265	.124	.207	2.131	.035
	Abundant Labour	.136	.099	.133	2.367	.014
a. Dependent Variable: Migratory Behaviour						

Source: Author's analysis
Y (Migratory Behaviour) = 1.945+ 0.245(Wage Discrimination) + 0.265(Discontinuation of Income) + 0.136 (Abundant Labour) + e (errors)

As the ANOVA significance value is lower than 5%, the model is fit to run the multiple regression model. The result is discussed in Table 7.4.

The result supports all the hypotheses. It can be seen that wage discrimination and discontinuation of income are the two most important reasons for migratory movement. Abundant labour has less of an effect on migratory movement. Another point to note is that, out of the two hypotheses, "discontinuation of income" has a stronger impact on migratory movement than wage discrimination. Thus, it is mainly loss of income that affects migratory movement.

Conclusion

COVID-19 had a major influence on the lives of migrants in our selected communities. Many of them had to return because they were unable to maintain themselves at their destinations. They did not receive the rest and assistance at their destination that would have been required for them to stay. Furthermore, those who returned were mostly from poor communities. As a result of the loss of earnings, the families have suffered. As a result of this, rural hardship has gotten worse. There is a surplus of wage employees as a result of return migration, which has impacted earnings and increased intra-worker rivalry over the few local employment possibilities. The situation was exacerbated during the rainy season, when the MGNREGA programme was suspended. It was also a problem because migrants did not have access to other government aid or assistance programmes, largely because they did not sign up. All assertions that the government was proactive in offering acceptable livelihood choices to the returning migrants during the lockdown were overstated. Return migrants from resource-poor areas required immediate assistance in the form of direct cash transfers, food subsidies, and rural job development. Without such assistance, migrants found it impossible to live a decent life and preserve whatever modest living standards they had before the pandemic.

References

Adhikari, S., Mandal, A., & Guha, S. (2021). Place attachment and decisions to move: A study of Indian migrants during Covid-19 pandemic and directions to future research. *Journal of Medicinal and Chemical Sciences*, 4(5), 444–451. https://doi.org/10.26655/JMCHEMSCI.2021.5.5

Ahmed, I., Das, N., Debnath, J. et al. (2018). Erosion induced channel migration and its impact on dwellers in the lower Gumti River, Tripura, *India. Spat. Inf. Res.* 26, 537–549.https://doi.org/10.1007/s41324-018-0196-9

Barhate, B., Hirudayaraj, M., Gunasekara, N., Ibrahim, G., Alizadeh, A., & Abadi, M. (2021). Crisis within a crisis: Migrant workers' predicament during COVID-19 lockdown and the role of non-profit organizations in India. *Indian Journal of Human Development*, 15(1), 151–164. https://doi.org/10.1177/0973703021997624

Blau, F. D., & Kahn, L. M. (2000). Gender differences in pay. *Journal of Economic Perspectives*, 14(4), 75–99. https://doi.org/10.1257/jep.14.4.75

Census Report, 2011, Ministry of Home Affairs, Government of India

Deshingkar, P., & Akter, S. (2009). *Migration and Human Development in India. Published in: Human Development Research Paper (HDRP) Series, 13,* https://mpra.ub.uni-muenchen.de/id/eprint/19193

Dhar, B., & Bhagat, R. B. (2021). Return migration in India: Internal and international dimensions. *Migration and Development*, 10(1), 107–121. https://doi.org/10.1080/21632324.2020.1809263

Gmelch, G. (1980). Return migration. *Annual Review of Anthropology*, 9(1), 135–159.

Goldin, C. (2014). A grand gender convergence: Its last chapter. *American Economic Review*, 104(4), 1091–1119. https://doi.org/10.1257/aer.104.4.1091

Guha, P., Islam, B., & Hussain, M. A. (2021). COVID-19 lockdown and penalty of joblessness on income and remittances: A study of inter-state migrant labourers from Assam, India. *Journal of Public Affairs*, 21(4), e2470. https://doi.org/10.1002/pa.2470

https://censusindia.gov.in/2011-common/census_data_2001.html

https://censusindia.gov.in/2011-common/censusdata2011.html

Khanna, A. (2020). Impact of migration of labour force due to global COVID-19 pandemic with reference to India. *Journal of Health Management*, 22(2), 181–191.https://doi.org/10.1177/0972063420935542

Kumar, S., & Anand, S. (2020). Perspectives on return migration and rural society during COVID-19 in Bhojpur District in Bihar. *Journal of Migration Affairs*, 3(1), 79–89. https://doi.org/10.36931/jma.2020.3.1.

Lakshmanasamy, T., & Maya, K. (2020). The effect of income inequality on happiness inequality in India: A recentered influence function regression estimation and life satisfaction inequality decomposition. *Indian Journal of Human Development*, 14(2), 161–181. https://doi.org/10.1177/0973703020948468

Panwar, N. S., & Mishra, A. K. (2020). Covid-19 crisis and urbanization, migration and inclusive city policies in India: A new theoretical framework. *Journal of Public Affairs*, 20(4), e2249. https://doi.org/10.1002/pa.2249

Ravenstein, E. G. (1885). The laws of migration. *Journal of the Statistical Society of London*, 48(2), 167–235. https://doi.org/10.2307/2979181

Sengupta, S., & Jha, M. K. (2020). Social policy, COVID-19 and impoverished migrants: Challenges and prospects in locked down India. *The International Journal of Community and Social Development*, 2(2), 152–172. https://doi.org/10.1177/2516602620933715

Stranded Workers Action Network (SWAN) 3 Reports. (2020, June 8). *Toleave or not to leave: Lockdown, migrant workers and their journeyshome*. https://watson.brown.edu/southasia/news/2020/leave-or-not-leave-third-report-swan-migrant-worker-crisis-and-their-journey-home.

Sumalatha, B. S., Bhat, L. D., & Chitra, K. P. (2021). Impact of Covid-19 on informal sector: A study of women domestic workers in India. *The Indian Economic Journal*, 00194662211023845. https://doi.org/10.1177/00194662211023845

Thankur, A. (2020). Economic implications of reverse migration in India. *Journal of Migration Affairs*, III(1), 16–31. https://doi.org/10.36931/jma.2020.2.2.16-31

Chapter 8

Forms of Online Lectures
A Key Factor in Making Online Education a Sustainable Future Option for Lifelong Learning

Lalima Mukherjee, Smita Datta

Introduction

The outbreak of the Coronavirus pandemic in 2019 (COVID-19), which started in China in December 2019, has proved to be a catastrophic calamity that has spread across the world at a very fast pace. Along with all other societal aspects, education was also forced to undergo an abrupt transformation. The pandemic forced institutions to move from offline (physical) to online (digital) modes of imparting education. This forced shift to online education has highlighted the unlimited potential benefits of online learning. Growing competition and a desire for an improved standard of living, as well as the necessity of being updated professionally, have made lifelong learning (LLL) essential (Beller 2006). As students can learn from a convenient place, at a convenient time, and at their own pace, online education is the most appropriate mode for lifelong learning. E-learning allows users to achieve an optimal balance between their learning activities, work, free time, and family (Sun et al., 2008).

However, recent evidence from students' e-learning experiences during the COVID-19 pandemic has revealed several major issues, including problems with internet connection (Agung et al., 2020; Basuony et al., 2020), a lack of requisite IT equipment (Bączek et al., 2021; Niemi & Kousa, 2020), and restricted interactive learning environments (Bączek et al., 2021; Yates et al., 2020). These shortcomings have been found to expose e-learners to several vulnerabilities, including declining academic performance (Molnar et al., 2019), a sense of isolation (Song et al., 2004), and decreased learning motivation (Muilenburg & Berge, 2005).

The potential for online education to become a sustainable solution for lifelong learning can only be realized when these adverse impacts on students are mitigated. Therefore, the concern is not whether or not online teaching and learning methods can provide a means for lifelong learning, but whether or not we can transform structured learning platforms in an efficient manner (Carey, 2020), so that this new education paradigm becomes sustainable. This can be done by designing online learning experiences in such a manner

DOI: 10.4324/9781032640488-10

that the problems associated with the current online education system are resolved to a greater extent. The mode of content delivery is the most crucial component of an online learning platform, which, if appropriately chosen, has the potential to address two of the major problems of e-learning – internet connectivity problems and a lack of collaborative learning environments. Thus, an appropriate form of imparting education in a digital mode can reduce negative psychological impacts on the students and make it a sustainable solution for lifelong learning.

Thus, there is a need to study and find a relationship between the different means of imparting education n online and students' psychological stability, as associated with institutional strategies, students' optimism and pessimism, engagement in academic work, depression, and well-being. The objectives of this study are to identify the form of online lectures that promotes the greatest level of psychological stability in students, and to offer some policy recommendations regarding relevant changes to structured learning environment, to make them a sustainable solution for lifelong learning.

The structured learning environment is synchronized, in the sense that students need to attend live lectures and that there are also real-time interactions between educators and learners. In this arrangement, there is a possibility of instant feedback. Asynchronous teaching and learning environments, on the other hand, are not properly structured, learning content thus not being available in the form of live lectures or classes, being available rather on different learning systems and forums. It has been also observed that due to the lack of physical presence on the part of teachers, instant feedback is not possible in such an environment. Apart from any obvious change to academic challenges, students being expected to behave in an autonomous manner in their studies, individuals are free to relocate to another geographical location within the same country or state as well as at times, internationally. This transition from the offline to the online mode represents a monumental shift in mobility and independence. For many new students, absolute control over their behavioural choices has become the norm for the first time, with the potential for either positive or negative change. Thus, synchronous learning is able to provide huge opportunities for social interaction. Amidst the spread of COVID-19, online platforms are needed where (a) video conferencing with at least 70 to 80 students is possible, (b) discussions can be done with students to keep the respective online classes organic, (c) there is stable internet connectivity, (d) lectures can be such that they are accessible through mobile phones as well as laptops, (e) there is the possibility of watching recorded lectures not in real-time, and (f) getting instant feedback from students is possible, along with assignments. Mostly, students find online education to be extremely boring and restless. However, online learning is very flexible, meaning students never find time to do it, and stricture and sincerity are at times a serious issue. Personal attention is also at risk as well, and is a huge problem facing online education in the current context. While students look forward to two-way interaction, sometimes it can be difficult to implement. Moreover, learning processes fail to reach their full potential unless students practice what they learn. It has often been noted that online content is absolutely theoretical in nature and does not help students practice and learn effectively. Students feel that lack of communication, technical problems, and difficulties in understanding instructions have emerged as the major barriers to online learning (Song et al., 2004). In a relevant study, students were not found to be sufficiently prepared to balance their work, family, and social lives, and to maintain an equilibrium with their so-called "student lives" in an online learning environment. Students were also found to be poorly prepared with regard to several e-learning competencies and academic competencies. Also, there is a low level of preparedness among students concerning the use of Learning Management Systems. The learning crisis, intensified by this pandemic, needs to be addressed prudently. In the short term, taking into account the mental and physical health of students and educators, online education should be streamlined. This also means ensuring access to the Internet in every corner of the country. Such measures will prepare the education sector for further COVID-19 infections, and will prevent students from dropping out of institutions. Meanwhile, preparations must begin for opening education institutes, with safety protocols in place.

Methods

The study tries to understand the importance of the form of online learning as it affects the psychological stability of higher education students throughout a pandemic crisis such as that of COVID-19. The problems associated with online learning and possible solutions are also identified, based on previous studies.

First, the ANOVA and then the Tukey-Kramer tests were conducted to allow us to understand which form of online lecture was the best for students' psychological stability, as it allows for the continuation of online modes of learning during this critical situation. The data used was collected through a web-based questionnaire with 150 responses from students across various private colleges and universities in Kolkata, West Bengal. Data could not be collected from students face-to-face. Currently, Kolkata has many new private institutions and universities. Public universities have not been considered due to a lack of information on regular online classes.

The paper employs both a quantitative and a qualitative approach to study the perceptions of students toward online teaching and learning modes, and also to highlight the implementation processes of online teaching and structured learning environment. The analysis has been carried out with careful implication on the feedback sources of the data collected. Relevant literature

Results & Discussions

A one-way ANOVA was performed to compare the effect of the form of education delivery on the psychological stability of students in higher education. The one-way ANOVA revealed a statistically significant difference in the mean psychological stability of students [$F(4,149) = 7.18$, $p = 0.000$] between at least two forms of online lectures.

Since the ANOVA was significant, a Tukey-Kramer test was carried out to examine which two forms of online classes differ with regard to the mean psychological stability of students. The results of the Tukey HSD test are displayed in Table 8.1 below.

The different forms of online lectures considered for this study are:

1. Online in real-time (video conference).
2. Online with a video recording (not in real-time).
3. Online with an audio recording (not in real-time).
4. Online by sending presentations to students.
5. Written communication (forums, chat, etc.).

From the results presented in Table 8.1, it is evident that Form 2 resulted in a statistically significant higher psychological stability on an average than

Table 8.1 Results of Tukey Honest Significance Difference Test

(I) Form of online class	(J) Form of online class	Mean difference (I − J)	Sig.	95% Confidence Interval Lower Bound	95% Confidence Interval Upper Bound
2	1	10.098	0.000*	3.59	16.60
3	1	8.598	0.026*	0.69	16.50
4	1	-1.113	0.930	-4.95	2.72
5	1	-2.402	0.975	-13.49	8.69
3	2	-1.5	0.994	-11.54	8.54
4	2	-11.211	0.000*	-18.50	-3.93
5	2	-12.5	0.056*	-25.20	0.20
4	3	-9.711	0.018*	-18.27	-1.15
5	3	-11.0	0.166	-24.47	2.47
5	4	-1.289	0.998	-12.86	10.28

Note: * The mean difference is significant at the 0.1 level. Source: Author's analysis

Form 1 (10.098), a statistically significant higher mean psychological stability than Form 4 (11.211), and also a statistically significant higher psychological stability than Form 5 (12.5). Form 3 also resulted in a higher psychological stability on an average of 8.598 over Form 1 and a higher psychological stability of 9.711 over Form 4. The mean psychological stability between no other pair of forms of online lectures is statistically significant. It has thus been found that Form 2 promotes better psychological stability among students compared to three other alternative forms of online classes, and Form 3 results in higher mean psychological stability than two other forms of online classes, while Form 1, Form 4 and Form 5 do not result in statistically significant higher psychological stability than any of the other forms of online lectures. Since Form 2 is statistically more significant than both Form 1 as well as Form 3, as shown in Table 8.1, it appears to be the best form in which to conduct online classes in terms of promoting psychological stability among students.

Conclusion

As the pandemic forced institutions to move from offline (physical) to online (digital) modes of imparting education, the unlimited potential benefits of e-learning were highlighted. Growing competition and desires for an improved standard of living, as well as the necessity of being updated professionally, have drastically changed the lifelong learning (LLL) mode of education, and made it essential. Due to the various benefits of online learning identified during the pandemic, it appears to be a very appropriate tool for lifelong learning. But online education cannot become a sustainable solution for lifelong learning until its adverse impacts on the student community are mitigated. Given this background, this paper has attempted to explore the issues related to new modes of education delivery, the psychological challenges as well as the social sustainability hindrances faced by higher education students who are the victims of socio-economic injustice in the context of a huge digital divide. It also attempted to delve deep into the students facing problems with internet connectivity, as well as with internet access with regard to real-time video conferencing, due to which they have opted for video recording which is not in real-time. In many cases, even when the educator is capable of imparting lectures through the online mode of video conferencing (in real-time), students are unable to be a part of the lecture due to their lack of internet access. Moreover, since for a major portion of the world population seamless internet access is still a distant dream, education cannot be delivered to those students residing in remote areas as they either lack connectivity, devices, or the proper environment required for continuous online learning. It has also been observed that students are immensely affected psychologically due to the absence of the collaborative learning opportunities that are present in physical classes, which at times makes them reluctant to attend online classes, leading to declining academic performance.

This study reveals that online lectures with a video recording (not in real-time) promote better psychological stability among students compared to three other alternative forms of content delivery through online learning platforms. This finding is not surprising, as this mode of lecture delivery overcomes the problem of intermittent internet connectivity, as students have access to the recorded lecture, which ought to reduce their anxiety around missing out on important topics. At the same time, the presence of peers and of the instructor during the live session provides an opportunity to virtually interact and collaborate with them.

Thus, online learning models that employ online lectures with a video recording (not in real-time) as their primary mode of content delivery can provide a sustainable solution to the global and urgent need for lifelong learning.

References

Agung, A. S. N., Surtikanti, M. W., & Quinones, C. A. (2020). Students' perception of online learning during COVID-19 pandemic: A case study on the English students of STKIP Pamane Talino. *SOSHUM: JurnalSosial Dan Humaniora*, 10(2), 225–235. 10.31940/soshum.,10i2.1316

Basuony, M. A. K., EmadEldeen, R., Farghaly, M., El-Bassiouny, N., & Mohamed, E. K. A. (2020). The factors affecting student satisfaction with online education during the COVID-19 pandemic: An empirical study of an emerging Muslim country. *Journal of Islamic Marketing*. 10.1108/JIMA-09-2020-0301

Bączek, M., Zagańczyk-Bączek, M., Szpringer, M., Jaroszyński, A., &Wożakowska-Kapłon, B. (2021). Students' perception of online learning during the COVID-19 pandemic: A survey study of Polish medical students. *Medicine*, 100(7), e24821. 10.1097/MD.0000000000024821

Beller, J. (2006). The Cinematic Mode of Production: Attention Economy and the Society of the Spectacle. 32(2), Hanover, NH: Dartmouth College Press. https://doi.org/10.1177/0196859907312288

Carey, K. (2020). Everybody ready for the big migration to online college. *Actually*. The New York Times, 13, 1–4.

Molnar, A., Miron, G., Elgeberi, N., Barbour, M. K., Huerta, L., Shafer, S. R., & Rice, J. K. (2019). Virtual schools in the US 2019. National Education Policy Center. 125,http://nepc.colorado.edu

Muilenburg, L. Y., & Berge, Z. L. (2005). Student barriers to online learning: A factor analytic study. *Distance Education*, 26(1), 29–48. 10.1080/01587910500081269

Niemi, H. M., & Kousa, P. (2020). A case study of students' and teachers' perceptions in a finnish high school during the COVID pandemic. *International Journal of Technology in Education and Science*, 4(4), 352–369. 10.46328/ijtes.v4i4.167

Song, L., Singleton, E. S., Hill, J. R., & Koh, M. H. (2004). Improving online learning: Student perceptions of useful and challenging characteristics. *The Internet and Higher Education*, 7(1), 59–70. 10.1016/j.iheduc.2003.11.003

Sun, P. C., Tsai, R. J., Finger, G., Chen, Y. Y., & Yeh, D. (2008). What drives a successful E-Learning? An empirical investigation of the critical factors influencing learner satisfaction.*Computers & Education*, 50(4),1183–1202. DOI:10.1016/j.compedu.2006.11.007

Yates, A., Starkey, L., Egerton, B., & Flueggen, F. (2020). High school students' experience of online learning during Covid-19: The influence of technology and pedagogy. Technology, Pedagogy and Education, 9, 1–15. 10.1080/1475939X.2020.1854337

Chapter 9

Influencers of Online Education and Social Sustainability of Blended Learning

Arijit Ghosh, Anirban Sarkar, and Suchitra Kumari

Introduction

The COVID-19 pandemic has drastically changed our lives, with offline classes not being held due to the multiple waves of the pandemic. Traditionally, offline classes have been the trend, but they have limitations with regard to inculcating critical thinking power among students (Means et al., 2009). Daily offline classes lead to droning; consequently, student attendance gradually diminishes, and non-participation and behavioural problems increase (Okaz, 2015). Moreover, over-dependence on technology often lowers students' attention spans (Okaz, 2015). Thus, there is a need for a change in pedagogy, allowing for the presentation of appropriate content in the proper form (Singh, 2003), a need that gave birth to the concept of socially sustainable blended learning, which joined technology and the warm-heartedness of offline classes to offer an attractive learning environment for students and a meaningful learning outcome for educators (Rooney, 2003; Garrison et al., 2004). Furthermore, a diverse combination of delivery media such as virtual classrooms, recorded live events, instant messaging, live chats, applications, social networking platforms, blogs and forums, and simulations augment learning (Singh, 2003). It is thus imperative to know what influences of online education, and what the predominant outlooks are toward socially sustainable Blended Learning. This paper will add to the previous literature by identifying the different factors of online education prevailing in India and, on a consolidated scale, predicting the propensities of stakeholders toward socially sustainable blended learning through Binary Logistic Regression.

Dziuban et al. (2005) studied the impact of generation markers on their blended learning experience. They used a principal components analysis and identified two satisfaction dimensions: interaction value and learning engagement. The outcome showed that millennials responded least positively to their blended learning experience. Lim et al. (2009) studied the learner antecedents among college students. The learner antecedents were the average study time, preference in delivery format, prior experience with distance learning outcomes, and age. Using regression analysis, it was found that the motivational

DOI: 10.4324/9781032640488-11

and instructional variables and the influence of the learner summed up to one variable in the learning application. Finally, Filippidi et al. (2010) studied the impact of nine variables on students' practices while using Moodle, and the regression analysis showed that blended learning significantly impacted their performance.

Lopez-Pérez et al. (2013) used students' perceptions regarding the blended learning activities performed and found that blended learning had a positive effect on the improvement of marks and led to a reduction in dropout rates. Martinez-Caro et al. (2011) did a two-year field study to determine the differential impact of satisfaction across traditional and blended learning methods. He found that student satisfaction was higher in blended learning than in face-to-face. This was due to greater motivation, greater online class attendance, and better collaboration with classmates in a blended learning classroom. Demirer et al. (2013) did fourteen weeks of pre- and post-test experimental study and found that blended learning positively affected knowledge transfer. Lopez-Pérez et al. (2013) found that the tasks being completed and the students' participation in the blended learning activities positively impacted the students' final marks. Moskal et al. (2013) did a continuous evaluation on the effects of blended learning on institutions, faculty and students. He stated that blended learning would result in positive institutional transformation with proper planning and support. Grabinski et al. (2015) used a survey method on Kraków University students and found that the students perceived blended learning positively. Kwak et al. (2015) used the difference-in-difference method, which controls the differences arising in course delivery methods and student characteristics, to appraise the impact of blended learning on student performance. The effect was found to be strongly negative. Jou et al. (2016) designed a blended learning environment and conducted a semester-long experiment to evaluate this learning environment. It was found that the approach improved knowledge transformation among students, and they were satisfied and motivated by it. Manwaring et al. (2017) used structural equation modelling and experience sampling to investigate the student engagement in blended learning settings and found that the perception of the student's activity had a strong influence on the engagement. Nguyen (2017) applied formative assessment to evaluate student learning outcomes using different learning activities and a learning management system (LMS). Baragash et al. (2018) surveyed 196 undergraduate students and found that the face-to-face (F2F) learning mode influenced students' performance in completing online assignments, and using learning management system (LMS) affected the performance in the final examination. Dziuban et al. (2018) opined that the evolution of blended learning was bound to contemporary information communication technologies. This study aims to understand:

a. What the influencers of online education are.
b. Whether accessing online education is convenient for students.

c. Whether the students are committing malpractice in online examinations.
d. Whether there is stress due to overemphasis on online education.
e. Whether students feel a need for socially sustainable blended learning.

Methods

Primary data was collected online between 15 March 2021 and 15 May 2021. A pilot survey was performed to pre-test the questionnaire before the final data collection. Data collection was based on the purposive sampling method, used within India. The majority of papers reviewed for this study used this sampling method. The framed questionnaire was distributed through email, and Google Survey form links captured information on demographics and various aspects of online education from 766 Indian students. Some of the questions were open-ended, and some of the questions requested answers given on an ordinal scale ranked on a 5-point Likert scale between 0 and 4, due to the country's vast geographical spread. There were 40 questions, and the methodology for data collection was adapted from the study by Bashir et al. (2015). After completing the descriptive analysis, a variable reduction technique, Exploratory Factor Analysis, was employed after checking its suitability.

Results and Discussions

The demographics study included gender, with 59% females and 41% males; location type, with 77% of respondents living in Urban areas and 23% in rural areas; income, which was spread across the categories 0–10k, 11k–25k, 26k–50k, 51k–100k, and above 100k; age, with 81% respondents in the 19–25 age group, followed by 12% in 11–18, 5% in 26–35, 2% who are 36 and above, with 1% of respondents being aged ten and below. In addition, respondents had the following levels of education: basic primary school, high-school, undergraduate, postgraduate, and doctorate.

The researchers used principal components analysis (PCA), a variable reduction technique similar to exploratory factor analysis. It aims to reduce a more extensive set of variables into a smaller group of "artificial" variables, called "principal components", which account for most of the variance in the original variables. An exploratory factor analysis using principal component analysis has been done to extract the factors impacting Indian students with regard to COVID-19.

The internal consistency has been checked using Cronbach's alpha (>0.7) (Gliem & Gliem, 2003). The Kaiser-Meyer-Olkin Measure of Sampling Adequacy (KMO) is 0.656, as depicted in Table 9.1; therefore, we proceed with our factor analysis.

Bartlett's Test of Sphericity is significant, concluding that there are relationships between the variables. So, the factor analysis technique is appropriate.

Table 9.1 KMO and Bartlett's Test

Kaiser-Meyer-Olkin Measure of Sampling Adequacy		.656
Bartlett's Test of Sphericity	Approx. Chi-Square	1357.764
	df	36
	Sig.	.000

Source: Author's analysis

Using our criterion of selecting Eigenvalues over 1, we can see from Table 9.2 that three components (or factors) have Eigenvalues greater than 1. For example, we can see that factor 1 has an Eigenvalue of 2.411, which is 26.785% of the variance. Thus, three factors explain a cumulative 61.142% of the variance in the data.

From the rotated component matrix depicted in Table 9.3, it can be observed that three factors explain the effect of COVID-19 on Indian students. Factor 1 is termed as "E-Comfort", which includes four variables. Factor 2 is termed "E-stress", which contains three variables. Finally, factor 3 is termed "E-malpractice", consisting of two variables.

Here, the researchers used binary logistic regression, as multiple independent variables and a single binary dependent variable are considered in the study. A binary logistic regression (often referred to simply as logistic regression) predicts the probability of an observation falling into one of two categories of a dichotomous dependent variable based on one or more independent variables that can be either continuous or categorical.

A 5-point Likert scale has been used for measuring responses on independent variables. In this analysis, the dichotomous dependent variable, an inclination toward blended learning, has two categories: "0" for "Yes" and "1" for "No".

The Hosmer–Lemeshow Goodness of Fit Test is the best test available to evaluate the fit of the logistic regression model. For this test to provide evidence of a good fit, we need to fail to reject the null hypothesis. Therefore, we want values greater than .05 in the significance column. For example, the above table shows a chi-square value of 5.015 at 8 DF with a significance level of .756. Therefore, we have added evidence that our model is reliable (Table 9.4).

The classification table depicts the outcomes when the independent variables are inserted into the equation. Here, TP means True Positive, FP means False Positive, TN means True Negative, and FN means False Negative. From the classification table, we find the sensitivity and specificity are 99.7% and 15.8%, respectively, coming in with an overall accuracy of 91.4% (TP + TN)/Total classifications (Table 9.5). Therefore, it can be seen that the majority of the respondents do not favour blended learning.

Table 9.2 Total Variance Explained

Component	Initial Eigen values			Extraction Sums of squared loadings			Rotation Sums of squared loadings		
	Total	% of Variance	Cumulative %	Total	% of Variance	Cumulative %	Total	% of Variance	Cumulative %
1	2.411	26.785	26.785	2.411	26.785	26.785	2.243	24.922	24.922
2	1.805	20.059	46.844	1.805	20.059	46.844	1.650	18.328	43.250
3	1.287	14.298	61.142	1.287	14.298	61.142	1.610	17.892	61.142

Source: Author's analysis

Table 9.3 Rotated Component Matrix

Variables	Factor Loading		
	1	2	3
The entire offline schedule should be converted to an online one	.651		
Submission of assignments is easy through online mode	.635		
It is possible to have a fair and Transparent Online exam from the comfort of home	.848		
It is possible to have a fair and Transparent Online Evaluation	.816		
Your friends are availing external help while preparing online assignments			.876
Your friends are availing external help while giving online examination			.887
Stress arises in a virtual class since you are unable to have face-to-face interaction with your teachers		.758	
In an online mode of education you are unable to interact with your friends which leads to stress.		.769	
Following an entire offline class schedule to an online one will create stress		.649	

Source: Author's analysis

Table 9.4 Hosmer and Lemeshow Test

Step	Chi-square	df	Sig.
1	5.015	8	.756

Source: Author's analysis

Table 9.5 Classification

Observed			Predicted		
			The Future of Education is Blended Learning (Online + Offline)		Percentage Correct
			No	Yes	
Step 1	The Future of Education is Blended Learning (Online + Offline)	No	688 (TN)	2 (FP)	99.7
		Yes	64 (FN)	12 (TP)	15.8
	Overall Percentage		91.4		

Conclusion

The ongoing pandemic has crippled our education system. All schools, colleges, and universities have started online classes and received mixed responses from their stakeholders. During the pandemic, the online education system was a safer medium than the offline education system. The driving factor for this was its connectivity to all the stakeholders without any health hazards. This study shows that "E-Comfort", "E- stress", and "E-malpractice" influence and play a significant role in online education. Even though students are availing themselves of external help to complete the assignments, it is felt that evaluation can be done reasonably. The comfort provided by online classes and the equal attention given to each student is essential for online classes, making it beneficial. On the other hand, "E-stress" and "E-malpractice" negatively influence online education, keeping people wary of the online component of blended learning. Socially sustainable blended learning is the way forward if we want to sustain all stakeholders in education: students, society, educators and institutions.

The data for this study was gathered solely from India, and it was done so through online channels. Offline data from around the world can be included in future studies. It would also be possible to conduct a state-by-state comparison to determine which states lag behind the rest. It is possible to consider different countries as well as the impact of nationality on education. Additionally, the long-term implications of blended learning on education may be investigated. Since stress is a significant component of everyone's life, there is room for further investigation into the topic. Further research is required to stop fraudulent practices in online education.

References

Baragash, R. S., & Al-Samarraie, H. (2018). An empirical study of the impact of multiple modes of delivery on student learning in a blended course. *Reference Librarian*, 59(3), 149–162. https://doi.org/10.1080/02763877.2018.1467295

Bashir, I., & Madhavaiah, C. (2015). Consumer attitude and behavioural intention towards Internet banking adoption in India. *Journal of Indian Business Research*, 7(1), 67–102. https://doi.org/10.1108/JIBR-02-2014-0013

Demirer, V., & Sahin, I. (2013). Effect of blended learning environment on the transfer of learning: An experimental study. *Journal of Computer Assisted Learning*, 29(6), 518–529. https://doi.org/10.1111/jcal.12009

Dziuban, C. D., Moskal, P., & Hartman, J. (2005). Higher education, blended learning, and the generations: Knowledge is power-No more. In C.J. Bonk & C.R. Graham (Eds.), *Handbook of Blended Learning Environments: Global perspectives, local designs*. San Francisco, CA: Pfeiffer Publishing.

Dziuban, C., Graham, C. R., Moskal, P. D., Norberg, A., & Sicilia, N. (2018). Blended learning: The new normal and emerging technologies. *International Journal of Educational Technology in Higher Education*, 15(1), 3. https://doi.org/10.1186/s41239-017-0087-5

Filippidi, A., Tselios, N., &Komis, V. (2010). Impact of Moodle usage practices on students' performance in the context of a blended learning environment. In *Proceedings of the social applications for lifelong learning* (pp. 2–7).

Garrison, D. R., & Kanuka, H. (2004). Blended learning: Uncovering its transformative potential in higher education. *Internet and Higher Education*, 7(2), 95–105. https://doi.org/10.1016/j.iheduc.2004.02.001

Gliem, J. A., & Gliem, R. R. (2003). Calculating, interpreting, and reporting Cronbach's alpha reliability coefficient for Likert-type scales. *Midwest research-to-practice conference in adult, continuing, and community education*. Ohio State University: Columbus, OH, USA.

Grabinsk, K., Kedzior, M., & Krasodomska, J. (2015). Blended learning in tertiary accounting education in the CEE region-A Polish perspective. *Accounting and Management Information Systems*, 14(2), 378.

Jou, M., Lin, Y. T., & Wu, D. W. (2016). Effect of a blended learning environment on student critical thinking and knowledge transformation. *Interactive Learning Environments*, 24(6), 1131–1147. https://doi.org/10.1080/10494820.2014.961485

Kwak, D. W., Menezes, F. M., & Sherwood, C. (2015). Assessing the impact of blended learning on student performance. *Economic Record*, 91(292), 91–106. https://doi.org/10.1111/1475-4932.12155

Lim, D. H., & Morris, M. L. (2009). Learner and instructional factors influencing learning outcomes within a blended learning environment. *Journal of Educational Technology and Society*, 12(4), 282–293.

Lopez-Pérez, M. V., Pérez-Lopez, M. C., Rodríguez-Ariza, L., &Argente-Linares, E. (2013). The influence of the use of technology on student outcomes in a blended learning context. *Educational Technology Research and Development*, 61(4), 625–638. https://doi.org/10.1007/s11423-013-9303-8

Manwaring, K. C., Larsen, R., Graham, C. R., Henrie, C. R., & Halverson, L. R. (2017). Investigating student engagement in blended learning settings using experience sampling and structural equation modeling. *Internet and Higher Education*, 35, 21–33. https://doi.org/10.1016/j.iheduc.2017.06.002

Martínez-Caro, E., & Campuzano-Bolarín, F. (2011). Factors affecting students' satisfaction in engineering disciplines: Traditional vs blended approaches. *European Journal of Engineering Education*, 36(5), 473–483. https://doi.org/10.1080/03043797.2011.619647

Means, B., Toyama, Y., Murphy, R., Bakia, M., & Jones, K. (2009). *Evaluation of evidence-based practices in online learning: A meta-analysis and review of online learning studies*. United States Department of Education.

Moskal, P., Dziuban, C., & Hartman, J. (2013). Blended learning: A dangerous idea? *Internet and Higher Education*, 18, 15–23. https://doi.org/10.1016/j.iheduc.2012.12.001

Nguyen, V. A. (2017). The impact of online learning activities on student learning outcome in blended learning course. *Journal of Information and Knowledge Management*, 16(4). https://doi.org/10.1142/S021964921750040X, PubMed: 1750040

Okaz, A. A. (2015). Integrating blended learning in higher education. *Procedia - Social and Behavioral Sciences*, 186(13), 600–603. https://doi.org/10.1016/j.sbspro.2015.04.086

Rooney, J. E. (2003). Knowledge infusion. *Association Management*, 55(5), 26–26.

Singh, H. (2003). Building effective blended learning programs. *Educational Technology-Saddle Brook Then Englewood Cliffs NJ*, 43(6), 51–54.

Chapter 10

Two-Part Public Policy to Balance Technological External Diseconomies

A normative approach

Rabin Mazumder

Introduction

Technological externalities are created when the producer of a given operation is unable to understand all of its benefits or is not required to absorb all of the costs that are borne in relation to it by other companies or members of society (Due and Friedlander, 2002). External economies or external diseconomies arise from such situations. These require governmental intervention. This study focuses only on external diseconomies which come into being through waste materials and pollution. In a time of environmental concern, the issue of technical inefficiencies or spill-over effects becomes crucial. Chemical plants pollute the water, rendering it unfit for leisure and consumption; oil spills wreak havoc on beaches and destroy fish and wildlife. Pesticides that boost agricultural output kill fish, animals, and, on rare occasions, people. Airports produce unnecessary noise, which congests the highways and raises the cost of travel for everyone else. Noises, odours, delays, and other disturbing occurrences continuously bombard us, and we have no control over them. The manufacturers are only concerned about their own prices. The social costs are borne by industrial waste and smoke pollution. Industrial waste and smoke emissions bear the social costs.

In assessing pollution, the total costs and benefits of pollution control must be taken into account, as well as the marginal costs and benefits (Brasington & Hite, 2005). A hypothetical example can be used to illustrate the significance of this argument. Consider the case of a school coaching centre that relocates to a location adjacent to a paper board manufacturing plant (Coase, 1960). The coaching centre's ability to instruct the students is hampered by the noise from the factory's computer. The coaching centre then files an injunction in court to halt the production of the paper board manufacturing plant, arguing that the factory owner prohibits them from attending classes. However, an injunction will prevent the paper board manufacturing factory from operating. Furthermore, before the coaching centre was built next to the plant, the paper board manufacturing factory imposed no costs on society. The most effective remedy can be determined based on who has been harmed the most.

DOI: 10.4324/9781032640488-12

If the manufacturing factory's loss of income is greater than the coaching centre's loss of income, the latter will be compensated enough by the manufacturer to relocate. If the coaching centre's loss of income is greater than the manufacturing factory's, the coaching centre will pay the manufacturing factory to relocate. Compensation will be dispensed as long as the gains to the staying party outweigh the losses to the moving party, leaving all parties at least as well-off as before. Government interference is not needed when bilateral externality exists.

When the externality's effects are dispersed, the issue becomes more difficult. To put it another way, the extent of an act's external impact can be determined not only by the decisions of the performer, but also by the acts of those who are affected. Externalities would not be imposed by a power plant in the desert, but they would be imposed by one in a heavily populated area. If, however, the power plant was there before the population now surrounding it, the causality of the externality is not completely unambiguous (Baumol, 1965).

The control of negative externalities is a complex phenomenon. Following Pigou (1920), the first best scheme for controlling negative externalities is to set marginal taxes equal to marginal external harms (Kaplow, 2012). In 1896, Vilfredo Pareto introduced the concept of Pareto optimality to the field of economics. According to his description, a society is Pareto optimum (Pareto efficient) when no member improves their condition while lowering the condition of another member. Externalities make Pareto efficiency impossible to achieve. Externalities can thus be managed to restore optimality and potentially increase social welfare. The option of externality controls is discussed in a wide body of literature, most of which focuses on environmental externalities and security. In some cases, Pigouvian taxes can viably manage the issue of negative externalities. Some of the advantages of Pigouvian taxes are that they advance market productivity by consolidating the extra costs forced by negative externalities.

The objective of the present study is to outline the externality model and the government's position in reducing negative externalities through a two-part tax policy. The complete method of the study has been described in the following section with the model and the optimization strategy. This segment looks at the circumstances under which the proficient scheme can be implemented. A conclusion is drawn in Section 4, and the limitations and scope of the analysis are discussed in the final section.

Methods

1. The model

Let there exist two firms, X and Y. Both firms use a common factor of production, labour (L). Firm X also uses energy (E) for the production of goods. E is considered bad, as it generates smoke (S). Let us assume that

(1) Firm X uses L and E only, whereas firm Y uses L and S, generated by X's E use.
(2) Firm Y cannot escape from S generated by X's E uses. So, in the production process, firm Y is actually using L and S, where S = S(E). Here, S is the negative externality of firm Y.
(3) Firm X does not deal with the negative externalities.
(4) The legal system of their country is set up in such a way that X can generate as much as S as it likes without Y's consent.
(5) The government adopts a two-part policy to mitigate the extent of any negative externalities. T is the tax per unit of input E imposed on firm X and d is the subsidy per unit of output produced by firm Y.

The production function of firm X is
$q^x = q^x(L, E)$ where q^x stands for the total production of firm X

Keeping the output level unchanged, the rate of change in energy due to additional labour is called the marginal rate of technical substitution between E and L ($MRTS_{EL}$).

$$(MRTS_{EL}) = -\frac{MP_E}{MP_L} = \frac{dL}{dE} < 0 \ (\because \text{Slope of the isoquant is negative})$$

$\because MP_L > 0$ and $MP_E > 0$

MP_L is the marginal productivity of labour and MP_E is the marginal productivity of energy.

The isoquant is the locus of a different combination of two inputs where the output remains constant with given technology. So, for firm X, the slope of the isoquant (IQ^x) is negative and $\frac{d^2L}{dE^2} > 0$ (IQ^x is convex to the origin).

Similarly, for firm Y, the production function is $q^y = q^y(L, S(E))$

where q^y stands for the total production function of firm Y and S is considered as a public ill which occurs due to the use of E by firm X.

$$MRTS_{SL}^Y = -\frac{MP_S}{MP_L} = \frac{dL}{dE} > 0 \ (\because MP_S < 0 \text{ and } MP_L > 0)$$

Thus, IQ^Y is positively sloped. $\frac{d^2L}{dS^2} > 0$ indicating that IQ^Y is convex to the origin.

Thus, the IQ curves of the two firms will be as shown in Figure 10.1.

3. Optimization Technique

We can set the optimization of firm X as
Max $q^x = q^x(L, E)$

88 Rabin Mazumder

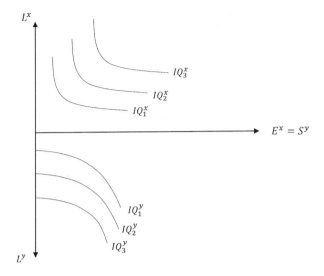

Figure 10.1 Isoquant of the firm.
Source: Author's analysis

Subject to the cost constraint, $C = wL + aE$
∴ The Lagrange equation is

$$Z_1 = q^x(L, E) + [C - wL - aE]$$

λ is the Lagrange multiplier.
Partially differentiating Z_1 with respect to L, E and λ

$$\therefore \frac{\partial Z_1}{\partial L} = q_L^x - \omega \left[q_L^x = \frac{\partial q^x}{\partial L} = \text{Marginal productivity of labour} \right]$$

$$\frac{\partial Z_1}{\partial E} = q_E^x - \omega \left[q_E^x = \frac{\partial q^x}{\partial E} = \text{Marginal productivity of energy} \right]$$

$$\frac{\partial Z_1}{\partial E} = c - wL - aE$$

According to the first-order condition (FOC) of optimization

$$\frac{\partial Z_1}{\partial L} = \frac{\partial Z_1}{\partial E} = \frac{\partial Z_1}{\partial} = 0$$

Therefore,

$$q_L^x - W\lambda \Rightarrow \lambda = \frac{q_L^x}{w} \quad \text{...............................Equation (1)}$$

$$q_E^x - a\lambda \Rightarrow \lambda = \frac{q_E^x}{a} \quad \text{...............................Equation (2)}$$

$$C - wL - aE \quad \text{...............................Equation (3)}$$

From equation (1) and (2), we get

$$\lambda = \frac{q^x_L}{w} = \frac{q^x_E}{a}$$

$$\text{Or,}\ \lambda = \frac{a}{w} = \frac{q_E^x}{q_L^x} > 0 \quad \text{...............................Equation (4)}$$

Hence, $\text{MRTS}_{EL} = (-)\dfrac{q_E^x}{q_L^x} < 0$

Now, firm X wants to maximize the level of production.

For maximization, the IQ must be convex to the origin. We checked the second-order condition and in such cases, the Boarder Hessian determinant (D) should be positive.

$$|D| = \begin{vmatrix} z_{LL} & z_{LE} & z_{L\lambda} \\ z_{EL} & z_{EE} & z_{E\lambda} \\ z_{\lambda L} & z_{\lambda E} & z_{\lambda\lambda} \end{vmatrix}$$

$$= \begin{vmatrix} q_{LL} & q_{LE} & -w \\ q_{EL} & q_{EE} & -a \\ -w & -a & 0 \end{vmatrix}$$

$$= q_{LL}(-a^2) - q_{LE}(-aw) - w(-aq_{EL} + wq_{EE})$$

$$= -q_{LL}\frac{q_E^2}{\lambda^2} + \frac{q_L}{\lambda} \cdot \frac{q_E}{\lambda} \cdot q_{LE} + \frac{q_L}{\lambda} \cdot \frac{q_E}{\lambda} \cdot q_{EL} - \frac{q_L^2}{\lambda^2} q_{EE}$$

$$= -\frac{1}{\lambda^2}\left[q_E^2 q_{LL} - 2q_L q_E q_{LE} + q_L^2 q_{EE}\right] \text{ (here, } q_{LE} = q_{EL} \text{ as per Young's theorem)}$$

For, $|\bar{D}| > 0$, $(q_E^2 q_{LL} - 2q_L q_E q_{LE} + q_L^2 q_{EE}) < 0$ (here, q_{LL} and $q_{EE} \langle 0$ and q_L and $q_E \rangle 0$ and we also assume that $q_{LE} > 0$

Hence, the MRTS is diminishing and IQ^x is convex to the origin.

Proposition 1: In the absence of a Pigouvian production tax on commodity, firm X can produce the maximum amount of output by using the factor of production L and E. Negative production externalities reduce the social welfare.

The production function of firm Y is $q^y = q^Y(L, S(E))$

Therefore, the objective function is Max $q^y = q^Y(L, S(E))$

Subject to the cost constraint: $C = wL + bS(E)$, where b is the cost per unit of smoke borne by firm Y (created through the production of firm X).

Therefore, the Lagrangian equation is
$Z_2 = q^Y(L, S(E)) + \mu[C - wL - bS(E)]$
μ is the Lagrangian multiplier.

Partially differentiating Z_2 with respect to "L", "S" and "μ"

$$\frac{\partial z_2}{\partial L} = q_L^Y - \mu w \quad (q_L^Y = \frac{\partial q^y}{\partial L} = \text{marginal productivity of labour})$$

$$\frac{\partial z_2}{\partial s} = q_s^y \frac{\partial s}{\partial E} - \mu b \cdot \frac{\partial s}{\partial s} \cdot \frac{\partial s}{\partial E} = (q_s^y - \mu b) \frac{\partial s}{\partial E}$$

$$\frac{\partial z_2}{\partial \mu} = C - wL - bS(E)$$

According to the first-order condition of optimization

$$\frac{\partial z_2}{\partial L} = \frac{\partial z_2}{\partial s} = \frac{\partial z_2}{\partial \mu} = 0$$

Therefore, $\mu = \dfrac{q_L^Y}{w}$ ....Equation (5)

$\mu = \dfrac{q_s^y}{b}$ ....Equation (6),

(since, $\dfrac{\partial s}{\partial E} > 0$)

$C - wL - bS(E)$ ....Equation (7)

From equation (5) and equation (6) we get

$$\frac{q_L^y}{w} = \frac{q_s^Y}{b} = \mu \Rightarrow \frac{q_s^y}{q_L^y} = \frac{b}{w} = \mu \quad \text{........................Equation (8)}$$

It is implied that the second-order condition is fulfilled for the maximization of output. IQ^x is convex to the origin.

Proposition 2: In the absence of a Pigouvian production tax on the commodity and the subsequent subsidy provided to the affected firm, IQs for firm Y will be upward sloping convex to the origin, because one bad input, S, reduced the output of the firm.

In the following figure, we show the Iso-cost line of our hypothetical economy. In Figure 10.2, the ordinate = $\sum_{i=x}^{y} B^i$, which measures a private factor of production. The abscissa is $E^X = s^Y$. Therefore, it measures public ills. Now combining Figure 10.1 and Figure 10.2, we get an Edgeworth triangle (see Figure 10.3).

In Figure 10.3, q_i^x (i = 1, 2, 3) are the isoquant curves of X and q_i^y (i = 1, 2, 3) are the isoquant curves of Y. CC is the contract curve joining all the tangency points of q_i^x and q_i^y. Along the CC curve, Pareto optimality condition is maintained, where,

Slope of the IQ^x = Slope of the IQ^Y

MRTS$^x_{EL}$ = MRTS$^Y_{SL}$

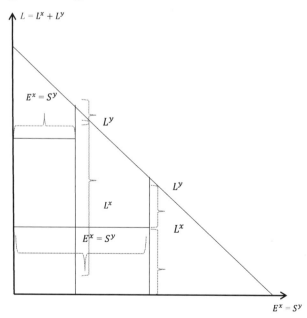

Figure 10.2 Iso-cost line.

Source: Author's analysis

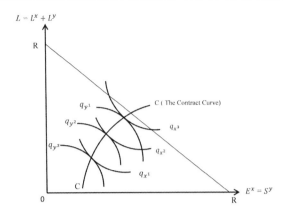

Figure 10.3 Contract curve.
Source: Author's analysis

Proposition 3: During externalities, there is a divergence of social costs from private costs and social benefits from private benefits. Externalities lead to poor allocation of resources and cause production to fall short of Pareto optimality. Equations (4) and (8) represent the equilibrium conditions of firms X and Y, where IQ is convex to the origin. But, $\dfrac{a}{w} = \dfrac{q_E^x}{q_L^x} \neq \dfrac{q_s^y}{q_L^y} = \dfrac{b}{w}$, so no Pareto optimal solution is found for the externality situation.

To mitigate the extent of the negative externalities the government adopts a two-part tax policy. Tax (t) per unit of input E is imposed on firm X and subsidy (d) is provided per unit of output produced by firm Y. Therefore, the modified optimization function will be $Q^* = Q^*(L, E)$ subject to the cost constraint C = wL + (a + t)E. The absolute slope of the iso-cost line $\left(\dfrac{a+t}{w}\right)$ will swing down, as shown in Figure 10.4. The new iso-cost line is AB′. Therefore, the equilibrium point will change from F to G. The PP line shows the post-tax equilibrium of firm X. In this scenario, firm Y has produced the same level of output as in the no-externality situation. But clearly G is not a Pareto optimal situation.

In the two-part tax policy, the government provides subsidy (d) per unit of output to firm Y, such that $tE = dq^Y$. After receiving the subsidy, the production of goods by firm Y will increase. Thus, firm Y has to be placed on a higher quantity level than in the no-externality situation. This is shown in Figure 10.5. Here, $q_1^x < q_2^x$ and $q_2^Y > q_1^Y$. Hence, an effective two-part tax policy can be Pareto optimal.

Proposition 4: The two-part tax policy is effective and Pareto optimal when the amount of tax imposed on the bad factor of production is equal to the subsidy provided to the affected firm.

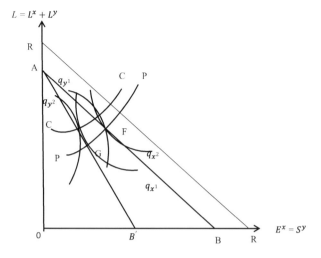

Figure 10.4 Equilibrium without Pareto optimal.
Source: Author's analysis

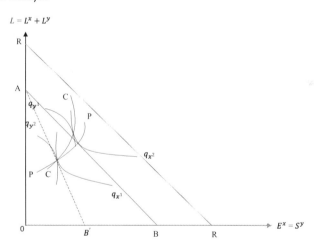

Figure 10.5 Pareto optimal.
Source: Author's analysis

Conclusion

In this theoretical note, it is observed that when negative externalities exist and the government's two-part tax policy is absent, one firm benefits by increasing production while the other is negatively affected. When negative externalities occur, resources are poorly allocated, causing output to fall short of Pareto optimality. Pigouvian taxation combined with subsidies would be effective in addressing negative externalities and improving social welfare. The Pareto optimal condition is achieved when a tax levied on one firm whose output generates negative externalities is fully balanced by offering a subsidy to the affected firm.

Since calculating the degree of pollution and the socially desirable tax rate is difficult in practice, the Pigouvian production tax may not be the best tool for dealing with negative externalities and improving social welfare. In an ideal world, the Pigouvian tax would be set at the same level as the costs of the negative externality. When Pigouvian taxes are levied, the supply of negative externality–producing economic activity decreases. As a result, the quantity demanded will fall while the price rises. The imposition of Pigouvian taxes is often linked to political difficulties. Attempts by the government to impose such taxes are often met with opposition from lobbyists who support parties that might be impacted by the taxes (e.g., tobacco producers). As a result, certain taxes are not always the best option from a political standpoint.

References

Baumol, W. J. (1965). *Welfare economics and the theory of the state*. Harvard University Press.

Brasington, D. M., & Hite, D. (2005). Demand for environmental quality: A Spatial Hedonic analysis. *Regional Science and Urban Economics*, 35(1), 57–82.

Coase, R. H. (1960). The problem of social cost. *Journal of Law and Economics*, 3, 1–44. https://doi.org/10.1086/466560

Due, J. F., & Friedlander, A. F. (2002). *Government finance, economics of public sector*. AITBS Publishers.

Kaplow, L. (2012). Optimal control of externalities in the presence of income taxation. *International Economic Review*, 53(2), 487–492.

Nemoto, J., & Goto, M. (2004). Technological externalities and economies of vertical integration in the electric utility industry. International Journal of Industrial Organization, 22(1), 67–81.

Pigou, A. C. (1920). The economics of welfare. *The Economic Journal*, 31(122), 206–214.

Part 2

Economic Sustainability

Chapter 11

Socio-economic Repercussions of COVID-19 and Economic Sustainability in the Aftermath

An Indian Perspective

Amitava Basu, Sugato Banerjee, Amalendu Samanta, Subhamay Panda, and Rakhi Chowdhury

Introduction

COVID-19, a pandemic which brought the whole world to a standstill, was not only a new disease which baffled the world, but one that brought with it a whole raft of perils which the world had not considered for a long time. India has been no exception. Its economy, society, and health sector have been seriously affected. Its social and its economic sustainability were presented with a huge challenge. India, an emerging economy, had felt the jolt of demonetization and GST just before the pandemic. The situation went from bad to worse with the chaos of COVID-19. As far as the economy was concerned, it affected both the demand and supply fronts. As far as education was concerned, our country was not equipped to move from physical to digital learning. A viral disease is supposed to affect people's physical health, but with so many repercussions stemming from the disease, people's mental health also entered its ambit. The situation as a whole has become a problem for Indian policy makers, and has put the social and economic sustainability of the entire country in question.

COVID-19 and the Indian Economy: Burning Problems and Plausible Solutions

Despite the fact that world history has seen several economic crises before COVID-19, the magnitude of economic devastation that the world economy faced during the COVID-19 pandemic surpassed all earlier experiences. An IMF report (June, 2020) mentioned four main reasons for this unprecedented economic crisis. Firstly, during the lockdown period, economic activities in all sectors were reduced significantly. Secondly, social distancing policies also considerably impacted economic activities. Thirdly, even after the recommencement of operations, the productivity of different sectors faced a steep decline. Finally, huge uncertainty and fear in the economic environment drastically reduced new investment and very harshly affected the capital market.

DOI: 10.4324/9781032640488-14

Being a part of the global village and today's integrated world economy, the Indian economy has also been shattered in numerous ways, and appropriate measures must be adopted to get out of the crisis through a proper analysis of the problems and of potential cushioning strategies.

Indian Economy and COVID-19

This "Black Swan" event attacked India on both the demand and supply fronts. Huge losses of employment, and the fear of further losses, reduced the demand for different commodities and services to a great extent. The resulting shutdowns of firms, the suspension of different economic activities, and the reduced productivity caused by lockdowns and social distancing strategies, created a supply-side crisis. The financial market also saw severe panic due to the pandemic (Agarwal et al., 2020). This crisis in the Indian economy appeared all the more shocking because the attack came at a time when the economy was already on a downward trajectory with regard to GDP growth over the previous few years because of the malfunctioning of its finance sector, considered to be the brain of the economy, and due to some macroeconomic policy changes like demonetization and the implementation of GST, etc. The backdrop of this slowdown in demand spread the crisis to the supply side through disruptions to domestic and global supply chains and, on both fronts, the crisis was exacerbated by a global recession and further decline in domestic demand (Dev & Sengupta, 2020; Ghosh et al., 2020).

Marks of Devastation

According to a report published by the United Nations, considering its economic devastation, India is one of the top fifteen COVID-19 victims in the world, and its potential loss of trade is around US$348 million. Asian Development Bank

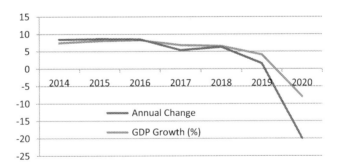

Figure 11.1 Trend in annual GDP growth percentage and the percentage of annual change of GDP growth.

Source: Handbook of Statistics on Indian Economy (RBI, September, 2021) and National Statistical Office (NSO)

estimates suggest, for their part, that the COVID-19 outbreak in India may result in a trade loss of US$387 million. The report also estimates a potential household consumption loss of US$30 billion due to reduced purchasing power on the part of consumers (Kumar et al., 2020). According to finance researchers and economists, the duration and depth of the crisis will have a far-reaching afterlife in the Indian economy. In order to bring coherence to our discussion, an analysis of sector-wise contribution to GVA by the different sectors of the economy, and of some major indicators reflecting the economic health of the country over the last few years, are required.

Figures 11.2 and 11.3 clearly show that, though the output of the Agriculture, Forestry and Fishing sector has grown over the years and even through the period of COVID-19, the growth of this output has a falling trend. This is mainly attributable to disruptions to transport, a decrease in demand, the complete shutdown of exports, and troubles in sowing and harvesting during the lockdown period (Sahoo & Samal, 2020).

A survey report from UNIDO (April, 2020) remarked that after the lockdown, Indian manufacturing faced severe turmoil. According to the report,

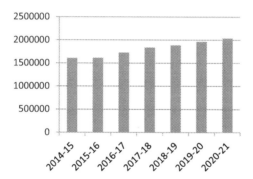

Figure 11.2 GVA by Agriculture, Forestry Fishing

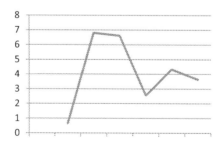

Figure 11.3 Rate of growth of GVA.

Source of Fig 11.2 and 11.3: Handbook of Statistics on Indian Economy (RBI, September, 2021) and National Statistical Office (NSO)

some of the most affected industries were the metal and chemical industries, the textile industry, and the automobile industry, etc. The figures published in the Handbook of Statistics on Indian Economy (2020–21) by the RBI also show a downfall in overall industrial output, as well as of the outputs of its different constituents. The steepest decline was noticed in the manufacturing sector, which accords with the UNIDO report. An insight into the figure reveals that, though the outputs of the different constituents of the manufacturing sector rose over the period 2014–2015 to 2017–2018, the slope of the curves clearly indicates a downward trajectory in the rate of growth of the output. So COVID-19 just exacerbated existing problems in the manufacturing industry.

The contribution of the service sector is considered to be an important indicator of economic development. Different subsectors of this sector include construction, travel/tourism, communication, medicine, public administration, and other services, etc. Except for the health and communication sectors, all other service sectors faced an austere crisis in their survival and growth. Tourism and construction, etc., faced a complete deadlock during different phases of the lockdown (Kumar & Nagrani, 2020). Figure 11.3, based on figures published in the Handbook of Statistics on Indian Economy (2020-21) by the RBI, shows the overall and sub-sectoral decline through the COVID-19 period.

Besides the sectoral decline and its adversities, this economic slump can clearly be seen in the trends of private final consumption, gross fixed capital formation, export, and import. Figure 11.4, based on reports published in the Handbook of Statistics on Indian Economy (2020-21) by the RBI, clearly reveals a downward trend in all parameters during the COVID-19 period. Here the only good sign is a decline in imports, which resulted in a positive current account balance in the BOP in 2020-21.

The overall employment situation in the organized and unorganized sectors has been in a dilatory state since 2015-16, and this situation was also worsened by the pandemic. The situation is evident from the data published

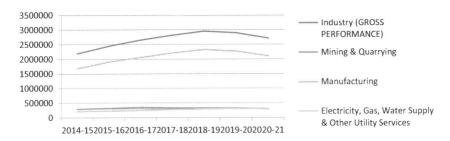

Figure 11.4 Gross and sector-wise performance of the industrial sector of the Indian economy.

Source: Handbook of Statistics on Indian Economy (RBI, September, 2021) and National Statistical Office (NSO)

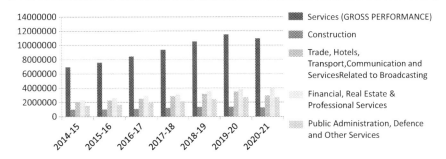

Figure 11.5 Performance of the service sector of the Indian economy.

Source: Handbook of Statistics on Indian Economy (RBI, September, 2021) and National Statistical Office (NSO)

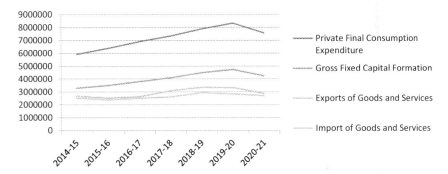

Figure 11.6 Trends in private final consumption, gross fixed capital formation, and the export and import of goods.

Source: Handbook of Statistics on Indian Economy (RBI, September, 2021) and National Statistical Office (NSO)

Note: (1) Data for 2017-18 are Third Revised Estimates, those for 2018–19 are Second Revised Estimates, and those for 2019-20 are First Revised Estimates.
(2) Data for 2020-21 are Provisional Estimates.
(3) All are at constant prices ((Base Year : 2011–12)

by the RBI regarding the organized public and private sectors. It is difficult to present a reliable picture, based on published sources, regarding the unemployment situation in the unorganized sector. However, researchers have reported that the unemployment rate in the unorganized sector rose from 6.7% to 26% during the second phase of the lockdown. (Arora & Gupta, 2020). Different newspaper reports also highlighted the adversities faced by migrant labourers, as well as the overall employment situation of the country.

COVID-19 not only affected the economy, but its ramifications spiralled into other spheres, notably the education and health sectors, and our society as a whole.

Societal Impact of the COVID-19 Pandemic in India

In India, precautionary protocols were enacted to contain the viral spread due to the severity of COVID-19, which led to restraints on all non-essential public movements (Saha et al., 2020). The necessity of moving from physical to digital learning became apparent with the closing of educational institutions (Kapasia et al., 2020). Virtual learning was identified as a potential substitute for conventional learning (Adnan, Anwar et al., 2020). In order to enhance e-learning, educational institutions have to adhere to the guidelines and suggestions of government entities, while encouraging students to be motivated to learn online in this challenging situation (Aucejo et al., 2020; Chaturvedi et al., 2021).

Over 1.2 billion students and young people across the world have been affected by the outbreak of the COVID-19 pandemic. In India, the different regulations and the national COVID-19 lockdown have affected more than 320 million students. According to the UNESCO estimate, about 140 million primary school children and 130 million secondary students are affected, representing the two most afflicted levels in India (Jena, 2020).

The COVID-19 pandemic has had a more detrimental impact on students from lower socio-economic backgrounds (Aucejo et al., 2020). Reduced family incomes, restricted access to electronic resources, and the high expense of internet connections have all interrupted students' academic lives. Furthermore, disruptions to daily schedules, such as a lack of outdoor movement, irregular sleeping habits, and social distancing, have impacted students' mental well-being (Cao et al., 2020; Chaturvedi et al., 2021). Many educational institutions and students in India are also unable to keep up with the swift transition between conventional education and the virtual learning system through digital resources.

Since most students have inadequate or no internet connection and many students cannot afford home computers, personal laptops or smartphones, online education has created a digital divide between students. According to numerous studies, the COVID-19 lockdown has severely affected impoverished students in India, because many students are unable to access the virtual learning sphere. As a result, during the COVID-19 pandemic, online teaching–learning techniques may have widened the gap between wealthy and poor, urban and rural (Jena, 2020; Nayek et al., 2021). The right to education is the most important right in the Indian constitution. According to the Indian constitution, the fundamental duty of parents/guardians is to send their children, if in the 6–14 age group, to school (Sindhu, 2014). In the context of the COVID-19 pandemic, then, these rights and duties have also been disrupted. Mid-day meals are an Indian government-sponsored school meal programme that aims to improve the nutritional status of school-aged children across the country. Because mid-day meal programmes have been temporarily closed due to the school closures, children's daily nutrition has been severely impacted (Upadhyay et al., 2020; Bahatheg, 2021). With minimal infrastructure exposure and maximum health risks, and at a time when India is making headlines every day for the highest daily COVID-19-positive cases across the globe, a debate has erupted about how final examinations should be held at educational institutions. In the event of a pandemic, India lacked the infrastructure to conduct the examination. Many students have failed to take their exams due to a lack of preparedness on the part of the government and exam authorities during the COVID-19 pandemic, leaving them with unfulfilled aspirations (Roy & Roy, 2021).

Public Health Burden of the COVID-19 Pandemic in India:

According to the World Health Organization (WHO), up to September 2021, more than 225 million people have been infected by the virus, killing more than 4.6 million worldwide. In India alone, more than 33 million cases and 440,000 deaths have been reported, and this number is on the rise as the pandemic continues. Individuals, irrespective of their sociodemographic positions, are equally susceptible to the disease (Park et al., 2020). The COVID-19 pandemic particularly affected health services in the low- and middle-income nations of South-East Asia, including India. HIV, TB, and malaria programmes run by the state and central governments have been affected (Di Gennaro et al., 2020). Maternal health services have been affected, and thus infant mortality and child health-associated mortalities have increased due to a lack of funding for maternal and child health services (Roberton et al., 2020).

Due to an increase in the disease, India experienced a shortage of medical equipment, hospital bed spaces, ICUs, respiratory ventilators, and personal protective gear like gloves, masks, and PPE kits (Armocida et al., 2020; Odone et al., 2020; Moatti, 2020; Hunter, 2020; Ranney et al., 2020). While developed nations like Germany have 29 ICU beds per 100,000 people, India has around 2.3 ICU beds per 100,000 individuals (Phua et al., 2020), which led to a serious crisis and high mortality among moderate to severe COVID patients, especially when the second wave of the pandemic hit India. It has been estimated that there are only 48,000 ventilators, which is considerably below the number necessary to serve the huge Indian population during any pandemic surge (Tirupakuzhi et al., 2020). To meet the country's demand, the government has roped in various Indian companies to rapidly manufacture and distribute endogenous ventilators. Finding adequate numbers of trained healthcare workers has also been a challenge during the pandemic. A major problem that India faced during the second wave of the COVID-19 pandemic was an acute shortage of medical oxygen. Indian railways have been running "OXYGEN Express" trains all across the country to supply medical-grade oxygen to meet the shortage. On April 21, the Dr. Zakir Hussain Hospital in Nasik reported 24 COVID-19 deaths due to a lack of medical oxygen.

With the increase in cases, the demand for medical-grade oxygen to support ICU patients jumped by 600%. India also received aid from various foreign nations: 23 oxygen-generation plants from Germany, 10,000 oxygen concentrators from the US, oxygen tankers from Singapore, and ventilators from the UK and Europe. Due to a lack of local production, the supply of medical oxygen to various parts of the country has always been dependent on how fast oxygen-supplying tankers could travel across the country (Changoiwala, 2021). After the oxygen crisis India has already ramped up its oxygen production and is targeting a production capacity of 15,000 tons per day, which is a 50% increase in production.

The Indian government not only plans to vaccinate its population against COVID-19 but also to provide the vaccine to less developed nations that cannot afford expensive vaccines. Primarily three vaccines are being used in the vaccination programme: Covishield, by the Serum Institute, Covaxine by Bharat Biotech, and the Russian vaccine Sputnik V, marketed by Dr Reddy's Laboratory. While the above vaccines are for individuals in the age group of 18 and above, ZyCoV-D, manufactured by Cadila Healthcare, has recently been introduced for 12–18-year-olds (Sharma et al., 2021). The government has also authorized Cipla to import Moderna's RNA vaccine. In the meanwhile, the Central Drugs Standard Control Organization (CDSCO) of the Government of India is in the process of approving other vaccines, like the Janssen COVID-19 single-dose vaccine. The Government of India–constituted National Expert Group on Vaccine Administration for COVID-19 (NEGVAC) is responsible for providing guidelines for vaccine administration in India. According to NEGVAC, the vaccines were initially offered to healthcare workers, frontline workers like police personnel, cleaning staff, military personnel, etc., and to individuals >50 years of age (prioritizing individuals >60 years old) followed by those of the >45 age group with co-morbidities. Expert committees were established to determine the clinical criteria based on which people with co-morbidities would attain priority for COVID-19 vaccination. According to the recommendations of the committee, individuals with congenital heart disease, end-stage kidney disease, cancer, liver cirrhosis, immune deficiency, and sickle cell anaemia are included in the priority list for vaccination. This is followed by the vaccination of individuals in the 18–45 age group (Kumar et al., 2021). The Indian Academy of Pediatrics (IAP)/IAP Committee on Vaccines & Immunization (ACVIP) has also recommended the vaccination for breastfeeding women (Kasi et al., 2021). It has also been demonstrated in the Indian population that two doses of Covishield have reduced mortality rates among moderate to severe COVID-19 hospitalized patients (Muthukrishnan et al., 2021). It has also been predicted that vaccination will play a major role in protecting the Indian population during the third wave of the pandemic (Rajgopal & Joseph, 2021). The major challenge in the vaccination programme was the storage and transportation of the vaccines, because of its specific storage temperature requirements. Some of the vaccines produced by foreign nations, requiring −80 °C storage, were of limited use in India because of the lack of infrastructure in the Indian vaccination distribution chain. Fortunately, the vaccines produced by India have a storage temperature requirement of 2–8°C. Temperature monitoring of 29,000 cold-chain points is being done in real time through a cloud-based digital platform, the COVID Vaccine Intelligence Network (Co-WIN). The initial batches of the COVID-19 vaccines have been administered through the Universal Immunization Program (UIP) mechanism already operational in India. The UIP is linked to the Co-WIN system (Kumar et al., 2021). However, there is a need to expand the cold-chain infrastructure for the storage and transport of vaccines. This will help in the expansion of COVID-19 vaccine coverage to the most remote Indian villages.

Cushioning Measures Adopted

The magnitude of the crisis demanded quick and steady measures from different corners of the economy. The Government of India declared a stimulus package for the revival of different sectors of the economy. It is also expected that this will improve the growth rate of India's GDP and will reduce the rate of unemployment (Ghosh et al., 2020). From the stimulus package, the greatest benefit will be felt by the MSME sector. The agricultural sector will receive benefits through Kissan credit cards and through improvements in agricultural infrastructure. Besides these, other sectors are also receiving different kinds of subsidies. Development measures are also being taken to protect the financial system of the country. Apart from fiscal support, the RBI has adopted a monetary policy to help fight against the crisis (Manjushree & Mavuri, 2020). To reduce the societal burden, the Government of India followed the stress management guide issued by the World Health Organisation. Different programmes on COVID-19 dos and don'ts were broadcasted and aired by different types of media. News agencies have also played a positive role during this period. The efforts of different NGOs have also been worth mentioning. No praise is sufficient for health workers and other public health stakeholders for their fight against the crisis. Aside from Government Initiatives, the private investment in the field of research and development aimed at discovering different medicines and vaccines is also noteworthy. Different state governments have also declared different types of support to ease the crisis.

Policy Recommendations and Economic Sustainability

Economic sustainability refers to the ability of the economy to maintain a particular desired level of economic operation over an indefinite period of time. The pandemic, the economic downturn, and the social and health crises are interrelated issues. Finance researchers and economists across the

106 Amitava Basu et al.

globe have given different suggestions related to strategies for fighting against crises and resolving the situation. These suggestions are multidimensional and multifaceted. Particular policies should be adopted depending on the situation of a particular economy. For a developing economy like India, the policies adopted must be inclusive, resilient, and flexible. There should be a proper integration of monetary policy, fiscal policy, and macro-prudential policy. (Padhan & Prabeesh, 2021). Besides providing appropriate subsidies depending on the needs of different sectors, improvisation in the supply network is needed. Tax relief should be provided not only to corporate houses but also to baseline consumers. Direct cash transfer benefits should be provided not only to landowners but also to landless labourers. The digital divide in "Digital India" has been very clearly noticed during the pandemic. It must be solved through proper budgetary support. To cure demand-side shock, increased liquidity and enhanced consumer confidence are very much required (Arora & Gupta, 2020). To reduce the societal impact, more front-line workers are required, and the related infrastructure must be improved considering the current inadequacies. A combined attack using these different suggested measures will certainly help to arrest recession in different sectors of the economy, increase demand, improve the GDP growth rate, increase

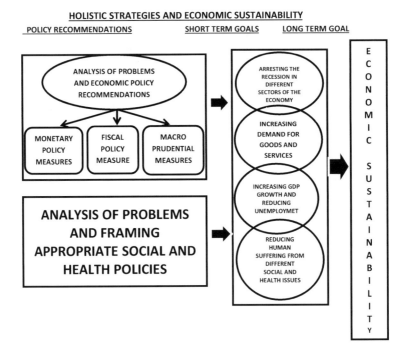

Figure 11.7 Holistic strategies and economic sustainability.

Source: Model developed by the authors

employment, and flatten human suffering from different social and health issues. These will certainly help the economy to achieve economic sustainability, as shown in Figure 11.6.

Conclusion

The COVID-19 pandemic has given enough lessons to the whole world, especially to developing nations like India, on gaps in our economic, social, and health infrastructures. A SWOC analysis of the entire system is needed to find an integrated solution to the problems arising from the pandemic. A holistic strategy should be framed after a proper analysis of economic, social, and public health problems to ensure growth. A critical analysis of the problems discussed, and the recommendations mentioned, in this article will make our recommendations more subtle and will reveal more productive combat strategies. These will lead our country and the world down the path of sustainable development by providing economic sustainability.

References

Adnan, M., Anwar, K., & Cheng, T. (2020). How students' perspectives about online learning amid the COVID-19 pandemic? *Studies in Learning and Teaching*, 1(3), 133–139. https://doi.org/10.46627/silet.v1i3.46

Agrawal, S., Jamwal,A., & Gupta, S. (2020). Effect of COVID-19 on the Indian economy and supply chain. *Preprints*, 2020050148. https://doi.org/10.20944/preprints202005.0148.v1.

Armocida, B., Formenti, B., Ussai, S., Palestra, F., &Missoni, E. (2020). The Italian health system and the COVID-19 challenge. *The Lancet Public Health*, 5(5), e253. https://doi.org/10.1016/S2468-2667(20)30074-8

Arora, N., & Gupta,V. (2020). Study on impact of COVID-19 on Indian economy. *International Journal of Science and Research*, 9(7, July), 20201516–20201519. https://doi.org/ 10.21275/SR20724142409

Aucejo, E. M., French, J., Ugalde Araya, M. P., & Zafar, B. (2020). The impact of COVID-19 on student experiences and expectations: Evidence from a survey. *Journal of Public Economics*, 191(11), 104271. https://doi.org/10.1016/J.JPUBECO.2020.104271

Bahatheg, R. O. (2021). Young children's nutrition during the COVID-19 pandemic lockdown: A comparative study. *Early Childhood Education Journal*, 49(5), 915–923. https://doi.org/10.1007/S10643-021-01192-3

Cao, W., Fang, Z., Hou, G., Han, M., Xu, X., Dong, J., & Zheng, J. (2020). The psychological impact of the COVID-19 epidemic on college students in China. *Psychiatry Research*, 287, 112934. https://doi.org/10.1016/J.PSYCHRES.2020.112934

Changoiwala, P. (2021). India at breaking point. *New Scientist*, 250(3332). https://doi.org/10.1016/s0262-4079(21)00715-6

Chaturvedi, K., Vishwakarma, D. K., & Singh, N. (2021). COVID-19 and its impact on education, social life and mental health of students: A survey. *Children and*

Youth Services Review, *121*, 105866. https://doi.org/10.1016/J.CHILDYOUTH.2020.105866

Deb, S. M., & Sengupta,R. (2020, April). "Covid-19: Impact on the Indian Economy" WP-2020-013. Indira Gandhi Institute of Development Research. http://www.igidr.ac.in/pdf/publication/WP-2020-013.pdf

Di Gennaro, F., Marotta, C., Locantore, P., Pizzol, D., & Putoto, G. (2020). Malaria and Covid-19: Common and different findings. *Tropical Medicine and Infectious Disease*, *5*(3), 141. https://doi.org/10.3390/tropicalmed5030141

Ghosh, A., Nundy, S., & Mallick, T. K. (2020, July). How India is dealing with COVID-19 pandemic. *Sensors International*. https://doi.org/10.1016/j.sintl.2020.100021

Hunter, D. J. (2020). Covid-19 and the stiff upper lip — The pandemic response in the United Kingdom. *New England Journal of Medicine*, *382*(16), e31. https://doi.org/10.1056/nejmp2005755

International Monetary Fund. (2020, June). A crisis like no other, an uncertain recovery. https://www.imf.org/en/Publications/WEO/Issues/2020/06/24/WEOUpdateJune2020

Jena, P. K. (2020). Impact of pandemic COVID-19 on education in India. *International Journal of Current Research*, *12*(7), 12582–12586. https://papers.ssrn.com/abstract=3691506

Kapasia, N., Paul, P., Roy, A., Saha, J., Zaveri, A., Mallick, R., Barman, B., Das, P., & Chouhan, P. (2020). Impact of lockdown on learning status of undergraduate and postgraduate students during COVID-19 pandemic in West Bengal, India. *Children and Youth Services Review*, *116*, 105194. https://doi.org/10.1016/J.CHILDYOUTH.2020.105194

Kasi, S. G., Dhir, S. K., Shivananda, S., Marathe, S., Chatterjee, K., Agarwalla, S., Verma, S., Shah, A. K., Srirampur, S., Kalyani, S., Pemde, H. K., Balasubramanian, S., Basavaraja, G. V., Parekh, B. J., Kumar, R., & Gupta, P. (2021). Breastfeeding and coronavirus disease 2019 (COVID-19) vaccination: Position statement of Indian Academy of Pediatrics advisory committee on vaccination and immunization practices. *Indian Pediatrics*, *58*(7), 647–649. https://doi.org/10.1007/s13312-021-2261-z

Kumar, P. S., & Nagrani, K. (2020). A study on Covid effect on Indian service sector. *Seshadripuram Research Foundation*, 14–23. Vol. Oct, 2020. https://www.researchgate.net/publication/344873679_A_STUDY_ON_COVID_EFFECT_ON_INDIAN_SERVICE_SECTOR

Kumar, S.,Thombare, P. B., & Kale, P. A. (2020, April) Impact of coronavirus (COVID-19) on Indian economy. *AGRICULTURE & FOOD: e-Newsletter*, *2*(4). https://kvkkolhapur2.icar.gov.in/PDF/Impact%20of%20coronavirus%20COVID19%20on%20Indian%20economy.pdf

Kumar, V. M., Pandi-Perumal, S. R., Trakht, I., &Thyagarajan, S. P. (2021). Strategy for COVID-19 vaccination in India: The country with the second highest population and number of cases. *NPJ Vaccine*, *6*(60). https://doi.org/10.1038/s41541-021-00327-2

Manjushree, P., Sudha, M., & Lalitha, N. (2020). Economic impact of COVID-19 on Indian economy - Government measures to contain the pandemic. *Journal of Critical Reviews*, *7*(19), 5903–5913. https://doi.org/10.31838/jcr.07.19.683

Moatti, J. P. (2020). The French response to COVID-19: Intrinsic difficulties at the interface of science, public health, and policy. In *The Lancet Public Health*, 5(5), E255. https://doi.org/10.1016/S2468-2667(20)30087-6

Muthukrishnan, J., Vardhan, V., Mangalesh, S., Koley, M., Shankar, S., Yadav, A. K., & Khera, A. (2021). Vaccination status and COVID-19 related mortality: A hospital based cross sectional study. *Medical Journal Armed Forces India*, 77 (Suppl. 2), S278–S282. https://doi.org/10.1016/j.mjafi.2021.06.034

Nayak, J., Mishra, M., Naik, B., Swapnarekha, H., Cengiz, K., & Shanmuganathan, V. (2021). An impact study of COVID-19 on six different industries: Automobile, energy and power, agriculture, education, travel and tourism and consumer electronics. *Expert Systems*, 1–32. https://doi.org/10.1111/EXSY.12677

Odone, A., Delmonte, D., Scognamiglio, T., & Signorelli, C. (2020). COVID-19 deaths in Lombardy, Italy: Data in context. In *The Lancet Public Health*, 5(6), E310. https://doi.org/10.1016/S2468-2667(20)30099-2

Padhan, R., & Prabheesh, K. P. (2021, February). The economics of COVID-19 pandemic: A survey. *Economic Analysis and Policy*. https://doi.org/10.1016/j.eap.2021.02.012 pp.-230–237

Park, M., Cook, A. R., Lim, J. T., Sun, Y., & Dickens, B. L. (2020). A systematic review of COVID-19 epidemiology based on current evidence. *Journal of Clinical Medicine*, 9(4). https://doi.org/10.3390/jcm9040967

Phua, J., Faruq, M. O., Kulkarni, A. P., Redjeki, I. S., Detleuxay, K., Mendsaikhan, N., Sann, K. K., Shrestha, B. R., Hashmi, M., Palo, J. E. M., Haniffa, R., Wang, C., Hashemian, S. M. R., Konkayev, A., Mat Nor, M. B., Patjanasoontorn, B., Nafees, K. M. K., Ling, L., Nishimura, M., … Fang, W. F. (2020). Critical care bed capacity in Asian countries and regions. *Critical Care Medicine*, 48(5), 654–662. https://doi.org/10.1097/CCM.0000000000004222

Rajgopal, T., & Joseph, B. (2021). Vaccination as a strategy to prevent or mitigate a potential COVID-19 third wave in India. *Indian Journal of Occupational and Environmental Medicine*, 25(2), 55–59. https://doi.org/10.4103/ijoem.ijoem_193_21

Ranney, M. L., Griffeth, V., & Jha, A. K. (2020). Critical supply shortages — The need for ventilators and personal protective equipment during the Covid-19 pandemic. *New England Journal of Medicine*, 382(18), e41. https://doi.org/10.1056/nejmp2006141

Reserve Bank of India (2021). Handbook of statistics on Indian economy" September,2021. https://www.rbi.org.in/scripts/annualPublications.aspx%3Fhead%3DHandbook%20of%20Statistics%20on%20Indian%20Economy

Roberton, T., Carter, E. D., Chou, V. B., Stegmuller, A. R., Jackson, B. D., Tam, Y., Sawadogo-Lewis, T., & Walker, N. (2020). Early estimates of the indirect effects of the COVID-19 pandemic on maternal and child mortality in low-income and middle-income countries: A modelling study. *The Lancet Global Health*, 8(7), E901–E908. https://doi.org/10.1016/S2214-109X(20)30229-1

Roy, B., & Roy, A. (2021). Conducting examinations in India: Emergency, contention and challenges of students amidst Covid-19 pandemic. *Children and Youth Services Review*, 120, 105768. https://doi.org/10.1016/J.CHILDYOUTH.2020.105768

Saha, J., Barman, B., & Chouhan, P. (2020). Lockdown for COVID-19 and its impact on community mobility in India: An analysis of the COVID-19 Community Mobility Reports, 2020. *Children and Youth Services Review*, 116, 105160. https://doi.org/10.1016/J.CHILDYOUTH.2020.105160

Sahoo, P. J., Samal, K., & Chandra. (2020, July). Impact of COVID-19 on Indian agriculture. *Agriculture Letters*, *01*(03), 45–47. https://doi.org/10.13140/RG.2.2.19521.68969

Sharma, J., Sharma, D., Tiwari, D., & Vishwakarma, V. (2021). The challenges and successes of dealing with the COVID-19 pandemic in India. *Research and Reports in Tropical Medicine*, *12*, 205–218. https://doi.org/10.2147/rrtm.s274673

Sindhu, S. (2014). Fundamental right to education in India: An overview. *Global Journal of Interdisciplinary Social Science*, *3*(5), 92–95.

TirupakuzhiVijayaraghavan, B. K., NainanMyatra, S. M., Lodh, N., VasishthaDivatia, J., Hammond, N., Jha, V., & Venkatesh, B. (2020). Challenges in the delivery of critical care in India during the COVID-19 pandemic. *Journal of the Intensive Care Society*, *2020*, 1–7. https://doi.org/10.1177/1751143720952590

United Nations Industrial Development Organisation (2020, April). *India's manufacturing reels from the impact of COVID-19*. https://www.unido.org/stories/ indias-manufacturing-reels-impact-covid-19

Upadhyay, M. K., Patra, S., & Khan, A. M. (2020). Ensuring availability of food for child nutrition amidst the COVID-19 pandemic: Challenges and Way forward. *Indian Journal of Community Health*, *32*(2 Suppl.), 251–254. https://doi.org/10.47203/IJCH.2020.V32I02SUPP.015

Chapter 12

Toward Sustainable Livelihood Promotion for Artisans – A Holistic Marketing Framework for Improving the Indian Handicraft Sector

Arunava Dalal, Subrata Chattopadhyay, and Subhajit Bhattacharya

Introduction

The handicraft industry is primarily an unorganized sector, providing livelihoods to over 7 million people. This sector is the second largest employment generator in India after agriculture. The majority of the craftspeople belong to the weaker section of society (Ministry of Textiles, Government of India, 2020), spread across different locations in India. Due to the poor economic conditions of these artisans, they are forced to take to other professions that are completely different from the traditional arts and crafts work inherited from their ancestors.

The handicraft sector has grown over the years. The export value of Indian handicrafts grew from Rs. 34.63 billion during FY 2011 to Rs. 128.35 billion in FY 2019 (Statista, 2019). This shows the acceptability of these products on a global scale. But when this is compared with the value of the global handicrafts market of US$ 526.5 Billion in 2017 (IMARC Group, 2020) the percentage share of Indian handicrafts in the global market is minuscule. The USAID Global Market Assessment for Handicrafts report (2006) mentioned India's potential for increasing its share in the global handicraft market, but the constraints faced by this industry will need to be mitigated first. This will help in providing sustainable livelihoods to the artisans, leading to a balance of socio-economic development and inclusive growth.

In the field of Indian handicrafts, studies have been carried out related to the field of marketing and how the internet and e-commerce can be leveraged to popularize the Indian handicraft industry in the domestic and international markets. Kumar and Rajeev, 2013; Kumari and Srivasatava, 2016; Oza, 2019; and Yadav & Mahara, 2018 have worked in the domain of handicraft marketing and of e-commerce in the handicraft sector. Research papers by Srivastav and Rawat 2016; Vats, 2014; and Ghouse, 2017 have focused on the export market of Indian handicrafts due to globalization. But very little work has been done looking at the handicraft sector holistically, covering all the major elements of the value chain.

DOI: 10.4324/9781032640488-15

Considering the current situation, the purpose of this study is to conceptualize a model based on the identified roadblocks. This will ensure a wider reach for organizations to procure different varieties of unique handicrafts across locations, and to overcome geographical constraints using technology as an enabler. Besides bringing these crafts before the world, this model will also help to uplift a major segment of artisans who are unable to showcase their talents and sell their crafts to prospective buyers without having to go through multiple intermediaries.

Methods

This paper follows a systematic literature review framework and, on the basis of existing work, attempts to reveal the theoretical gap that exists with regard to the conceptualization of a holistic framework. The identification of the constraints to the sector, as carried out through the literature review, is discussed below.

Consumers and the Craft Producers

Campbell (2005) has identified "craft consumers" as a category of customer. These people consume crafts, as this act gives them an outlet for their creative acts of self-expression. Craft consumption happens when consumers adopt products that are in line with their preferences. A study conducted by Dasgupta and Chandra (2016) identified aesthetics as the most influential factor for handicraft purchasers, along with other important factors like utility, sustainability, and cultural connections. Knowledge of the customers' preferences is an important aspect of designing crafts. The handicraft industry faces the challenges of a lack of market knowledge, of marketing activities, and of agility and scalability in craft design (Yihao & Yuning, 2010). The same concern regarding a lack of communication between artisans and their end customers has been highlighted by many researchers like Banik, 2017; Kumari & Srivasatava, 2016; and Menon, 2010. So, the following constraint can be put forward:

C1: Lack of knowledge of customers' needs and preferences.

Internet technology could effectively address this issue in the handicraft sector. According to Kumar and Rajeev (2013), online marketing plays a crucial role, as it gives the necessary information to the customers and motivates them to buy the products. Due to this, the first proposition for the handicraft industry is:

P1: Use of online platforms/technology by the handicraft sector to reach their target customers.

For small businesses, the internet can connect producers with their customers easily and can help organizations become aware of their customers' changing behaviours. This will help them to develop products that meet customers' requirements (Migiro & Ocholla, 2005).

Intermediaries in the Handicraft Sector

The majority of India's artisans live in remote locations, where they are deprived of the facilities of large towns or cities and so have to depend on third parties. The problem of middlemen in the handicraft industry has been expressed by many authors, such as Pathak et al. (2017); Tiwari and Dutta (2013); and Yadavand Mahara (2018) in their research, thus exposing the second constraint of the sector:

C2: Influence of middlemen in the handicraft supply chain.

The proposition for addressing the above constraint is

P2: Elimination or minimization of the layers of intermediaries.

The Sourcing of Raw Materials

Raw materials play an important part in any production process, and researchers have highlighted their importance in papers like those of Kamble and Raut, 2019; and Agrawal 2014. In his paper, Agrawal (2014) mentions the significance of the procurement of the right quality and quantity of raw materials to achieve finished products of the right quality and price. Therefore, the identification of the right suppliers for the input materials, and the formation of appropriate relationships with them, is critical for the effective and efficient functioning of a supply chain (Mukhamedjanova, 2020). In the handicraft sector, too, the procurement of raw materials is an important function for the artisans. In the past, artisans used raw materials that were locally available to produce their crafts, but now artisans find it difficult to access quality raw materials. The issues related to the supply of raw materials have been put forward by Venkataramanaiah and Kumar (2011) in their research paper. Thus, the third constraint, and the corresponding proposition, to be addressed by the proposed model are:

C3: Difficulty in the procurement of quality raw materials at a suitable price.
P3: Streamlining the process of procuring raw materials for the effective functioning of the handicraft sector.

Other Constraints in the Handicraft Sector

Ernst and Young (2012), in one of their reports on the Indian handicraft sector, have highlighted a few issues, namely a lack of access to credit, inadequate raw material input, inadequate infrastructure and technology, and limited access to the market. A report by the Ministry of Textiles, Government of India (2012), also corroborates this. Different schemes launched by the government for the benefit of the handicraft sector seem to have failed to reach their target audience. In her article, Kumari (2016) mentions the low education levels of artisans, as well as regulations, as impediments to the complete dissemination of all the required information.

The constraints of "the lack of knowledge of new technologies and methods of production" and "lack of access to credit" can be summed as:

C4: Lack of coordination with external parties (NGOs or government training centres for artisans, and banks or financial institutions for credit access).

The possible proposition for the above constraints (C4) is:

P4: Making possible and aiding the connection of artisans with external parties (NGOs or government training centres for artisans, and banks or financial institutions for credit access).

Results and Discussions

Based on the constraints (C1 to C4) that have been identified from the literature review, the current study looks to develop a conceptual model to minimize the gap between the value created and the value delivered. Figure 12.1 puts forward the "enablers" (P1 to P4) that will mitigate the identified issues (C1 to C4), resulting in benefits for all the stakeholders. The four enablers that have been identified are: bonding with customers using technology (P1), breaking the chain of intermediaries (P2), bridging the raw materials sourcing issue (P3), and building awareness of external enablers like training agencies and financial institutions (P4). Figure 12.1 depicts how the enablers (the four Bs) can lead to the five Rs (Right product, Right design, Right time, Right customer, Right price), thus benefiting all the stakeholders in the handicraft industry.

Customers will be happy to have access to beautifully crafted products according to their choices and tastes. This will ensure higher and more regular demand for the crafts. This continuous demand for and sale of handicrafts will in turn ensure that the artisans are able to sell their products throughout the year and earn appropriate prices for their skills and craftsmanship. This will help with the expansion of the handicraft market, thus helping handicraft organizations increase their sales and earn higher profits.

Sustainable Livelihoods for Artisans 115

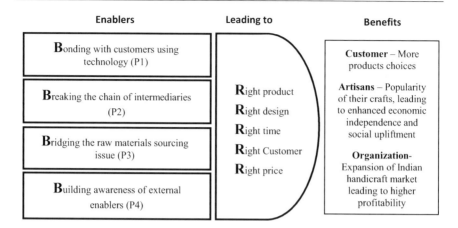

Figure 12.1 Four Bs to five Rs model.
Source: Prepared by authors

Based on the "four Bs to five Rs" model (Figure 12.1), an operational model has been conceptualized, as seen in Figure 12.2. The most important elements in the proposed model are the "Hub and Distribution (HD) Cell", the "Design and Development (DD) Cell" and the "Artisans' Support (AS) Cell". The HD cell has been considered as a means of performing functions catering to multiple channels for the distribution of crafts. The cell receives the finished goods from the artisans, artisan clusters, or artisan cooperatives. From this central hub, the products will be distributed through different online and offline channels, and can also be delivered directly to customers for requests received through the organization's online portal or mobile app. This is the application of P2, which is "breaking the chain of intermediaries", as an enabler mentioned in the four Bs to five Rs model.

The DD Cell is the answer to P1, which is "bonding with customers through technology". This cell connects the customers with the artisans and ensures seamless interactions between them. This cell will ensure that the artisans are aware of market realities, customers' needs, likings, and feedback, and in turn, customers will find their craft purchases in line with their tastes and preferences.

The AS cell is for "building awareness of external enablers" (P4). This cell will be in contact with other external agencies related to the training and skill development of the artisans – non-governmental organizations (NGOs), financial institutions, and other institutions working for the betterment of the handicraft sector. They will also be responsible for handholding the artisans so that they can reap the benefits of the different government schemes floated from time to time. This cell will also interact with the DD Cell to identify the artisans' training and skill development requirements.

116 Arunava Dalal et al.

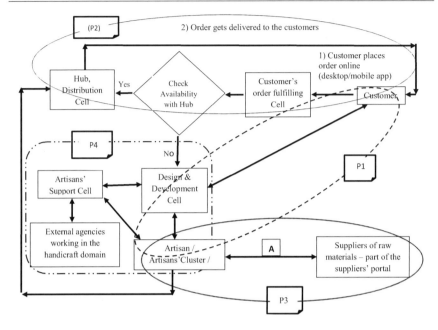

Figure 12.2 The operational model.
Source: Prepared by authors

To address C3, relating to the availability of raw materials for the artisans, the model has incorporated a portal for the onboarding of suppliers. This is independent of the customer-facing portal. An intelligent system (marked as "A" in Figure 12.2) will ensure the connection of the artisans with the correct suppliers, thus implementing the enabler P3, "bridging the raw materials sourcing issue".

The arrows in the model are indicative of the flow of information or products between entities or cells.

Conclusion

Our conceptual model looks at the handicraft value chain holistically; this can be beneficial for organizations engaged in the handicraft sector. This was based on the identification of the individual connectors which, when joined together, can address the problems that are presently being faced by the handicraft sector. This model will be beneficial for all the stakeholders in developing and underdeveloped countries involved in the handicraft sector, and particularly for the sustainable improvement of the socio-economic status of artisans. The model will also ensure the preservation of the originating country's culture and heritage which is an important aspect integrally linked with handicrafts.

The findings of this study suggest that organizations dealing in handicrafts should take a holistic view of handicraft operations. The study has identified various factors impacting the handicraft sector that have been addressed in the conceptual model. The implementation of the model is applicable to all businesses involved in the handicraft sector. The model should benefit these organizations in terms of sales volumes and profitability, along with building a strong relationship with the artisans, on one hand, and the customers on the other.

The conceptual model demonstrated in this paper could help researchers understand the integrated value chain process, helping them boost business outcomes in a positive direction. This article can be seen as taking a holistic view of the handicraft industry, which could lead toward improved strategies and process development which could revive and restructure the unorganized handicraft marketing setups present in developing and underdeveloped countries, and ensure sustainable livelihoods for craftspeople.

The model, being conceptual, lacks validation in a real setting. Thus, future research needs to be conducted to test it empirically, and help convert it into a robust business model. The study could be tested in other developing and underdeveloped countries to check its validity and to make it more generalizable.

References

Agrawal, A. (2014). Managing raw material in supply chains. *European Journal of Operational Research, 239*(3), 685–698.

Banik, S. (2017). A study on financial analysis of rural artisans in India: Issues and challenges. *International Journal of Creative Research Thoughts (IJCRT), 5*(4), 1–6.

Campbell, C. (2005). The craft consumer: Culture, craft and consumption in a postmodern society. *Journal of Consumer Culture, 5*(1), 23–42.

Dasgupta, A., & Chandra, B. (2016). Evolving motives for fair trade consumption: A qualitative study on handicraft consumers of India. *Anthropologist, 23*(3), 414–422.

Ernst and Young. (2012). *Competitive study on Handicrafts Sector in China.* http://www.epch.in/ChinaStudy/Report.pdf

Ghouse, S. M. (2017). Export challenges to MSMEs: A case study of Indian handicraft industry. *International Journal of Applied Business and Economic Research, 15*(6), 339–349.

https://niti.gov.in/planningcommission.gov.in/docs/aboutus/committee/wrkgrp12/wg_handi1101.pdf

IMARC Group. (2020). *Handicrafts market: Global industry trends, share, size, growth, opportunity and forecast 2019–2024.* https://www.imarcgroup.com/global-handicrafts-market

Kamble, S. S., & Raut, R. D. (2019). Evaluating the factors considered for procurement of raw material in food supply chain using Delphi-AHP methodology-a case study of potato chips processing company in India. *International Journal of Productivity and Quality Management*, 26(2), 176–189. https://doi.org/10.1504/IJPQM.2019.097765

Kumar, D., & Rajeev, P. V. (2013). Present scenario of Indian handicraft products. *Asian Journal of Managerial Science*, 2(1), 21–27.

Kumari, G. (2016). Marketing support and services schemes for Indian handicraft. *Journal of Rural and Industrial Development*, 4(2), 27–35.

Kumari, G., & Srivasatava, A. R. (2016). Role of E-tailing in boosting the Indian handicraft. *International Journal of Marketing & Financial Management*, 4(4), 27–36.

Menon, V. (2010). Art of marketing village crafts; challenges in applying quantitative marketing to resist recession. *International Review of Business Research Papers*, 6(5), 196–205.

Migiro, A., & Ocholla, D. N. (2005). Information and communication technologies in small and medium scale tourism enterprises in Durban, South Africa. *Information Development*, 21(4), 283–294.https://doi.org/10.1177/0266666905060089

Ministry of Textiles, & Government of India. (2012). *Working group report on handicrafts for 12thfive year plan*. Retrieved from https://niti.gov.in/planningcommission.gov.in/docs/aboutus/committee/wrkgrp12/wg_handi1101.pdf

Mukhamedjanova, K. A. (2020). Concept of supply chain management. *Journal of Critical Reviews*, 7(2), 759–766.

Ministry of Textiles, Government of India. (2020). *Compendium of Handicrafts Schemes for 12th five year plan*. http://handicrafts.nic.in/pdf/Scheme.pdf#page=139

Oza, M. S. (2019). Study of handicraft industry strategies and its implications in marketing. *International Journal of Research and Analytical Reviews*, 6(2), 874–877.

Pathak, R., Sharma, M., & Sujatha, R. (2017). RC²@ Craftsvilla. Com Craftsvilla is revolutionizing through co-creation: Creating value for stakeholders. *Journal of Business and Retail Management Research*, 12(1), 49–61.

Srivastav, G., & Rawat, P. S. (2016). Indian handicraft and globalization: The export context. In S. Joshi & R. Joshi (Eds.), *Designing and implementing global supply chain management* (pp. 175–184). IGI Global. https://doi.org/10.4018/978-1-4666-9720-1.ch009

Statista. (2019, October 23). India's handicrafts exports from FY 2011 to FY 2019. https://www.statista.com/statistics/624202/export-value-of-handicrafts-india/

Tiwari, A., & Dutta, B. (2013). Indian handicrafts industry: Evaluating inclusivity of current business models. https://tejas.iimb.ac.in/articles/Tejas_September%20Edition_Article%202.pdf

USAID (2006). Global market assessment for handicrafts. https://www.marketlinks.org/sites/marketlinks.org/files/resource/files/ML4636_global_market_assessment_for_handicrafts.pdf

Vats, N. (2014). Indian handicrafts and globalization: A review. *Journal of Humanities and Social Science*, 19(1), 40–43.

Venkataramanaiah, S., & Kumar, N. G. (2011). Building competitiveness: A case of handicrafts manufacturing cluster units. *Indore Management Journal*, 3(2), 27–37.

Yadav, R., &Mahara, T. (2018). An exploratory study to investigate value chain of Saharanpur wooden carving handicraft cluster. *International Journal of System Assurance Engineering and Management*, 9(1), 147–154.

Yihao, Z., & Yuning, Z. (2010, November 17–19). *The strategic research of traditional handicraft products' modern development bases on consumer psychology* [Paper presentation]. 2010 IEEE 11th International Conference on Computer-Aided Industrial Design & Conceptual Design 1. Yiwu, China. https://doi.org/10.1109/CAIDCD.2010.5681353

Chapter 13

Perceptions of Financial Literacy among Students in Higher Education

Gargi Das Bhattacharya and Anirban Sarkar

Introduction

Financial literacy is an individual's capacity to use their understanding of money to make wise decisions about saving, investing, and budgeting, boosting the flow of money throughout the economy. Making wise financial decisions can help a person and their family become more financially secure. Because practical financial competence enhances a family's financial well-being, boosts the liquidity of the financial market, and supports the nation's economy, it is necessary for individuals and the country as a whole to have correct financial knowledge. Thus, a lack of financial literacy would lead to reduced use of financial products, which would impede the nation's economic progress (Mahapatra et al., 2017).

The financial market has expanded, which has led to a recent increase in the complexity of the economic and product markets. Thus, improving one's financial literacy in such situations has become increasingly crucial. The findings of this study will enable people to make more knowledgeable financial decisions, including matters of investing, retirement planning, and borrowing. Also, as financial institutions compete for a larger share of the market, credit has become much easier to obtain, as financial products have become more broadly accessible as a result of extensive marketing (Kiliyanni & Sivaraman, 2018).

The financial product market has become more sophisticated, and because young people now have to deal with more complicated and diversified financial products, financial literacy – which is crucial for people of all ages – is especially important for teenagers. The level of financial literacy among students in underdeveloped and underprivileged nations varies (Oseifuah et al., 2018). One of the causes of the financial crisis is identified as a lack of financial literacy. India is a developing country, and we are entering into our second phase of financial sector reforms. The integration of our economy into the world economy will increase further, and so will the risk of worldwide crises impacting the Indian economy. In India there is a large unorganized sector, and the Government is withdrawing from pension schemes even in

DOI: 10.4324/9781032640488-16

the organized sector. In the absence of any social security scheme, our economy may be in for major instability after the demographic dividend starts waning after 20–25 years. Thus, the improvement of financial literacy in the country is imperative for the financial well-being of individuals, as well as for the economy. The significance of financial literacy as a transformative agent on the financial inclusion agenda of the nation is undisputed in academic as well as practitioner circles. This paper performs a literature review of definitional and measurement aspects of financial literacy (Ambarkhane & Venkataramani, 2015). In "A Study of the Level of Awareness of Financial Literacy among Management Undergraduates", the investigators sought to understand the level of financial literacy among undergraduate students at the University of Mauritius, as well as the relationship between financial literacy and demographic factors such as age, gender, and programme of study. In general, students had a satisfactory degree of financial awareness. The lack of relevant government programmes and access to financial journals, on the other hand, were highlighted by the students as barriers to financial literacy. Furthermore, there was no statistically significant association between gender and age group and financial literacy (Ramasawmy et al., 2013). The study "Measuring the Level of Financial Literacy among Management Graduates," aims to examine graduates' abilities to handle finances, the restrictions of financial literacy, and the steps that must be taken to promote financial literacy among students. The information for the study was gathered from both secondary and primary sources. A structured questionnaire was issued to 100 post-graduate students at the Central University of Kashmir to collect primary data. The respondents in the study were found to be lacking in fundamental financial literacy. Basic financial concepts, money management, and financial decision-making capacity were all inadequate among the respondents. There is a shortage of financial understanding among students in the educational system. Financial literacy is also poorly promoted by the government and financial institutions. Financial literacy should be promoted through television, radio, and other forms of media (Altaf, 2014).

Financial literacy is increasingly important, as it has become essential that individuals acquire the skills to be able to survive in modern society and cope with the increasing diversity and complexity of the financial products and services available. Financial literacy is the ability to make informed judgments and to make effective decisions regarding the use and management of money. It enables individuals to improve their overall well-being and to plan for their future security. The main objective of this study is to analyze the level of financial literacy among college students, and to determine the need for financial literacy programmes on college campuses, as well as assessing current students' desires for these programmes. Both primary and secondary data has been used in this study. The convenience sampling method has been used to collect the data, and this study surveys 30 college students to examine their personal financial literacy. This paper seeks to examine the role of

Jnana Jyothi Financial Literacy Trust and their literacy programmes in developing financial knowledge among the college students (Rizwan et al., 2015).

Financial literacy is increasingly important as it has become essential that individuals acquire the skills to be able to survive in modern society and cope with the increasing diversity and complexity of financial products and services available. Financial literacy is the ability to make informed judgments and to take effective decisions regarding the use and management of money. It enables individuals to improve their overall well-being and to plan for their future security. The main objective of this study is to analyze the level of financial literacy among college students by evaluating the influence of various demographic factors like gender, age group, discipline of study, level of study, annual household income, parent's occupation, and the students' source of income (Dhawan, 2017).

The objectives of the study are to assess the level of financial literacy of students in Kolkata, to find out the factors influencing students' perception of financial literacy, and to predict the students' inclination toward financial literacy.

Methods

This study aims to analyze the level of financial literacy among graduate and post-graduate students in Kolkata, as well as the factors impacting the students' financial literacy. Primary and secondary data were employed in this investigation. The primary data were collected from June to July 2021 using a Google Survey questionnaire with a purposive sample size of 211 respondents from Kolkata, West Bengal, of which 205 responses were complete and used for analysis. The framed questionnaire was distributed via email, and Google Survey form links captured information on demographics and various aspects of financial literacy from 205 students. Some of the questions were open-ended, and some of the questions were on an ordinal scale ranked on a 4-point Likert scale between 1 and 4. Due to the COVID-19 pandemic prevailing in the country, the online survey was our preferred choice. To assess financial literacy, basic questions about interest rates, inflation, and risk diversification were posed. The research identifies a number of elements that influence students' perceptions of financial literacy. After finishing the descriptive analysis, a variable reduction technique, exploratory factor analysis, was used, after determining its applicability. Furthermore, the researchers used binary logistic regression, as multiple independent variables, along with a single binary dependent variable, were considered in the study, to predict students' attitudes toward financial literacy.

Results and Discussions

The demographic study included gender, with 152 female respondents and 53 male respondents, indicating a representation of both genders in the collected sample. In addition, 61 respondents were 18–19 years old, 114 respondents belonged to the age bracket of 20–21, and 30 respondents were 22–23. Furthermore, 135 of the respondents were undergraduate students, 62 of them were graduates, and eight respondents were in the post-graduate level of education. In addition, 185 of the respondents studied Commerce subjects, 15 respondents studied Science subjects, and five respondents were associated with the Arts. 47.4% of the respondents had an annual family income below Rs 250,000, and 28.9% had an annual family income between Rs 250,000 to Rs 500,000.

The researchers used Cronbach's alpha, a measure of consistency; the alpha coefficient for the thirteen items was .823, as depicted in Table 13.1 below, which is acceptable for further analysis (Bonett & Wright, 2014).

The researchers utilised principal components analysis (PCA), a technique for reducing variables that is comparable to exploratory factor analysis. Its goal is to condense a large number of variables into a smaller number of "artificial" variables known as "principal components", which account for the majority of the variance in the original variables. In the context of COVID-19, an exploratory factor analysis using principal component analysis was conducted to uncover the determinants influencing financial literacy among students in Kolkata.

The Kaiser-Meyer-Olkin Measure of Sampling Adequacy (KMO) was 0.827, as depicted in Table 13.2; therefore, we were able to proceed with our factor analysis. Furthermore, Bartlett's Test of Sphericity was significant (<0.05); hence we were able to conclude relationships between the variables. So, the factor analysis technique was appropriate.

Factor Analysis has been applied to identify the factors influencing students' perceptions of financial literacy. The statements are further combined

Table 13.1 Reliability Statistics

Cronbach's Alpha	N of Items
.823	13

Source: Author's analysis

Table 13.2 KMO and Bartlett's Test

Kaiser-Meyer-Olkin Measure of Sampling Adequacy.		.827
Bartlett's Test of Sphericity	Approx. Chi-Square	881.115
	Df	78
	Sig.	.000

Source: Author's analysis

Table 13.3 Total Variance Explained

Component	Initial Eigenvalues			Extraction Sums of Squared Loadings			Rotation Sums of Squared Loadings		
	Total	% of Variance	Cumulative %	Total	% of Variance	Cumulative %	Total	% of Variance	Cumulative %
1	4.607	35.441	35.441	4.607	35.441	35.441	3.368	25.909	25.909
2	1.803	13.869	49.310	1.803	13.869	49.310	2.333	17.946	43.855
3	1.083	8.329	57.640	1.083	8.329	57.640	1.792	13.785	57.640

Source: Author's analysis

Table 13.4 Rotated Component Matrix Depicting Factor Loading

	Component		
	1	2	3
Financial literacy helps you to purchase the right kind of insurance to protect you in case of future contingencies.	.834		
Financial literacy helps you to make the right investment decisions.	.765		
Adequate financial knowledge helps you to compare returns before investment.	.671		
Financial literacy helps one avoid being victimized by financial scams.	.641		
Personal financial literacy and planning will help to improve your family's well-being.	.607		
It would help if you learned more about dealing with credit cards.		.807	
You feel that you need to be more informed regarding proper debt management.		.660	
You need to have more knowledge before investing your money.		.635	
Financial literacy motivates you to keep a budget of day-to-day expenses		.554	
You face difficulty in understanding market risks before investing.			.824
Investing in shares, mutual funds, and insurance is always confusing to you.			.807
You prefer to save money in fixed deposit and other savings schemes in banks to avoid the risks of investment.			.630

Source: Author's analysis

into three distinct factors with an Eigenvalue of no more than 1. These factors together explain 57.64% variability, as depicted in Table 13.4.

The rotated component matrix is depicted in Table 13.4. It can be observed that three factors explain students' perceptions of financial literacy. Factor 1 is referred to as "Financial Security", and it consists of five variables. Factor 2 is referred to as "Financial Knowledge", and it has four components. Finally, Factor 3 is referred to as "Financial Risk Appetite" and comprises three elements.

The null hypothesis that all regression coefficients are 0 is tested in Table 13.5. We can reject the null hypothesis and accept the alternative hypothesis, which states that at least one of the b's (regression coefficients) is not zero and can be used to form the regression model, because the p-value is less than 0.05. A goodness of fit test with a chi-square statistic of 32.481 and 13 degrees of freedom (df) and a significance level of p<.05 can be obtained from this table. The p-value of .002 indicates that the goodness of fit test findings are reliable, therefore our model is reliable.

The Hosmer–Lemeshow Goodness of Fit Test is the most accurate way to assess the logistic regression model's fit. We must fail to reject the null hypothesis for this test to show evidence of a good match. As a result, we want numbers in the significance column to be more than .05. Table 13.6

Table 13.5 Omnibus Tests of Model Coefficients

		Chi-square	df	Sig.
Step 1	Step	32.481	13	.002
	Block	32.481	13	.002
	Model	32.481	13	.002

Source: Author's analysis

Table 13.6 Hosmer and Lemeshow Test

Step	Chi-square	Df	Sig.
1	11.462	8	.177

Source: Author's analysis

Table 13.7 Classification Table

Observed			Predicted		Percentage Correct
			Inclination toward Financial Literacy		
			No =0	Yes =1	
Step 1	Inclination toward Financial Literacy	No =0	TN = 22	FP =43	33.8
		Yes =1	FN = 11	TP =129	92.1
	Overall Percentage				73.7

Source: Author's analysis

reveals that at eight df, the chi-square value is 11.462, with a significance level of .177. As a result, we have further proof that our model is accurate.

The classification table this time shows the results when the independent variables are inserted into the equation. Here, TP means True Positive, FP means False Positive, TN means True Negative, and FN means False Negative. Thus, we find the sensitivity and specificity from the classification table are 33.8% and 92.1%, respectively, with an overall accuracy of 73.7 (TP + TN)/Total classifications (Table 13.7).

The final regression output that we present is called "variables" in the equation table, which shows how each independent variable contributes to the equation. When looking at this table, we should pay special attention to the significance column. For example, "financial literacy can help you avoid being a victim of financial scams"; "it can help you purchase the right kind of insurance to protect you in the event of a future contingency"; "it can help you make the right investment decision"; "it can help you understand market risks before investing"; and "you believe you need to be more knowledgeable about effective debt management" are the variables that drive students'

Table 13.8 Variables in the Equation

		B	S.E.	Wald	df	Sig.	Exp(B)
Step 1	Financial literacy helps one avoid being victimized by financial scams.	.782	.326	5.766	1	**.016**	2.186
	Financial literacy helps you to purchase the right kind of insurance to protect you in case of future contingencies.	-.822	.415	3.917	1	**.048**	.440
	Financial literacy helps you to make the right investment decisions.	.855	.444	3.708	1	**.044**	2.351
	Adequate financial knowledge helps you to compare returns before investment.	-.504	.398	1.603	1	.206	.604
	Personal financial literacy and planning will help to improve your family's well-being.	-.190	.417	.208	1	.649	.827
	Financial literacy motivates you to keep a budget of day-to-day expenses.	.224	.410	.300	1	.584	1.252
	You need to have more knowledge before investing your money.	.245	.390	.395	1	.530	1.278
	Investing in shares, mutual funds, and insurance is always confusing for you.	-.131	.311	.179	1	.672	.877
	You face difficulty in understanding market risks before investing	-.977	.401	5.923	1	**.015**	.377
	You prefer to save money in fixed deposit and other savings schemes in the bank to avoid the risks of investment.	.214	.242	.781	1	.377	1.238
	You feel that you need to be more informed regarding proper debt management.	-.722	.367	3.877	1	**.049**	.486
	It is important for you to learn more about dealing with credit cards.	.084	.357	.055	1	.814	1.087
	Constant	1.999	1.585	1.589	1	.207	7.378

financial literacy, which can be evaluated by noting that the significance value is less than 0.05 in the above scenarios (Table 13.8).

Conclusion

Financial literacy assists individuals in making good financial planning, creating and diversifying their savings, comprehending market risks, and therefore boosting their financial and economic sustainability. A financially literate person can be more active in managing their finances appropriately in order to attain their financial goals, making them more financially and economically active. The study concludes that acquiring financial knowledge at an early age will help people become more financially active as adults. Young adults play an essential role in the development of a country's overall economy. However, students' financial literacy must be improved in order to help them make sensible financial decisions in the future and improve their economic well-being. Young people with strong financial literacy contribute to the country's economy. Furthermore, characteristics such as financial knowledge, financial security, and financial risk-bearing capabilities influence students' perceptions of financial literacy. As a result, we may conclude that youth financial literacy should be improved. The sample for this purpose was solely collected from Kolkata; data from no other districts in West Bengal could be taken. However, further research can be done, taking into consideration other districts of the state, as well as inter-city or inter-state comparisons.

Reference

Altaf, N. (2014). Measuring the level of financial literacy among management graduates. *Abhinav National Monthly Refereed Journal of Research in Commerce & Management*, 3(6), 29–36.

Ambarkhane, D., & Venkataramani, B. (2015, April). Financial literacy index for college students. *Annual Research Journal of SCMS*, 3, 1–25.

Bonett, D. G., & Wright, T. A. (2014). Cronbach's alpha reliability: Interval estimation, hypothesis testing, and sample size planning. *Journal of Organisational Behaviour*, 36(1), 3–15.

Dhawan, K. (2017). A study on financial literacy among college students in Delhi / NCR Ms . Mani Goswami Karan Dhawan. *XVIII [Annual International Conference Proceedings]*, 97, 455–460.

Kiliyanni, A. L., & Sivaraman, S. (2018). A predictive model for financial literacy among the educated youth in Kerala, India. *Journal of Social Service Research*, 44(4), 537–547.

Mahapatra, M. S., Alok, S., & Raveendran, J. (2017). Financial literacy of Indian youth: A study on the twin cities of Hyderabad–Secunderabad. *IIM Kozhikode Society and Management Review*, 6(2), 132–147.

Oseifuah, E., Gyekye, A., & Formadi, P. (2018). Financial literacy among undergraduate students: Empirical evidence from Ghana. *Academy of Accounting and Financial Studies Journal*, 22(6), 1–17.

Ramasawmy, D., Thapermall, S., Dowlut, S. A., & Ramen, M. (2013, February). *A study of the level of awareness of financial literacy among management undergraduates proceedings of 3rd asia-pacific business research conference*.

Rizwan, M., Sadhik, M., & Kumar, K. K. (2015). *A study on financial literacy among college students with special reference to Jnana Jyothi Financial Literacy Trust*. In 2nd International Conference on Science, Technology and Management. University of Delhi.

Chapter 14

Impact of COVID-19 on the Share Prices of Life Insurance Companies

A Case of Economic Sustainability in India

Shalini Singh, Bhavna Sharma, and Garima Madaan Dua

Introduction

Covid 19 has shocked the insurance industry (Babuna et al., 2020) and affected the global economy as well. It brought a global economic crisis, starting in China and spreading all over the world, however it did not impact China's economy, despite the whole global trade network being affected by it (Vidhya and Prabheesh, 2020). COVID-19 has had a multi-sectoral impact and has affected the economic sustainability of India as well (Sharma et al., 2022). The market has been negatively affected by the pandemic and has shown falls in various sectors, with the insurance sector not remaining untouched. Economic sustainability means the policies that help the long-term growth of the economy without harming the cultural, environmental, and social facets of the economy (https://sustainability.umw.edu/).

With most people losing their jobs or even losing their loved ones, it creates a panic between them and forces them to think twice about insurance. The Indian insurance industry is comprised of 57 insurance companies, out of which 24 are in the life insurance business, and 34 in the non-life business (www.ibef.org, 2021). Life insurance is directly related to the performance of the business and to people's incomes (www.indiainfoline.com, 2020). COVID-19 has changed people's perceptions; previously they did not think that life insurance was essential, but due to the pandemic, people are buying more insurance policies, be it life or health insurance. Now they are shifting toward long-term plans rather than ULIPs (www.edelweisstokio.in). There is less demand for investment-linked products as consumers do not have confidence in the stock market (Sanghvi, 2020). People are now considering insurance as a risk cover and not as an investment. According to a study conducted by the PWC, it was found that only 15% of respondents agreed that they would buy life insurance (www.edelweisstokio.in).

Up to March 2021, the premium from new policies from the life insurance companies in India was US$ 31.9 billion. In March 2021, the health insurance sector increased by 41%, as there was a rise in the demand for health insurance products due to COVID-19 (www.ibef.org, 2021). There were

DOI: 10.4324/9781032640488-17

437,687 deaths by August 2021; due to this people have become more aware and started buying life insurance policies (www.worldometers.info, 2021). According to IRDAI data, during April–May 2021, 1,850,000 life insurance policies were sold, as compared to 2020 in which only 1,420,000 were sold (Sharma, 2021). Up to March 25 2021, life insurance companies paid out Rs 19.86 billion toward 25,500 COVID-19 death claims (Panda, 2021). According to McKinsey, in India between December 2019 and April 2020, the insurance sector dropped by 25.9%. Figure 14.1 shows that life insurance premiums have increased to 27.1% during April–May 2021 (Sharma, 2021). COVID-19 has impacted the sustainable growth of these countries. There is a visible difference in the economic sustainability of Asian economies before and after the pandemic (Jiang et al., 2021) (Figure 14.1)

According to general insurance companies, until May 5 2021, 1,139,000 cases were recorded related to COVID-19 worth Rs 159.88 billion, out of which the insurance companies have settled 951,000 cases worth Rs 91.41 billion. Now insurance companies are getting more careful with regard to new applications and are tightening their rules with higher premiums, longer waiting periods, etc. (Anshul, 2021). There is growth in the life insurance business in India; it increased by 7.5% in 2021 compared to 2020. In order to increase the sales of insurance policies, the industry must introduce innovative products, ensure that the claim settlement procedure is quick, and offer proactive customer support (www.bajajallianzlife.com, 2021). During 2020, life insurers issued 28.847 million new individual policies, out of which the LIC issued 75.9% of policies and the private life insurers issued 24.1% of policies (Dhanuka, 2021). Whenever someone is buying a life insurance policy, they should always look for

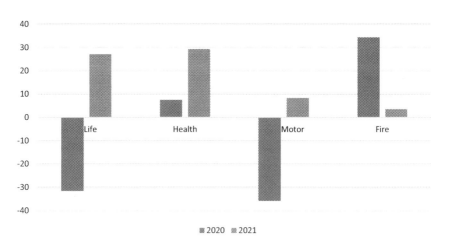

Figure 14.1 Percentage Growth in Premiums during April–May 2021.
Source: Sharma, 2021.

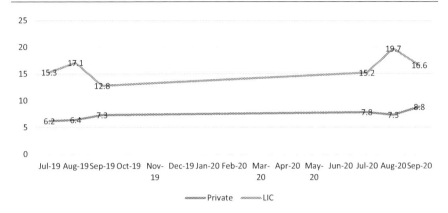

Figure 14.2 New Business Premiums 2019–2020 (Rs '000 crore).
Source: Maitra et al. 2021.

the claim–settlement ratio. This is a ratio that reveals the proportion of claims a company has settled against the number of claims it received. During the year 2019–2020, Max Life Insurance's claim–settlement ratio was 99.22%, followed by HDFC Life Insurance at 99.07%, and Tata AIA Life Insurance at 99.06% (Kumar, 2021). Figure 14.2 shows that the new business premiums in the private sector and of the LIC have increased to 8.8% and 16.6% respectively in September 2020, as compared to 7.3% and 12.8% in September 2019 (Maitra et al., 2021).

India's share in the global insurance market was a mere 1.92% in 2018 (Tripathy, 2021). Before COVID-19, people in their 20s did not buy life insurance policies, thinking that they were not required at that age, but due to COVID-19, people in the 25–35 age group are buying 30% more insurance policies. There is more awareness regarding financial safety due to COVID-19 (Thomas & NR, 2021). According to a McKinsey analysis, insurance share prices fell 25.9% from December 31, 2019, to April 9, 2020, and in their report, they expected this trend to continue until the fourth quarter of 2020. The objective of this study is to assess the impact of COVID-19 on the share prices of life insurance companies in India.

In India, the insurance industry was established before independence and gradually progressed from there. Today, there are both private and public players in the market. There are two categories in the insurance sector: life and non-life. Ghosh (2013), in his empirical study, found that growth in the insurance industry brought development to the Indian economy, which has given it a new dimension in the global market. Today India, with a huge population, stands in tenth position among 88 countries in the insurance industry. The Indian insurance industry can offer a bright future, and, globally, the Indian life insurance market share was 2.73% in 2019. In 2020 the world was confronted with COVID-19; the

WHO soon announced it as a pandemic and lockdowns were imposed in different countries, resulting in a shrinking down of the global economy. The insurance industry was not untouched by this, and the effects have been noticed in different countries. Worku et al. (2020), in their exploratory study on Ethiopia, found a clear impact of COVID-19 on life insurance, due to payment breaks and uncertainty, spending power being adversely affected, and the result of this, expense cutting. Harris et al. (2020), in their findings from an analysis of 100 companies and over 80000 US policies, explained that COVID-19 affected people's lifespans, but in the end, companies did not change their life insurance offerings and they did not increase their premiums or decrease their policy offerings. Babuna et al. (2020) investigated the influence of COVID-19 on the insurance market and discovered that premiums in both life and non-life insurance firms have decreased, while claims for both industries have grown. This resulted in a 17.01% decrease in premiums and a 38.4% increase in claims, resulting in a full loss for the Ghanaian insurance market between March and June 2020. According to an empirical study by Wang et al. (2020), COVID-19 has a considerable negative influence on China's insurance market in the short term, owing to insurance market channels and a reduction in demand for household insurance. However, personal insurance is more affected by COVID-19 than property insurance.

Purchasing decisions are influenced by financial health and company growth, but the key factor that affects the buying of insurance is the face value of the policy, its term length, and the purchaser's probability of death. The market trend in this industry has also evolved, and it has shifted from an offline to a virtual platform. Life Insurance Corporation is the biggest player in the insurance industry in India, the reasons for this being that people trust it, and that LIC is the oldest company in the industry (Sadhak, 2009). According to the IRDAI Annual Report (2019-20), Future Generali India Insurance Company Limited performed a survey of 600 consumers throughout India and reported that half of those polled who chose to purchase insurance from the company received information digitally. If technology is effectively employed in this scenario, insurance efficiency will increase, resulting in better conversations with clients (Wang et al., 2020). A study by Preda et al. (2021) claims that customer behaviours around purchasing insurance are currently influenced by two factors: preference shopping and social media behaviour. The pandemic and social distancing raise a need and value for digitalization. Life insurance is a nudge product; the pandemic has caused anxiety in people's minds, and so they want to protect their lives with insurance.

In a study of impact analysis in India's banking, insurance, and financial services industries (BFSI), Ramasamy (2020) discovered that COVID-19 has had a beneficial impact on the insurance business. This is the only industry that has made money while also attracting customers among the BFSI businesses.

Although it is well known that there is no cure for COVID-19, individuals are more concerned about the costs of everything from using a ventilator to paying hospital fees. The easiest way to avoid these costs is to purchase insurance.

Methods

This study has considered three life insurance scripts from NSE, namely SBI Life, HDFC Life, and ICICI PRU, for the period from April 2020 to July 2021; the data have been taken on a daily basis. We have adopted the methodology of moving average trading rules to ascertain the profitability of the rule. We continue with identifying possible moving average trading rules. According to the trading rule, one buys when the price exceeds some moving average historical prices, and one sells when the price falls below some moving average (Chakrabarti & Sen, 2013).

- A possible trading rule is formed with a moving average of 3 days, 7 days, 14 days, and 30 days.

$Rt = \ln(Pt/Pt - 1)$

- The return is calculated for the time series data, then the return is regressed on a constant and a lagged buy signal value. The estimated slope coefficient will give the possible profit. A significantly positive slope coefficient, which is higher than the intercept, as well as the coefficient of the general buy–sell regression, hints toward the existence of a profitable trading rule,

Results and Discussions

The daily return of life insurance scripts is regressed upon a constant and the result is summarized in Tables 14.1, 14.2 and 14.3. In the next step, lagging the buy rule signals by one period, several regression equations are generated. They are:

Table 14.1 Regression Result of SBI Life on a Constant (general buy and sell strategy) Dependent Variable: SBI Life

Variable	Coefficient	Std Error	t-statistic	Prob.
SBILife 3 C	0.000575	0.000415	1.384471	0.1672
SBILife 7 C	0.000647	0.000415	1.556605	0.1205
SBILife 14 C	0.000704	0.000405	1.741344	0.0826
SBILife 30 C	0.000692	0.000387	1.789458	0.0746

Source: Author's Calculations

Table 14.2 Regression of SBI Life Based on the Trading Rule

Variable	Coefficient	Std Error	t-statistic	Prob.		
C	0.000614	0.000585	1.049349	0.2948	**R-squared**	**Adjusted R-squared**
Buy3(−1)	−0.000104	0.000834	−0.124221	0.9012	0.000048	−0.003048
C	0.000917	0.000589	1.556047	0.1207	**R-squared**	**Adjusted R-squared**
Buy7(−1)	−0.000473	0.000832	−0.569024	0.5697	0.001014	−0.002118
C	0.000504	0.000565	0.891197	0.3735	**R-squared**	**Adjusted R-squared**
Buy14(−1)	0.000269	0.000802	0.335941	0.7371	0.000362	−0.002842
C	0.000542	0.000529	1.024362	0.3065	**R-squared**	**Adjusted R-squared**
Buy30(−1)	0.000272	0.000778	0.349119	0.7272	0.000412	−0.002965

Source: Author's Calculations

Table 14.3 Regression Result of HDFC Life on a Constant (general buy and sell strategy) Dependent Variable: HDFC life

Variable	Coefficient	Std Error	t-statistic	Prob.
HDFCLife 3 C	0.00046	0.000406	1.133321	0.2579
HDFCLife 7 C	0.000462	0.00041	1.128302	0.26
HDFCLife 14 C	0.000527	0.000397	1.329944	0.1845
HDFCLife 30 C	0.000498	0.00038	1.310387	0.1911

Source: Author's Calculations

Table 14.4 Regression of HDFC Life Based on the Trading Rule

Variable	Coefficient	Std Error	t-statistic	Prob.		
C	0.000454	0.000583	0.779308	0.4364	**R-squared**	**Adjusted R-squared**
Buy3(−1)	0.00002	0.000815	−0.023471	0.9813	0.000002	−0.003094
C	0.00026	0.000584	0.444532	0.657	**R-squared**	**Adjusted R-squared**
Buy7(−1)	0.0003	0.000818	0.367282	0.7137	0.000423	−0.002711
C	0.000541	0.000557	0.97114	0.3322	**R-squared**	**Adjusted R-squared**
Buy14(−1)	−0.000203	0.000776	−0.261858	0.7936	0.00022	−0.002985
C	0.000649	0.00055	1.180285	0.2388	**R-squared**	**Adjusted R-squared**
Buy30(−1)	−0.000332	0.000763	−0.435585	0.6635	0.000641	−0.002736

Source: Author's Calculations

Table 14.5 Regression Result of ICICIPRU on a Constant (general buy and sell strategy) Dependent Variable: ICICIPRU

Variable	Coefficient	Std Error	t-statistic	Prob.
ICICILife 3 C	0.00074	0.000535	1.445385	0.1493
ICICILife 7 C	0.000895	0.000535	1.673037	0.0953
ICICILife 14 C	0.000883	0.000517	1.708781	0.0885
ICICILife 30 C	0.000833	0.000484	1.719236	0.0866

Author's Calculations

Table 14.6 Regression of ICICIPRU Based on the Trading Rule

Variable	Coefficient	Std Error	t-statistic	Prob.		
C	0.001016	0.000723	1.405808	0.1607	**R-squared**	**Adjusted R-squared**
Buy3(−1)	−0.000388	0.001071	−0.36224	0.7174	0.000406	−0.002689
C	0.001394	0.000745	1.870685	0.0623	**R-squared**	**Adjusted R-squared**
Buy7(−1)	−0.001079	0.001072	−1.005739	0.3153	0.003161	0.000036
C	0.000836	0.000685	1.221156	0.2229	**R-squared**	**Adjusted R-squared**
Buy14(−1)	−0.000229	0.000991	−0.230982	0.8175	0.000171	−0.003034
C	0.001163	0.000674	1.725242	0.0855	**R-squared**	**Adjusted R-squared**
Buy30(−1)	−0.000718	0.000973	−0.737433	0.4614	0.001834	−0.001538

Source: Author's Calculations

return c buy3(−1), return c buy7(−1), return c buy14(−1), return c buy30(−1)

Each regression is estimated and the regression that gives the highest daily return, the coefficient, is considered. According to the values calculated, from Table 14.1, Table 14.2 and Table 14.3 it can be observed that the significant values are of more than 5% significance. The market return of life insurance companies is not satisfying for the investor. Due to the pandemic, the insurance sector has been one of the hardest-hit sectors due to claims and releases. Life insurance has performed poorly during the period of study. According to the data, if an investor has entered the market during that period, then their position will have been stable, but investors holding the stock would have suffered a huge loss during this period. Investors need to wait for better opportunities post COVID-19.

Regression is estimated for all the observations, and it is noted that the p-value is not significant for any of the trading rules. This indicates that the trading rules should be revised according to the period of study and a combination of rules considering short-run and long-run periods should be formed to assess the profitability of return.

Conclusion

The life insurance market in India's economy was steady and developing significantly before the COVID-19-induced shutdown. It not only unsettled individuals' pursuits but drastically affected economic activity. In January 2020, all key indicators grew by double digits year over year, including premiums. In January, new business premiums totalled $2.3 billion, up 24% year over year. COVID-19 came as a disaster to the country, swiping away all its business and earnings, leaving the nation helpless to cope with the situation of loss arising in different sectors. Assets under management declined due to COVID-19 which led to an increased redemption of claims by investors to fulfil their urgent needs and also due to a rise in death cases.

Reference

(2021). 4 ways the Pandemic Changed the Life Insurance Sector in India. (n.d.). www.edelweisstokio.in/. Retrieved August 18, 2021, from https://www.edelweisstokio.in/blogs/lifeinsurancesimplified/4-ways-the-covid-pandemic-impact-the-life-insurance-sector-in-india

(n.d.). https://sustainability.umw.edu/areas-of-sustainability/economic-sustainability/#:~:text= Econ omic%20sustainability%20refers%20to%20practices,cultural%20aspects%20of%20the%20community.

Anshul. (2021). COVID-19 second wave: Impact on insurance sector and policyholders. www.cnbctv18.com. Retrieved June 2, 2021, from https://www.cnbctv18.com/finance/covid-19-second-wave-impact-on-insurance-sector-and-policyholders-9467141.htm

Babuna, P., Yang, X., Gyilbag, A., Awudi, D. A., Ngmenbelle, D., & Bian, D. (2020). The impact of Covid-19 on the insurance industry. *International Journal of Environmental Research and Public Health*, 17(16), 5766. https://doi.org/10.3390/ijerph17165766

Dhanuka, R. (2021). *Insurance Market in India is Expected Reach $250 bn by 2025*. Retrieved July 6, 2021, from https://www.investindia.gov.in/sector/bfsi-insurance

(2020). How the Corona Pandemic has Impacted the Indian Insurance Sector. www.indiainfoline.com. Retrieved July 9, 2021, from https://www.indiainfoline.com/article/general-blog/how-the-corona-pandemic-has-impacted-the-indian-insurance-sector-120110900096_1.html

Chakrabarti, G., & Sen, C. (2013). *Momentum trading on the Indian stock market*. https://doi.org/10.1007/978-81-322-1127-3

Ghosh, A. (2013). Does life insurance activity promote economic development in India: An empirical analysis. *Journal of Asia Business Studies*. https://doi.org/10.1108/15587891311301007

Harris, T. F., Yelowitz, A., & Courtemanche, C. (2020). Did COVID-19 change life insurance offerings? *Journal of Risk and Insurance*.https://doi.org/10.1111/jori.12344

Jiang, J., Park, E., & Park, S. (2021). The impact of COVID-19 on economic sustainability—A case study of fluctuation in stock prices for China and South Korea. *Sustainability*, *13*(12), 6642. https://doi.org/10.3390/su13126642

Kumar, N. (2021). Latest life insurance claim settlement ratio of companies in 2021. www.economictimes.indiatimes.com. Retrieved July 30, 2021, from https://economictimes.indiatimes.com/wealth/insure/life-insurance/latest-life-insurance-claim-settlement-ratio-of-companies-in-2021/articleshow/80835626.cms?utm_source=contentofinterest&utm_medium=text&utm_campaign=cppst

Maitra, B. C., Gupta, A., Singh, M., & Nyati, Y. (2021). A bright future for life insurance in India in a post-pandemic world. Retrieved July 8, 2021, from https://www.adlittle.com/en/insights/report/bright-future-life-insurance-india-post-pandemic-world

Panda, S. (2021). Life insurers shell out Rs 2,000 crore as Covid-19 death claims, shows data. Retrieved July 6, 2021, from https://www.business-standard.com/article/economy-policy/life-insurers-shell-out-rs-2-000-crore-as-covid-19-death-claims-shows-data-121032800858_1.html

Preda, A., Popescu, M., & Drigă, I. (2021). The impact of Covid-19 on global insurance market. In *MATEC Web of Conferences* (Vol. 342). EDP Sciences. https://doi.org/10.1051/matecconf/202134208012

Ramasamy, D. (2020). Impact Analysis in Banking, Insurance and Financial services industry due to COVID-19 Pandemic. *Pramana Research Journal*, *10*(8). https://papers.ssrn.com/sol3/papers.cfm?abstract_id=3668165

Sadhak, H. (2009). *Life insurance in India: Opportunities, challenges and strategic perspective*. SAGE Publications.

Sanghvi, D. (2020). Covid-19-how it has impacted Indias insurance industry. www.livemint.com. Retrieved June 25, 2021, from https://www.livemint.com/money/personal-finance/covid-19-how-it-has-impacted-india-s-insurance-industry-11592387890202.html

Sharma, B., Budhiraja, A., Singh, S., & Bala, R. (2022). Responding to the pandemic-A case of Indian hotel industry. *Cases on Emerging Market Responses to the COVID-19 Pandemic*. IGI Global. https://doi.org/10.4018/978-1-6684-3504-5

Sharma, S. (2021). Indians more inclined towards life insurance during Covid's second wave. www.indiatoday.in. Retrieved July 21, 2021, from https://www.indiatoday.in/diu/story/indians-more-inclined-towards-life-insurance-during-covids-second-wave-1816701-2021-06-19

Thomas, C., &Sethuraman, N. R. (2021). Shocked by covid deaths indians rush for life insurance. www.livemint.com. Retrieved July 19, 2021,. from https://www.livemint.com/insurance/shocked-by-covid-deaths-indians-rush-for-life-insurance-11623832428821.html

Tripathy, S. (2021). Pandemic gives insurance a boost. www.thehindubusinessline.com. Retrieved July 26, 2021, from https://www.thehindubusinessline.com/opinion/pandemic-gives-insurance-a-boost/article34628591.ece

Vidya, C. T., & Prabheesh K. P. (2020). Implications of COVID-19 Pandemic on the Global Trade Networks, *Emerging Markets Finance and Trade*, *56*(10), 2408–2421. DOI: 10.1080/1540496X.2020.1785426

Wang, Y., Zhang, D., Wang, X., & Fu, Q. (2020). How does COVID-19 affect China's insurance market? *Emerging Markets Finance and Trade*, 56(10), 2350–2362. https://doi.org/10.1080/1540496X.2020.1791074

Worku, A., & Mersha, D. (2020). The effect of COVID-19 on insurance industry in Ethiopia. *Horn of African Journal of Business and Economics (HAJBE)*, Special Issue, 39–44.

Chapter 15

Sustainable Agronomic Practices

India's Efforts Toward Booming Agricultural Growth

Swati Mishra and Manjula Upadhyay

Introduction

Humans began to domesticate plants through agriculture about 12,000 years ago. In the beginning, agriculture was a means of satisfying daily food demands, and production was limited to the needs of the farmer's family. But with increased industrialization and urbanization, agriculture became a source of income generation for poor farmers beyond the satisfaction of their food needs. In developing countries, more than half of the population is poor, and these people rely on agriculture for their livelihood. Population growth and poverty are the two major reasons why agriculture has impacted the environment so badly. In India, which is the second most populous country in the world and is likely to pass China in the rankings (*Population by Country (2020) – Worldometer*, no date), agriculture is the largest source of livelihood. 70% of its rural households still depend primarily on agriculture for their livelihood, with an estimated food grain production of 275MT in the year 2017–18 (*India at a glance | FAO in India | Food and Agriculture Organization of the United Nations*, no date). While achieving food sufficiency in production, India still holds 102nd place out of 117 countries in the Global Hunger Index 2019 (Waghmare, 2019). On one hand, population and poverty are leading to an over-exploitation of the land's resources. In addition to this, climate change is contributing through desertification and land degradation, which again affects food production and thereby influences food security. Interestingly, agriculture emits significant amounts of greenhouse gas, and higher food demands greatly impact GHG emissions and climate ("Special Report on Climate Change and Land – IPCC site", no date). Climate change again influences the sustainability of land management and healthy agricultural growth.

The unsustainable agriculture practised over the years has degraded the land and the environment, affected human health, delayed the vision of a sustainable future, and will continue until necessary adaptation and mitigation measures have been accepted. To earn higher yields and greater income, humans become unconcerned by the consequences to their environment and health. To overcome such adversities, it is recommended that farmers opt into and practice sustainable agriculture methods, which undoubtedly allow for satisfactorily high production levels with no chemical use and low environmental unbalance (*Getting back to nature*, 2019).

Agriculture – A Dominant Sector Driving Land Degradation and Climate Change

- Tilling of the soil: the tilling of soil is an important and surprisingly harmful practice in agriculture (*Unsustainable Agriculture*, no date). Tilling soil incorporates more oxygen into the soil and enhances the biological and chemical processes of microorganisms, which in turn increases the decomposition rate of the organic matter within the soil (*Unsustainable Agriculture*, no date). This process makes nutrient-rich soil which allows for fast and bountiful production. Conversely, organic nutrients deplete very fast and the complex chemical structure of soil breaks down into a looser structure. Tillage makes soil structure more prone to erosion, eventually leading to unhealthy and sterile land.
- Mono-cropping or monoculture: mono-cropping refers to the plantation of a single crop throughout a field or growing area. This practice may cause crop infestation and a loss of underground water and soil nutrients. The planting of a single crop in close proximity over a large area increases the likelihood of mass crop failure due to insect and disease infestation. As a result, farmers use pesticides, fungicides, and herbicides to escape such possibilities. Also, to restore the soil composition, farmers use chemical fertilizers to feed the soil. Thus, increasing the extent and intensity of biomass production through fertilizer addition, irrigation, or monoculture energy plantation can result in local land degradation. Monoculture has led farmers to deplete finite water resources by watering hundreds of acres of land for food grain production. The literature shows that continuous and similar cropping patterns have reduced the quality and quantity of crop yields and led to a demand for fertilizer use after a few years (Yadav, 1998).
- Use of chemicals: farmers add fertilizers to enrich the soil composition, and add chemicals to avoid insect and disease infestation in the plants (Savci, 2012). The addition of chemicals not only affects the quality of the food produced, but also affects the environment in many ways. During heavy rains, the fertilizer may mix into the surrounding water bodies and soil through leaching. This is when fertilizer runs off the sowing field and pollutes water bodies resulting in eutrophication (or dead zones). Fertilizers mix with large water bodies and increase their nutrient contents, causing algae blooms. Algae blooms create low-oxygen areas within rivers (and oceans) and create uninhabitable environments for aquatic life (*Unsustainable Agriculture*, no date). Studies have shown a positive

association between pesticide exposure and diseases like solid tumours and cancer, especially in children and pregnant women who are exposed to pesticides at work (Bassil et al., 2007).
- Soil erosion: surface soil is rich in organic matter and plant nutrients. Soil particles are fine to retain nutrients and water into the roots of plants or trees. Soil erosion has several adverse impacts on the environment which result in catastrophic events such as floods, the destruction of habitats for aquatic life, etc. Leaching is caused by soil erosion and leads to the contamination of drinking water supplies, which may raise public health issues. Soil erosion deteriorates agricultural productivity and affects the environment in many ways. With the continuous increase in the population, soil erosion and land degradation are creating a challenge and raising concerns for the abilities of future generations to produce food. Deteriorating soil productivity is reducing agricultural land and providing less space for food production.
- Deforestation: land degradation caused by tilling, mono-cropping, and chemical usage makes soil inefficient. As a result, farmers migrate to new places where nutrient-rich soil is excessively present. Forests are places where soil is rich and high in humus and organic content underneath the canopy. This justified the cutting or burning of half the world's rainforests, affecting entire species living in these forests. Agriculture accounts for up to 80% of deforestation. In general, deforestation can be defined as the destruction of habitats for agricultural use. Deforestation has also limited vegetation, and the medicinal plants which were primarily found in forests have become scarce.
- Climate Change: agriculture systems have direct implications for climate change, as they also make substantial contributions to carbon emissions. Today, climate change is a major threat to the whole world, as it powerfully affects human life. The entire ecological system is facing the impacts of anthropogenic climate change. Erratic weather patterns, drought, floods, cyclones, and earthquakes are just a few of the common events that have killed many living creatures and will reach an increased severity in future if sustainable practices are not implemented in the present.

Sustainable Agriculture

In recent years, farmers have reported serious health problems which, in some cases, have resulted in death. Other big problems that farmers face every year are loan repayment, crops destroyed due to pest infestations, loss of crops and income, debts, and much more; all of these are related to pesticides (*Sustainable farming in India*, no date). Agro-ecosystem and food systems perspectives are very much essential when incorporating sustainability, because the survival of living beings without food is unimaginable. Sustainable agriculture integrates three main goals – environmental health, economic profitability, and social equity (*Sustainable Agriculture | Learn Science at Scitable*, no date).

Thus, agricultural practices should be followed with strict consideration of the following principles (Impulse, no date):

(i) An efficient, self-sufficient, and economical production system should be developed without compromising income.
(ii) Biodiversity should be conserved and protected.
(iii) The use of natural resources should be optimized.
(iv) Good air quality should be maintained and water and land should be managed sustainably.
(v) Food production and distribution should be increased using efficient energy methods.

Economy

We are talking about sustainable agriculture because it is necessary to maintain constant and healthy food production, for current and future generations. The question thus arises as to what possible agricultural practices could be followed to achieve the above principles. What are the methods that need to be adapted in order to mitigate the catastrophic consequences of agriculture on the environment and the land? The following sustainable agricultural behaviours could answer such questions. Additionally, these are some very effective and efficient processes which are nowadays followed by some farmers, but are not popular or country-wide due to a lack of awareness and knowledge.

- Non-pesticide management or use of natural deterrents: a sustainable approach to pest control is non-pesticide management. The use of natural deterrents such as neem and chilli pepper balance the ecosystem in such a

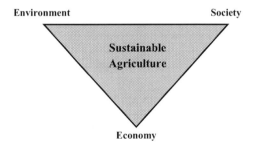

Figure 15.1 Sustainable Agriculture gives equal weight to environmental, social, and economic concerns in agriculture.

Source: Sustainable Agriculture-Scitable by Nature Education Environment Society

way that insects like ladybugs, dragonflies and spiders, which have important roles in nature that can benefit plants, leave in normal numbers without exceeding infestation levels (*Getting back to nature*, 2019). More jobs can also be created in relation to sourcing, grinding, and mixing repellants like neem seeds and chilli peppers.

- Trap crops: Trap crops are planted along the main crop as intercropping, as borders, or in strips (*Trap crops: A tool for managing insect pests damage | agropedia*, no date). Trap crops protect the main crop from pest infestations by attracting insects and pests for feeding, breeding, and survival. Some varieties of trap crops, along with main crops, methods of planting, and the pests they control, are given below in Table 15.1. (*Trap crops: A tool for managing insect pests damage | agropedia*, no date; Srinivasan & Moorthy, 1991; Badenes-Perez et al., 2005). Tobacco plants, which produce cembratrienol (CBToI) in their leaves, protect themselves from pests (*Organic insect deterrent for agriculture: Biodegradable crop protection products without risks or side effects*, no date). Researchers built tobacco plant genomes into the genome of coli bacteria, the result showing antibacterial effects and being usable as a disinfectant spray that acts actively against pathogens.

- Organic Farming: organic farming is a farming method that aims at land cultivation and crop production using organic waste or other biological materials and bio-fertilizers. Organic farming improves soil structures and biodiversity, improves land fertility, reduces erosion, and maintains a healthy environment and ecology with a reduced risk of exposing humans and animals to toxic materials. These nutrients are released to crops for increased sustainable production in an eco-friendly, pollution-free environment. The United States Department of Agriculture (USDA) defines "organic farming as a system which avoids the use of synthetic inputs (chemical fertilizers, pesticides, hormones, feed additives etc.) and relies maximum on crop rotation, crop residue, animal manures, off-farm organic waste, mineral grade rock additives and biological system of nutrient mobilization and plant protection" (*Organic Agriculture | National Institute of Food and Agriculture*, no date). The different components of organic farming are green leaf manures, crop rotations, biological management, animal husbandry, bio-fertilizers, manures, and vermicomposting (*ICAR-CCARI*, no date). The FAO says "Organic agriculture is a holistic production management system which promotes and enhances agro-ecosystem health, including biodiversity, biological cycles, and soil biological activity" (*Organic Agriculture: What is organic agriculture?*, no date).

- Agro-waste management: An agricultural waste management system consists of six basic functions: production, collection, storage, treatment, transfer, and use. Agricultural waste management systems may vary depending on the type of waste.

Table 15.1 Trap Crops for Managing Insect and Pest Damage

Trap crop	Main crop	Method of planting	Pest controlled
Alfalfa	Cotton	Strip intercrop	Lygus bug
Basil and marigold	Garlic	Border crop	Thrips
Castor plant	Cotton	Border crop	Heliotis sp.
Chervil	Vegetables, ornamentals	Among plants	Slugs
Chinese cabbage, mustard, and radish	Cabbage	Planted in every 15 rows of cabbage	Cabbage webworms, flea hoppers, mustard aphids
Beans and other legumes	Corn	Row intercrop	Leafhoppers, leaf beetles, stalk borers, fall armyworms
Chickpea	Cotton	Block trap crop at 20 plants/sq m	Heliotis sp.
Collards	Cabbage	Border crop	Diamondback moths
Corn	Cotton	Row intercrop, planted in every 20 rows of cotton or every 10-15 m	Heliotis sp.
Cowpea	Cotton	Row intercrop in every 5 rows of cotton	Heliotis sp.
Desmodium	Corn, cowpea, millet, sorghum	Row intercrop	Stemborers, strigas
Dill and lovage	Tomato	Row intercrop	Tomato hornworms
Green beans	Soybean	Row intercrop	Mexican bean beetles
Horseradish	Potato	Intercrop	Colorado potato beetles
Hot cherry pepper	Bell pepper	Border crop	Pepper maggots
Indian mustard	Cabbage	Strip intercrop in between cabbage plots	Cabbage head caterpillars
Marigold (French and African marigold)	Solanaceous, crucifers, legumes, cucurbits	Row/strip intercrop	Nematodes
Medick (*Medicago littoralis*)	Carrot	Strip intercrop in between carrot plots	Carrot root flies
Napier grass	Corn	Intercrop, border crop	Stemborers
Nasturtium	Cabbage	Row intercrop	Aphids' flea beetles, cucumber beetles, squash vine borers
Okra	Cotton	Border crop	Flower cotton weevils
Onion and garlic	Carrot	Border crops or barrier crops in between plots	Carrot root flies, Thrips
Radish	Cabbage family	Row intercrop	Flea beetles, root maggots
Rye	Soybean	Row intercrop	Corn seedling maggots
Sesbania	Soybean	Row intercrop at a distance of 15 m apart	Stink bugs
Sickle pod	Soybean	Strip intercrop	Velvet bean caterpillars, green stink bugs
Soybean	Corn	Row intercrop	Heliotis sp.
Sudan grass	Corn	Intercrop, border crop	Stemborers
Sunflower	Cotton	Row intercrop in every 5 rows of cotton	Heliotis sp.
Tansy	Potato	Intercrop	Colorado potato beetles
Tobacco	Cotton	Row intercrop, planted in every 20 rows of cotton	Heliotis sp.
Tomato	Cabbage	Intercrop (tomato is planted 2 weeks ahead at the plots' borders)	Diamondback moths
Vetiver grass	Corn	Perimeter crop	Corn stalk borers

Source: http://agropedia.iitk.ac.in/

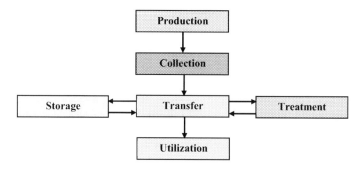

Figure 15.2 Agricultural waste management functions.

It is very important to know the nutritional content of the waste, i.e., its nitrogen, phosphorous, heavy metal, toxin, pathogen, oxygen-demanding material, or total solid content. Dry waste has a high nitrogen content, thus a suitable treatment process has to be adopted to reduce the nitrogen content if used on a limited land.

- Crop rotation and diversity: crop rotation is the repetitive growing of an ordered succession of crops on the same land over multiple years. Crop rotation improves agronomical production yields and is also well-established through multiple trials (*Diversify Crop Rotations | NRCS Pennsylvania*, no date). Today, agriculture systems are more focused on single-crop production due to infrastructure, machinery, and money constraints. Some benefits of diverse crop rotations include the following:

(i) Legume nitrogen in rotation can reduce the need for nitrogen fertilizers for non-leguminous crops and fix atmospheric nitrogen.
(ii) A diverse crop rotation controls weeds and acts as an important pest management tool.
(iii) Crop rotation results in more varied microbe food sources and a more diverse microbial community below the ground, as well as different root structures, which improves soil structure and health.

- Cover crops: cover crops favourably affect the physical, chemical and biological properties of the soil. Cover crops are grown during the season when cash crops are not grown. These are fast-growing crops and are planted to prevent soil erosion, improve soil nutrients, and provide organic matter (*Cover crop | agriculture*, no date). Cover crops also help maintain soil humidity by providing shade and controlling the thermal regime (they lower the temperature, therefore reducing the evaporation of water from the soil and increasing water infiltration). These conditions also favour greater biological activity

among the soil's flora and fauna (improving the modulation of legumes, increasing the quantity of earthworms, etc.).
- Integrated farming: integrated Farming is the integration of two or more activities that are sustainable in environmental terms and provide an additional source of income to poor farmers. These activities might be aquaculture, vegetable farming, livestock production, goat-keeping, poultry-keeping, mushroom cultivation, sericulture, horticulture, etc. The integration of these activities can be complementary to each other, such that the product of one process becomes an input into the other enterprise (*Integrated farming system and agriculture sustainability-Indian Journals*, no date). For example, fodder is food for cattle, which provide milk as an edible product and provide cattle dung, urine, and litter to be used as fertilizers to increase the land's nutritional value. Integrated farming ensures sustainable agriculture production by providing additional income to poor farmers. It takes environmental concerns into account along with good food quality (Morris & Winter, 1999).
- Renewable energy used for agriculture and gained from agriculture: sustainable agriculture promotes sufficient agricultural production for the population of a nation in such a way that it doesn't affect the food security of future generations, without damaging the environment. Today, climate change is our biggest challenge. Agriculture requires energy for growth and production. Fossil fuel-based energy is expensive and causes greenhouse gas emissions, which exacerbate climate change. Renewable energy sources mitigate these emissions to a permissible extent and promote sustainable agriculture through different applications. Some applications, such as solar-powered (photovoltaic) water pumps, off-grid solar electricity production, greenhouse technologies, solar dryers for post-harvest processing, solar water heaters, and organic fertilizers made from biomass can increase agricultural production while decreasing its contribution to climate change (Chel & Kaushik, 2011) and meeting energy requirements.

National Mission for Sustainable Agriculture (NMSA): An Initiative by the Indian Government

NMSA is one of the missions under the National Action Plan on Climate Change. This mission aims to promote sustainable development through a focus on ten key dimensions of Indian agriculture. The NMSA was formed by subsuming the Rain-fed Area Development Programme (RADP), the National Mission on Micro-Irrigation (NMMI), the National Project on Organic Farming (NPOF), the National Project on Management of Soil Health & Fertility (NPMSH&F), and the Soil and Land Use Survey of India (*Department of Agriculture Cooperation & Farmers Welfare | Mo A&FW |*

GoI,). The NMSA is transforming Indian agriculture into a climate-resilient production system. The NMSA primarily focuses on conservation and the sustainable use of natural resources for food and livelihood security.

Case Study of Sustainable Agronomic Practices in the Uttar Pradesh Region: A Review

- Aromatic and medicinal plant-based agricultural programme ("Jeevan Shakti Pariyojna"): under this programme, the Uttar Pradesh Bio-Energy Development Board has undertaken a move toward medicinal and aromatic plant cultivation to support sustainable agriculture. The state's climatic zone is highly conducive to the growth of these plants. The aim of this scheme is to allow for a managed cultivation and production of medicinal plants which are scarce due to deforestation. Simultaneously, it will also provide an additional income to poor farmers. In an attempt to successfully implement this project, 21 such medicinal and aromatic plants have been listed. These are: lemongrass, palmarosa grass, aloe vera, rauwolfia serpentine, wild asparagus, holy basil, khas, citronella, *Rosmarinus officinalis*, senna, *Gymnema sylvestre*, sweet flag, abelmoschus, piper longum, *Mucuna pruriens*, winter cherry, creat, psyllium, *Bergenia*, and garden cress. The objective of this scheme is to use waste lands; for example, water-logged lands or forest-covered lands where primary crop production is untenable. Such lands can be used for medicinal and aromatic plant cultivation, thus rejuvenating the degraded land. This agricultural method uses degraded land without disturbing primary crop production, thereby offering additional income to farmers. According to the Uttar Pradesh Bio-Energy Development Board, some studies gave the following results.
- Waste to energy: waste is present everywhere and has become a roadblock to the creation of a clean living environment. Bio-energy is the conversion of waste into useful fuel or energy products such as petrol, diesel, etc. Agricultural waste is either burnt to clear fields for the next crop, or it is collected and rots in villages, causing severe diseases in local villagers. Bio-energy produces green energy for rural electrification and cooking, generates organic fertilizer from discarded slurry, and keeps the environment clean. Agriculture residue, horticulture waste, food waste, cattle dung, etc. are the raw materials that are available in villages and are discarded as waste. The conversion of agricultural waste into biogas and organic fertilizer is a sustainable means of increasing crop production naturally without adding any pesticides or chemical fertilizers. The degradable waste, when it undergoes anaerobic decomposition in a biogas chamber, produces biogas as its product, which is rich in methane and is used for cooking and electrification, and it produces bio-slurry as waste, which is an excellent organic fertilizer. Biogas is a form of green energy, which has zero effect on climate change. Biogas has an energy capacity equal to that

Table 15.2 Medicinal and Aromatic Plants Cultivated in Few Regions of Uttar Pradesh under Crop Cluster

Crop Type	Climate	Usable Part	Total Expense (Rs/acre)	Total Production (kg/acre)	Total Income (Rs/kg)	Remarks
Aromatic Plants						
Lemongrass	10°C-45°C Temperature. Low water required; Feb-March/July-September are the best months for transplanting.	Leaves	35000-40,000 Rs/acre in 1st year. 6000-8000 Rs/acre in 2nd, 3rd, 4th and 5th years. (One crop can be reproduced for a maximum of 5 years).	60-80	800-900 Rs/kg oil on normal demand. 1000-1100 Rs/kg oil on high market demand.	Low maintenance, lower water requirement, protects from insects and animals, improves degraded land quality. Oil extracted from distillation process.
Palmarosa	10-45°C temperature, 60-100cm rainwater	Leaves	25,000-35,000 Rs/acre in 1st year. 6,000-8,000Rs/acre in 2nd years.	40-50	1000-1200 Rs/kg oil on normal market demand. 1500-2500 Rs/kg oil on high market demand.	Oil is extracted from distillation process.
Khas	Normal climate	Roots		1400-1600 kg/acre roots are produced. 8-10 kg/acre oil is produced.	15,000-20,000 Rs/kg oil on normal market demand. 20,000-25,000 Rs/kg oil on special market demand.	Can be cultivated on any land, one year cultivation plant.

Medicinal Plant

Plant	Temperature/Conditions	Parts Used	Yield	Price	Notes
Sarpgandha	10-38°C temperature, Dry land is required.	Roots, seed	800-900 kg/acre after 18 months. 1200-1400 kg/acre after 3 years.	2,00,000-2,50,000 Rs/acre roots are sold. 1,00,000 Rs/acre seeds are sold.	A total of 3,00,000-3,50,000 Rs/acre is earned by the farmers.
Shataavar	Starts flowering in Feb-March and fruits come in April month. 10-35°C temperature is good.	Roots	12-15 quintal/acre real production of roots.	400-500 Rs/kg roots on normal market demand. 700-800 Rs/kg roots on special market demand.	1.5-2 kg seed is required for cultivating in 1 acre of land. A healthy root is 20-30 cm long and 1-2cm wide. During seed plantation, high water quantity is required due to heavy seed layers. After germination no water is required.
Holy Basil (Tulsi)	70-90 days are required for 1st production.	Leaves, Seeds	50-60 kg/acre Tulsi oil	500-700 Rs/kg Tulsi oil	Oil is derived from distillation process. Remaining residue can be utilized as organic fertilizer.

Source: Uttar Pradesh Bio-Energy Development Board.

of petrol and diesel. It can be used for electricity, as cooking fuel, or as biofuel in automation.

The Uttar Pradesh Bio-Energy Development Board has claimed that a biogas digester of 10m^3 requires 200kg of carbonic waste in a week to generate enough biogas for 10 family members daily (*Bio-Energy Board-U.P.*). Lucknow, Balia, Kaushambi, and Hamirpur are some regions in which biogas plants are benefitting local people and farmers through the creation of biogas and organic fertilizer. Additionally, it helps in converting infertile, dried, and discarded lands into a green belt zone, along with generating employment for small and cottage industries.

Conclusion

The survival of any living being is unimaginable without food. Agriculture ensures the food security of a country and its population and is therefore known as the "backbone of the country". But climate change and social development have limited agricultural land, which has forced farmers to move toward unsustainable means of competing for societal existence. These unsustainable practices adversely affect the land and the environment in different ways. Agricultural practices such as the tilling of soil, the use of pesticides and chemicals, mono-cropping, etc. are driving land degradation and destroying the fertility and natural recharging ability of soil nutrients, which is again affecting agricultural productivity. Moreover, these practices are also causing climate change through significant greenhouse gas emissions. Sustainable agriculture gives an equal weight to environmental, social, and economic concerns in agriculture. Sustainable agriculture practices avoid the use of chemicals and pesticides through the adoption of natural alternatives such as trap crops, cover crops, organic farming, the use of renewable energy resources, etc. These practices maintain healthy crop productivity with minimal damage to land, the environment, and its feeders. But agro-ecosystems cannot be sustainable in the long run without the knowledge, technical competence, and skilled labour needed to manage them effectively. Therefore, it is essential for every country and its government to spread awareness about sustainable agriculture among farmers, both at the state and central levels. The Indian government has already initiated its push toward sustainable farming under the auspices of the National Mission on Sustainable Agriculture scheme.

References

Badenes-perez, F. R., Shelton, A. M., & Nault, B. A. (2005). Using yellow rocket as a trap crop for diamondback moth (Lepidoptera: Plutellidae). *Journal of Economic Entomology*, 98(3), 884–890. https://doi.org/10.1603/0022-0493-98.3.884

Bassil, K. L., Vakil, C., Sanborn, M., Cole, D. C., Kaur, J. S., & Kerr, K. J. (2007). Cancer health effects of pesticides. *Canadian Family Physician*, 53(10), 1704–1711.

Chel, A., & Kaushik, G. (2011). Renewable energy for sustainable agriculture. *Agronomy for Sustainable Development*, 31(1), 91–118. https://doi.org/10.1051/agro/2010029

Cover crop | agriculture. (n.d.) *Encyclopedia Britannica*. Retrieved August 23, 2020 https://www.britannica.com/topic/cover-crop

Diversify crop rotations | NRCS Pennsylvania. (n.d.). Retrieved August 23, 2020, from https://d.docs.live.net/72d21293ac4bcafd/Documents/SustainableAgronomic%20Practices-edited.docx

Getting Back to Nature. (2019). *Environment*. Retrieved August 18, 2020, from https://www.nationalgeographic.com/environment/2019/03/partner-content-getting-back-to-nature/

Home: Bio-Energy Board-U.P. (n.d.). Retrieved September 24, 2020, from http://bio-energy.up.nic.in/

Home, Department of Agriculture Cooperation & Farmers Welfare, Mo, A., F. W., & GoI. (n.d.). Retrieved September 24, 2020, from http://agricoop.nic.in/

Impulse, S. (n.d.). Sustainable agriculture: Solutions for the future of farming. Retrieved 19 August 2020, from https://solarimpulse.com/sustainable-agriculture-solutions

India at a glance | FAO in India | Food and Agriculture Organization of the United Nations. (n.d.). Retrieved August 16, 2020, from http://www.fao.org/india/fao-in-india/india-at-a-glance/en/

Indian Council of Agricultural Research. (n.d.). CCARI. Retrieved August 20, 2020, from http://agrigoaexpert.res.in/icar/OrganicFarming.html

Integrated farming system and agriculture sustainability-Indian Journals. (n.d.). Retrieved August 29, 2020, from http://www.indianjournals.com/ijor.aspx?target=ijor:ija&volume=54&issue=2&article=004

Morris, C., & Winter, M. (1999). Integrated farming systems: The third way for European agriculture? *Land Use Policy*, 16(4), 193–205. https://doi.org/10.1016/S0264-8377(99)00020-4

Organic Agriculture | National Institute of Food and Agriculture. (n.d.). Retrieved August 20, 2020, from https://nifa.usda.gov/topic/organic-agriculture

Organic Agriculture: What is organic agriculture? (n.d.). Retrieved August 20, 2020, from http://www.fao.org/organicag/oa-faq/oa-faq1/en/

Organic insect deterrent for agriculture: Biodegradable crop protection products without risks or side effects. *ScienceDaily*. Available at: https://www.sciencedaily.com/releases/2018/06/180606132729.htm (Accessed: 19 August 2020).

Population by country (2020) – Worldometer. (n.d.). Retrieved August 16, 2020, from https://www.worldometers.info/world-population/population-by-country/

Savci, S. (2012). Investigation of effect of chemical fertilizers on environment. *APCBEE Procedia*, 1, 287–292. https://doi.org/10.1016/j.apcbee.2012.03.047

Special Report on Climate Change and Land — IPCC site. (n.d.). Retrieved August 16, 2020, from https://www.ipcc.ch/srccl/

Srinivasan, K., & Moorthy, P. N. K. (1991). Indian mustard as a trap crop for management of major lepidopterous pests on cabbage. *Tropical Pest Management*, 37(1), 26–32. https://doi.org/10.1080/09670879109371532

Sustainable agriculture. Learn. Science at Scitable. Retrieved August 18, 2020, from https://www.nature.com/scitable/knowledge/library/sustainable-agriculture-23562787/

Sustainable farming in India. (n.d.). Retrieved August 18, 2020, from https://www.nationalgeographic.com/environment/2019/03/partner-content-getting-back-to-nature/

Trap crops: A tool for managing insect pests damage | agropedia. (n.d.). Retrieved August 19, 2020, from http://agropedia.iitk.ac.in/node/8450

Unsustainable Agriculture. (n.d.). *Citizens of Earth*. Retrieved August 15, 2020, from https://www.thecitizensofearth.org/unearthing-our-roots

Waghmare, A. (2019, October 15). India is 102 in Hunger Index of 117 nations, undoing decade of improvement. *Business Standard India*. Retrieved August 16, 2020, from https://www.business-standard.com/article/current-affairs/india-takes-the-low-rung-ranked-102-in-hunger-index-of-117-countries-119101501494_1.html

Yadav, R. L. (1998). Factor productivity trends in a rice–wheat cropping system under long-term use of chemical fertilizers. *Experimental Agriculture*, 34(1), 1–18. https://doi.org/10.1017/S0014479798001070

Chapter 16

Is Health Insurance a Sustainable Strategy for achieving Universal Health Coverage in India?

Archana Bakshi

Introduction

Health is the human resource that is valued the most across the globe. The role of health in influencing economic outcomes has been sufficiently investigated that we can claim it has a positive and statistically significant effect on the rate of growth of Gross Domestic Product (GDP). Pertinent literature (Schultz, 1961; Denison, 1962; Meier, 1990) suggests that investment in human capital along with physical capital can augment the process of economic development.

The introduction of the goal of Universal Health Coverage (UHC) by the World Bank (2013) served as a milestone in underlining the importance of health. UHC is defined by the WHO (2010) as "ensuring that all people can use the promotive, preventive, curative, rehabilitative and palliative health services they need, of sufficient quality to be effective, while also ensuring that the use of these services does not expose the user to financial hardship". In 2015, a "2030 Agenda for Sustainable Development" was envisioned in the form of 17 Sustainable Development Goals (SDGs) for achieving health objectives, both directly and indirectly.

In the beginning, India embraced a public sector–dominated model for providing health care guided by the Constitution of India, which made it obligatory for the State to ensure the proper health of its citizens. In spite of this ideal role of Government in the provision of health, a prudent policy for providing health care was missing. Public health programmes made a conscious effort, but inefficiencies diminished the ability of the public sector to catch up with the expanding medical requirements of the Indian masses. Even after seven decades of independence, the most crucial challenge to the Indian economy is the good health of its 1.2 billion citizens. India's health expenditure is less than 5% of its GDP, out of which only 1% is publicly financed. An imbalance between supply and demand for public health services provided an opportunity for the private sector to expand.

The graphical presentation of domestic health expenditure for the period 2000–2015, as given in Figure 16.1, shows that the public sector's share of

DOI: 10.4324/9781032640488-19

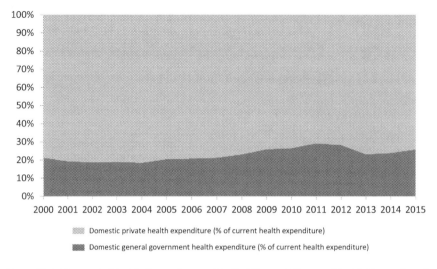

Figure 16.1 Domestic Health Expenditure of India (%age of Current Health Expenditure), 2015.

Source: Author's analysis

current health expenditure was never above 30%. Hooda (2015) states that the share of private hospitals increased from 18.5% per cent in 1974 to 74.9% in 2000. The private sector dominated the Indian healthcare market, accounting for more than three-fourths of health allocations. Healthcare was thus rendered too expensive for a large section of the population (Mavalankar & Bhat, 2000). Bhat and Saha (2004) have documented the acceleration of private health expenditures due to the emergence of the latest medical technologies and an ever-expanding middle class. Healthcare expenses have risen by 14% since 1994–1995, particularly in the case of in-patient treatment.

Healthcare needs are complex and dynamic, as they are affected by lifestyle and subjective behaviours. With the emergence of new diseases, the high cost of diagnosis and treatment and expensive procedures have made healthcare financing a challenge. Non-communicable diseases are major contributors to high morbidity and mortality in the country. With the increasing globalization and liberalization of the insurance market, health insurance has become an important pillar for health financing in India.

Several descriptive and empirical studies have examined the growth and significance of health insurance in the Indian economy.

Rao (2000) holds the opinion that with a dominant private sector and high out of pocket health expenditures, health insurance could be a good option for saving millions of lives. She also points out the reasons for the high priority given to health insurance in contemporary times, like pushes from within the private corporate sector, attempts at increasing foreign direct investment by promoting India as a health destination, and the deepening of the insurance market by TPAs and private HI companies through financial incentives such as tax exemptions and subsidies for premiums.

Ahuja and Jutting (2004) confirm that the demand for health insurance is limited because of the lack of standardization of health services, and also because of the absence of a database on the basis of which insurance companies could design health insurance products. They hold that healthcare infrastructure is positively related to the demand for health insurance by the poor, so it is necessary to address the demand side and at the same time design insurance schemes while taking into consideration the paying capacity of the poor.

Forgia and Nagpal (2012) undertook a study of the World Bank to evaluate the various types of publicly financed health insurance schemes in India. Specifically, they evaluated three central-level schemes – Employee's State Insurance Scheme (ESIS), Central Government Health Scheme (CGHS), and Rashtriya Swasthya Bima Yojana (RSBY) – in addition to six state Government Sponsored schemes. They documented that about a quarter of India's populace (300 million) were covered by health insurance by 2010; out of which 240 million were covered under Government financed health insurance schemes.

Kumar and Ramamoorthy (2014) observed that till 2000, only a limited number of health insurance plans were available, but in recent times there has been innovation in this sector. About 30 non-life insurance companies in India have made over 300 health insurance products available. Almost all private insurers witnessed satisfactory growth during this period. They suggested reform in the public health system to provide equity, affordability, and quality. They also recommended "market segment specific" insurance solutions and advanced networking technologies to expand the health insurance market in India.

In their article, Arivalagan and Perumal (2015) briefly describe the evolution of the Indian health insurance context as a result of the underfunding of health expenditure by the Government. They enumerated the various healthcare-financing models (single payer, employment-based, managed care, out of pocket expenditures) applied in different countries across the world. They mentioned that according to WHO data from 2010, the composition of global health was characterized as: private insurance (18%), social insurance (25%), public expenditure (35%) and OOP (18%). They documented that nearly 70% of healthcare in India was out of pocket. They stated that health insurance was a dominant segment (with a share of 30%) of the general insurance sector of India.

This paper aims to examine the pattern of health insurance in India, assess its scope in terms of population coverage, and identify the challenges to its growth.

Methods

This study is based on a descriptive research framework. Secondary data from the annual reports of the Insurance Regulatory and Development Authority (IRDA), the World Bank Database, WHO reports, and the publications of the MoHFW (Government of India) were used to achieve the objectives of the study.

Results and Discussions

In India, the concept of health insurance was still in its infancy till the end of the twentieth century. No mandatory subscription was provided to all citizens by the government. The evolution of health insurance in India after independence can be shown chronologically as follows:

1948: the Central Government initiated the Employees State Insurance Scheme (ESIS) for blue-collar workers.
1954: the Central Government Health Scheme (CGHS) was launched.
1973: the General Insurance Corporation (GIC) was established with four subsidiaries: the National Insurance Co., the New India Insurance Co., the Oriental Insurance Co., and the United Insurance Co.
1986: the four public sector general insurance companies introduced the "Mediclaim" policy.
1999: the Insurance Regulatory and Development Authority (IRDA) Act was passed.
2001: the Indian Insurance sector was opened to private companies.
2001: the introduction of Third Party Administrators (TPA's) in 2001 simplified the service delivery procedure to a cashless transaction.
2002: the parliament passed a bill de-linking the four subsidiaries from the GIC and restructuring them as independent companies, and at the same time the GIC was converted into a National Re-Insurer.
2003: the Universal Health Insurance Scheme (UHIS), a hospitalization indemnity scheme, was started by the government to introduce health insurance to the informal sector. The UHIS provides financial risk protection. This scheme was made available only to families below the poverty line.
2008: the Rashtriya Swasthaya Bima Yojana (RSBY) programme was inaugurated to provide health protection to Below Poverty Line (BPL) families.
2012: standalone health insurance companies were permitted to operate.
2014: the government increased the maximum Foreign Direct Investment cap in insurance sector to 49%.

The health insurance landscape in India covers different type of provisions and can be categorized as:

1. Government Schemes: the Ministry of Health and Family Welfare initiated the CGHS– and Ministry of Employment and Labour-launched ESIS and the RSBY. State specific schemes include the Yeshasvini scheme in Karnataka (2003), the Kudumbasree scheme in Kerala (2006), and the Rajiv Aarogyasri scheme in Andhra Pradesh (2007).
2. Market-based systems (private and voluntary): in private voluntary health insurance, the consumer can choose a plan directly or indirectly through an employer. The plan may be individual or a family floater plan. "Mediclaim" was the only health insurance policy sold by the four general insurance public sector companies. Post-2000, several private HI companies, including a few standalone companies, emerged on the insurance scene offering innovative product variants.
3. Community based schemes: these are typically targeted at poorer sections of the population. By and large, these voluntary but not-for-profit insurance schemes in India cater to the rural and informal sectors and include micro-insurance and mutual health organizations. The local community or society often plays an important role in generating awareness, collecting premiums, or managing claims. These are heterogeneous with regard to size, benefit packages, geography, and beneficiary groups. The number of members may vary from one thousand to two million.

Health insurance has been gradually emerging as a tool to manage the financial needs of the Indian people. The number of persons covered under it has improved over the years. Table 16.1 presents the population coverage in millions.

A World Bank report (La Forgia & Nagpal, 2012) observed that the total population covered by health insurance increased more than 5 times, from 55 million to 300 million, during the period 2003–2004 to 2009–2010. They pointed out that it was the government sponsored schemes to which this spectacular growth could be attributed.

The IRDA also stated that, if the population of India were 1.2102 billion, and assuming that only one policy has been issued to one person, it may be estimated that approximately 24% of India's total population has been covered under any of the health insurance policies during the FY 2014–2015, as compared to 3% in 2004.

Table 16.2 shows that during the time period 2010–2011 to 2016–17, the number of persons covered under any type of health insurance increased by 1.7 times. The proportion of the population covered increased from 21% to 33% in 2016–2017. Nearly three-fourths of the insured persons were covered under government sponsored schemes and the rest under market-based voluntary health insurance schemes. In the category of private insurance, group insurance policies had a wider coverage (16%) than individual policies (7%).

Table 16.1 Population Coverage under Health Insurance (in millions)

Scheme	2003-04	2009-10	2015*
Central Government Schemes			
1. Employees' State Insurance Scheme (ESIS)	31	56	72
2. Central Government Health Scheme (CGHS)	4,3	3	3
3. RSBY	n.a	70	300
State Government Schemes			
Andhra Pradesh, AP (Aarogyasri)	n.a	70	75
Tamil Nadu, TN (Kalaignar)	n.a.	1.4	33
KA (Yeshasvini)	1.6	3	3.4
Total Government Sponsored	37.2	243	528.4
Commercial insurers	15	55	90
Grand total (includes others not listed above) **	55	300	630

Sources: Forgia and Nagpal (2012); elaboration based on scheme data. Note: n.a = not applicable, scheme not yet in existence. * = estimated.
**Includes other health protection and health insurance schemes.

The future of the health insurance sector seems to be bright in the wake of the role assigned to "strategic purchasing" in The National Health Policy of India, 2017. The Government specified the aim of improving the health outcomes of the Indian populace by reducing out of pocket expenses. With the success of the RSBY and Arogyashri programmes, the policy advocated private sector participation through insurance so as to fill critical gaps in the provisioning of public health. It also provided for collaboration with private entities for CGHS empanelment. Further, the Ayushman Bharat, the National Health Protection Scheme announced in 2018, is the world's largest health insurance plan, which offers healthcare access to 500 million people.

In spite of the conspicuous role that health insurance can play, it has not realized its potential in India. The major challenges facing the rapid growth of health insurance in India have been identified as the following:

1) Ignorance among the masses about the role of this segment of insurance. Several empirical studies have recognized low levels of awareness as a vital challenge to the adoption of HI.
2) Low levels of disposable income among Indian families with which to afford premium payment.
3) Health insurance companies struggle to exist due to an absence of information regarding healthcare use, which could enable them to set premium levels and resolve the issues of adverse selection and moral hazards.

Table 16.2 Population Coverage under Different Categories of Health Insurance Business (in lakh)

Category	2010-11	2011-12	2012-13	2013-14	2014-15	2015-16	2016-17
Government Sponsored including RSBY	1891(75)	1612(76)	1494(72)	1553(72)	2143(74)	2733(76)	3350(77)
Group (other than Govt. Business)	226(9)	300(14)	343(17)	337(15)	483(17)	570(16)	70.5(16)
Individual Business	419(16)	206(10)	236(11)	273(13)	254(9)	287(8)	370(7)
Grand Total	2535	2118	2073	2162	2880	3590	4375

Note: figures in parenthesis show % to total of respective columns
Source: IRDA Annual Reports

4) This concept can thrive only if adequate hospitals and health care centres are available in which people would be able to claim their policies when required. Its demand is derived from the demand for health services.
5) The lack of standardization regarding the cost of health services in the private sector reduces its reliability.
6) Mis-selling is another problem that reduces its credibility. Agents and marketing professionals paint a very rosy picture of the benefits, but at the time of a medical exigency, claims get refused due to the existence of riders or due to insufficient coverage under the policy.

Policy Recommendations

1. Awareness of health insurance should be increased through public campaigns in rural and semi-urban areas. A sufficient budget should be allocated to health insurance programmes.
2. A cess (a levy) may be introduced for the purpose of funding health insurance premiums for economically challenged citizens.
3. To broaden coverage under health insurance, social insurance can be further deepened and broadened. White-collar employees in the unorganized sector can be incentivized to purchase health insurance through further tax incentives. It is recommended that GST on health insurance should be reduced. Permission for hybrid products could make this instrument lucrative to small investors.

Conclusion

Good health is an aspiration universal to human beings. In India a large informal sector, coupled with a large population base, limits the public health financing system's ability to realize the dream of universal health coverage. By the turn of the 21st century, the concept of health insurance had not gained much ground in India, although it formally existed through a number of arrangements. This movement gathered steam only after economic reforms affecting the liberalization, privatization and globalization of the Indian economy, which affected the financial sector and more specifically the insurance area. Furthermore, the IRDA Act of 2000 ushered in fundamental changes to this sector. It allowed private insurers to enter the Indian market, thus paving the way for its enlargement. It is expected that this momentum will continue, so as to make health access more equitable and realize the dream of Universal Health Coverage.

References

Ahuja, R., & Jütting, J. (2004). *Are the poor too poor to demand health insurance?* (No. 118). Working paper. http://icrier.org/pdf/wp118.pdf

Arivalagan, K., & Perumal, R. (2015). Health insurance in India. *International Journal of Advanced Research in Management and Social Sciences*, 4(10), 84–104.

Bhat, R., & Saha, S. (2004). Health insurance: Not a panacea. *Economic and Political Weekly*, 39(33), 3667–3670.

Denison, E. F. (1962). Education, economic growth, and gaps in information. *Journal of Political Economy*, 70(5, Part 2), 124–128.

Forgia, G., & Nagpal, S. (2012). *Government-sponsored health insurance in India: Are you covered?* https://openknowledge.worldbank.org/ handle/10986/11957

Hooda, S. K. (2015). Government spending on health in India: Some hopes and fears of policy changes. *Journal of Health Management*, 17(4), 458–486.

Insurance Regulatory And Development Authority. (2012). (Health Insurance) regulations, Irda exposure draft, Chapter 1. www.irda.gov.in

Kumar, S. S., & Ramamoorthy, R. (2014). Health insurance market in India–the way forward. *Health and Medical Care Services: Claims on National Resources*, pp.178.

Mavalankar, D., & Bhat, R. (2000). Health insurance in India: Opportunities, challenges and concerns. In D. C. Srivastava & S. Srivastava (Eds.), *Indian insurance industry transition and prospects*. Delhi: New Century Publications.

Meier, G. M. (1990). *Leading issues in economic development. Studies in international poverty* (2nd ed.). Oxford University Press.

Ministry of Health and Family Welfare. (2014–15). National health accounts - Estimates for India 2014–15. https://mohfw.gov.in/ newshighlights/national-health-accounts-estimates-india-2014-15

Rao, S. (2004). Health insurance: Concepts, issues and challenges. *Economic and Political Weekly*, 39, 3835–3844.

Schultz, T. W. (1961). Investment in human capital. *The American Economic Review*, 51(1), 1–17.

World Health Organization. (2010). *The world health report: Health systems financing: The path to universal coverage: Executive summary*. http://www.who.int/health_financing/universal_coverage_definition/en/

World Bank Database. https://data.worldbank.org/indicator

Part 3

Strategic Sustainability

Chapter 17

Inorganic Modes – An Inevitable Choice for the Sustainable Growth of RIL During the COVID-19 Pandemic

Manish Sharma, Komal Mishra, Dinesh Sharma, and Akriti Srivastava

Introduction

COVID-19 Pandemic as an Opportunity: Turning the Tide in One's Favour

"Never let a good crisis go to waste". This remark by Winston Churchill offers a ray of optimism in the current situation, as the whole world faces a turbulent and testing time during the COVID-19 pandemic. For corporations across the globe, mergers and acquisitions, along with innovations, could be the driving force allowing them to sail through.

This research paper examines the role of the digital enablement revolution – which encompasses such ideas as the use of ICT, blockchain technology, automation, AI, and data analysis – along with the inorganic mode of expansion resorted to by organizations wishing to reconfigure their strategies to make them resilient and stay competitive in the present crisis. This paper has examined the strategy of one of India's big bull companies, Reliance Industries Limited (RIL), which has proved that adversity can be turned into opportunity, and that remodelling and syndication can be effective tools for withstanding any adverse scenario. The adoption of such experimental strategies, which often involve high risks, in such a pessimistic environment could result in the firm's exorbitant growth. When successful, they not only provide opportunities for capturing the market for high-end vertically differentiated products, but they also facilitate the firm's horizontal product differentiation within its previous technical capabilities. Despite facing an unknown adversity, boardrooms around the globe have altered their priorities in the past to make a turnaround. CEOs, nowadays, are adapting more rapidly, and reconfiguring their business models according to the evolving situation. This "reconfiguration" phase is likely to include strategic initiatives such as alliances and partnerships aimed at augmenting capabilities, the optimization of operations and supply chains, and the reconfiguration of channels of distribution and manpower skilling.

DOI: 10.4324/9781032640488-21

The results of our research suggest that, in the long run, there is a significant change to the financial performance of the corporate sector in India after mergers and acquisitions, and the innovative visions of the management add fuel to such performances. This study has been undertaken to contribute to the following broad objectives: to make a segment-wise comparative analysis of the selected entity with its peers, to examine whether mergers and acquisitions should form part of corporate strategy in the near future to act as a shield against this pandemic, and to gain perspective as to whether innovation in technology has added value to the organization in the pandemic era. Combining technological competitiveness with an inorganic mode of expansion has surged as an expansion strategy in the last decade and a half. This has happened because of the digital enablement revolution, which encompasses such ideas as the use of ICT, blockchain technology, automation, AI, and data analysis in businesses. A company can face any adversity if it is well equipped with technology, along with strategies of furtherance, and dynamism in its approach.

Mantravadi and Reddy (2008) have studied the impact of mergers on the operating performance of acquiring corporations in different industries, by examining some pre-merger and post-merger financial ratios, with a sample of firms covering all mergers involving public limited and traded companies in India between 1991 and 2003. Their results suggest that there are minor variations in terms of the impact on operating performance following mergers in different industries in India.

Marina Martynova and Luc Renneboog in their study investigated why and when merger waves occur, be it because of technological, industrial, political, and social shocks. They propose a classification of merger waves into five phases, and then offer their outlook, concluding that takeovers toward the end of each wave are usually driven by non-rational, frequently self-interested, managerial decision making.

Md. Alam Ansari and M. Mustafa have conducted an analytical study of the impact of mergers and acquisitions on financial performance in the corporate sector in India, and the results of the research suggest that there is no significant change to the financial performance in the corporate sector in India after mergers.

- Several waves of M&A have occurred in the past that have helped corporations around globe to tide over adversity and also to expand their businesses across borders. The pandemic has paved the way for yet another such wave in the corporate world.
- Technological upgrading and innovation represent the most dynamic facets of corporate strategy. This study has been undertaken taking these important facts into consideration.

The recent PWC COVID-19 survey, which took the opinion of more than 900 global CFOs, reflected that M&A features as a preferred strategy in companies' recovery strategies. The PWC analysis found that companies that made acquisitions during the 2001 US recession saw around 7% higher shareholder returns than industry peers during a span of only one year. This supports the present study's proposition.

The World Economic Forum's Global Competitive Index 4.0 ranked India at 68th place among the 141 countries surveyed. India's rank slipped 10 spots compared to last year's rank of 58th. Analysis of the report reveals that, despite performing better, India slipped by 10 positions owing to its slow pace of development in comparison to other developing countries, be it in the adoption of ICT, in trade openness, or in the protection of intellectual property rights.

Methods

Our study analyzes the strategy adopted by the big bull company Reliance Industries Limited (RIL) as an ideal case, and as a leader driving the market for all. The success of Reliance in every sphere into which it has ventured in the past few years sets an example for achieving success through the use of dynamic strategy formulation, the adoption of innovative technology, and quick adaption to an Ever-changing environment. Diversification remained a key component of every move by RIL, and has added billions of dollars to its shareholders' wealth. Reliance's success in building up communication technology, specifically according to India's demand, and its ability to proliferate across the country in only a short span of time, reflect the company's enduring strategic robustness, and have therefore attracted global technology leaders like Whatsapp, Google, etc., to enter into an alliance with RIL in the recent past. Its recent acquisition of Kishore Biyani's Future Group and Food Bazaar business for approximately Rs 234 billion further reveals the company's future plans to integrate the advanced technology of Whatsapp and Google with traditional businesses in retail, grocery, food, and beverages, plans which show the entrepreneurial element in RIL's strategic decision making. This early adoption of technology could make the company's balance sheet strong, and its enhanced future cash flow will add value to the enterprise. Figure 17.1 details the investment of global leaders in RIL's Jio platform.

In 2019, RIL announced its strategic partnership with Microsoft. RIL management aimed to adopt the latest innovations in technologies like AI interfaces and the use of data analytics tools in assessing demand for their products. Together with SME partners, through the adoption and implementation of these technologies, RIL aimed at the inclusive all-round growth and development of Indian companies. Simultaneously, it will help the acceleration of technology-led GDP growth in India, and drive the adoption of next-generation technology solutions at scale.

The diversified portfolio of the RIL group includes companies operating in oil refining, petrochemicals, oil and gas, organized retail, digital services, financial services, etc. Reliance is ushering in the Fourth Industrial

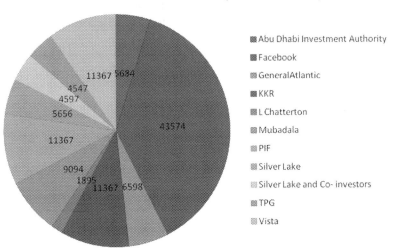

Figure 17.1 Stake Sale in RIL Jio in 2020.
Source: Reliance Annual Report

Revolution (4IR) within India. As a leader in the space, Reliance has capitalized on megatrends in the digital, physical, and biological spheres: trends such as the use of advanced technologies and equipment, global movements from a physical to a digital economy, advancements in biotech integrated within businesses, and a circular business model that derives value from waste. Table 17.1 depicts how Reliance is enabling the 4IR in India.

The table above contains only an indicative list; RIL is using many technologies besides these. Looking at RIL's Research and Development (R&D) expenditure, the company has reported an increase in expenditure of 6.77% from the previous year, which shows that the company is adopting a dynamic approach toward its changing environment and relying heavily on its R&D capabilities to use future-driven technology to develop core competencies.

The Reliance group is betting heavily on new age technologies for their expansion and sustainable growth.

RIL's Core Segment Analysis

On carrying out our comparative study of Reliance with its competitors, it was found that in most of its segments, the group is performing far better than its competitors owing to its adoption of innovative technologically-enabled strategies combined with M&A.

Table 17.1 RIL Technological Advancements and their Applications

KEY TECHNOLOGICAL TRENDS	RELIANCE PRESENCE
Artificial Intelligence and Machine Learning	Facial recognition used to comply with DOT KYC norms while onboarding telecom customers. Haptik: using AI for the GOI's official WhatsApp-based helpdesk for COVID-19 Embibe: AI-based education analytics enabling personalized education for every student for school and competitive exams. Machli App by Jio: helping fishermen by providing accurate weather information. Using Artificial Intelligence to scrutinize letters of credit, supplying shipping information, and managing cycle times in petro-chemical exports. ML is used extensively to improve effective and efficient operations in manufacturing.
Cloud Computing and Big Data	Jio operates one of the largest big-data lakes for telecom in the world. Jio, in collaboration with Microsoft, will set up data centres in locations across India, consisting of next-generation computing, storage, and networking capabilities.

Source: Reliance Annual report

Retail Segment

Reliance Retail, in comparison with Avenue Supermarket Limited, performed far better than its peer as illustrated in Figure 17.2.

Reliance Industries acquired Reliance Retail on 20 November 2006 and, in the long run, Reliance Retail has over-performed in terms of financials, and has added value to the organization as a whole, which is very well reflected in the figure above, which shows the standalone figures of Reliance Retail in comparison to Avenue Supermarket. Recently, Reliance Retail has made an announcement that it will acquire a 60% stake in NetMeds with an investment of Rs 620 million, which shows that the company is continuing its diversification strategy amidst the pandemic. NetMeds is an online pharmaceutical drug delivery company. Reliance's move to acquire this company came after Amazon opened up in this area, thus acting to offer Amazon strong competition.

Reliance Retail's strategy for fighting this black swan event (the pandemic) includes the roll-out of a digital commerce initiative that will open up further growth opportunities for the organized retail business, leveraging the best of their consumer and digital platforms.

Reliance's commercial agreement with Whatsapp was aimed at expanding its digital commerce business arm JioMart, so as to reach out to its clients through technological tools.

Figure 17.2 RIL retail segment growth in comparison with Avenue Supermarket.
Source: moneycontrol.com

Table 17.2 Reliance Retails Store and EBITDA (in Rs. crores)

YEAR	EBITDA(CRORE)	REVENUE(CRORE)	NO. OF STORES
2019-20	Rs 9654	Rs 162936	11784
2018-19	Rs 6201	Rs 130566	10415
2017-18	Rs 2529	Rs 69198	7573
2016-17	Rs 1179	Rs 33765	3616
2015-16	Rs 857	Rs 21075	3245
2014-15	Rs 784	Rs 17640	2621

Source: Reliance Annual report

Digital Segment

Similarly, on analyzing the number of subscribers to Reliance Jio (387 million), it happens to be at first position with regard to subscription numbers, with Bharti Airtel lagging at 329 million subscribers. In a short span of time it has overcome years of domination of the telecommunication sector by companies like Vodafone and Bharti Airtel and has become the market leader. This was due to the company's agility in scaling and adapting in an orderly manner and offering affordable and simple pricing plans. Figure 17.3 shows that RIL Jio is giving tough competition to its peers.

Analysis of the financials reveals that the revenue posted by Bharti Airtel, of Rs 2843.82 billion, lagged behind Reliance Jio's which stood at Rs 3875.22 billion, and the same declining trend was observed in earnings before interest and taxes (EBIT), due to declining numbers of subscribers to Bharti Airtel.

Inorganic Modes and Sustainable Growth   171

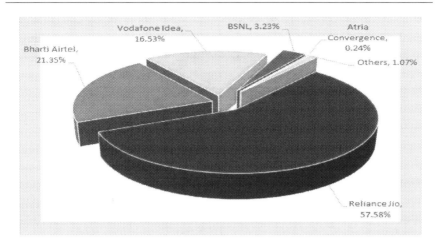

Figure 17.3 Market shares of key service providers.
Sources: Data released by TRAI as of 31.05.2020

The use of ML/AI applications, blockchain technologies, supercomputers, and the latest IoT technologies, have put RIL ahead of its competitors in a short span of time. Jio is set to launch virtual reality, high speed gaming, and 5G services in India in coming years. The advent of Amazon and Tesla satellite internet services and the entry of Bharti Airtel into 5G will surely open doors to new connectivity possibilities in the country.

Refining and its Marketing Segment

Comparative revenue analysis of Reliance, BPCL, EBIT can be observed from Figure 17.4.

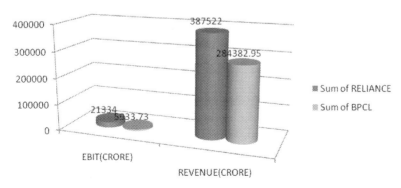

Figure 17.4 BPCL & RIL Comparative.
Source: RIL Annual Financial Report

RIL has rolled out state-of-the-art, new age fuel dispensers across its network. GPS enabled monitoring of its fleet, the launch of virtual card-enabled transactions, the digitalization of key processes, and the adoption of innovative R&D by RIL have resulted in delivery value to customers (See Figure 17.5).

SIDBI microfinance pulse reported in favour of using blockchain technology in the insurance business. It keeps track of a health database that can be accessed anywhere, anytime. With the launch of a digital health card by the Government of India in the third quarter of 2021, this will surely pave the way for a systematic and robust healthcare system in a populous country like India. No wonder healthcare in India is reportedly growing at 15% and is expected to be worth Rs 620 billion as compared to Rs 449 billion in 2018–2019.

Companies in India are experiencing better free cash flow positions in comparison to the last decade. This has paved the way for them to further expand their businesses, via all-cash deals, in service-enabled sectors in India and abroad.

With the advent of IBC (Insolvency and Bankruptcy) Code, 2016, there has been speedy trials for companies that have gone into liquidation, and it has been seen that big corporations like Reliance, Patanjali, etc. are coming forward to take up these insolvent entities, as their valuations are quite attractive for the bidders. In case of Ruchi Soya, the insolvent entity was taken up by the Patanjali group, and the share price surged from Rs 17 to Rs 1500 within a few months of its listing. The same story was repeated with RIL's acquisition of Alok Industries, with share prices rising from Rs 5 to Rs 55 within six months. RIL's infusion of capital and technology has resulted in Alok Industries setting an example through which India has become the second largest exporter of PPE kits in the world.

By the latest count, around $14.3 billion worth of M&A deals in distressed assets have been carried out since the code became functional in December 2016. Distress M&As account for 12% of the total M&A value in 2019–2020, led by deals including that of Bhushan Steel ($7.4 billion). In other words, it is a buyer's market in the M&A context. Some other notable distress M&A deals were Reliance Communications and Fortis Healthcare.

About two-thirds of these distress M&A deals were direct, in which the asset itself was distressed, while the remaining one-third were indirect transactions, which resulted in a sale because the parent organization was in distress.

Swift, time-bound resolutions to or liquidations of stressed assets will be critical for de-clogging bank balance sheets and for the efficient reallocation of capital. Stressed assets are found in multiple sectors, so M&As are expected to happen in multiple sectors.

CONCLUSION

The study we have conducted, and our analysis, show that it is quite evident that surplus cash positions, the adoption of innovations, and diversification strategies like M&A, could result in the achievement of a milestone,

Inorganic Modes and Sustainable Growth 173

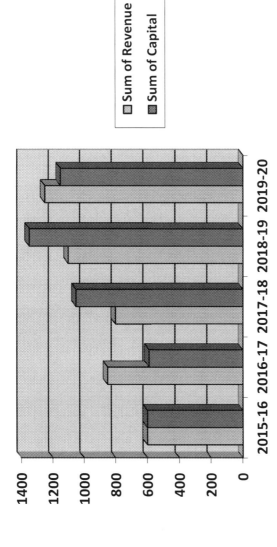

Figure 17.5 Value Creation through Innovation and R&D.
Source: RIL Annual Financial Report

Table 17.3 Comparison of Cash Flow Yields

COMPANY	FY 2020-21
Reliance Industries	7%
Infosys	6%
Bharti Airtel	7%
ITC	6%
Power Grid	11%
Tata Power	18%

Source: FactSet, Goldman Sachs Global Investment Research, NSE.

and could sustain growth in an atmosphere of uncertainty like that of the COVID-19 pandemic. In this study, Reliance Industries Limited has adopted innovative technology at a pioneer stage, which made it resilient against this pandemic. Therefore, in a way, RIL is establishing a benchmark for success and setting an example of technology-enabled sustainable growth in its diversified portfolios of companies.

The time is nigh for a kind of revolution in technologically driven M&A to sweep the corporate world globally. With the advent of 5G and 5G-enabled services and of innovation in allied product development, market development may also be technologically driven.

CEOs who adopt innovative and technology-embedded strategies will survive, sustain, or even grow in future, and those who fail to adopt and adapt will perish. Lastly, this increased dependency on technology comes with risks of cyber threats, and this will further push the use of technology to new heights. With Indian corporations adopting the latest technology and innovation, we can hope that India will attain a higher and higher rank in the GCI Rankings in coming years.

Bibliography

Ansaril, Md. A., & Mustafa, M.(2018). On An analytical study of impact of merger & acquisition on financial performance of corporate sector in India.

Bell, E. (2013). *How to evaluate a merger using financial statements*. Demand Media.

Chandra, P. T. *Financial management: Theory and practice*. McGraw Hill Publication.

Durity, H., & Goldman, M. (2013). *A vision for M&A: Best practices for creating a winning acquisition strategy*. The M&A Advisor and Merrill Datasite.

Fairburn, J. A., & Kay, J. A. (1989). *Mergers and merger policy* (1st ed.). Oxford University Press.

Fama, E. F., Fisher, L., Jensen, M. C., & Roll, R. (1969). The adjustments of stock prices to new information. *International Economic Review*, 10(1), 1–21.

Gray, A. (2003). Why do firms carry out mergers and acquisitions, and how can the difficulties involved be overcome? www.andrewgray.com.

Harris, R., & Ravenscraft, D. (1991). The role of acquisitions in foreign direct investment: Evidence from the U.S stock market. *Journal of Finance, 46*(3), 825–844.

Mantravadi, P., & Reddy, A. V. (2008). On post-merger performance of acquiring firms from different industries in India.

Martynova, M., & Renneboog, L. (2005) On a century of corporate takeovers: What Have we learned and where do we stand?

Miller, M. H.,& Modiglian, F. (1961). Dividend policy, growth and the valuation of shares. *Journal of Business, 344*, 411–433.

Rami, S. S. (1998). *Corporate growth through mergers & acquisitions* (1st ed.). SAGE Publications, Pvt. Ltd.

Ravenscraft, D. J., & Scherer, F. M. (1987). *Mergers, sell-offs and economic efficiency.* The Brookings Institution.

Sharma, R. K., & Gupta, S. K. (1997). *Financial management theory and practice.* Kalyani Publisher.

Sirower, M. L. (1997). *The Synergy trap: How the company loose the acquisition game.* The Free Press.

Chapter 18

Is the Premier League Really Balanced? Evidence From Multiple Measures

Mithun Kumar Guha and Somroop Siddhanta

Introduction

Sports have been one of the main forms of entertainment for human society since time immemorial. The context in which sports are viewed has transformed across the globe, with viewing limitations being mitigated by the advent of public broadcast systems. Today, sporting leagues across the globe are considered to be part of a highly profit-oriented industry that is not only related to entertainment but also to business organizations and media houses, putting huge investments at stake. Therefore, sporting leagues nowadays try to maintain a generous level of uncertainty in their outcomes so as to attain better target rating points (TRPs).

Since its inception in 1992, the English Premier League (EPL) has been the most popular football league in the world, according to the Global Football League Rankings (Matchet, 2017; Tansey, 2014), attracting sizeable investments from sponsors. It is not only the most popular football league in the world, but also the wealthiest of them all. Consequently, it is important to identify the analytical tools that can make the league more competitive in nature, thus maintaining its popularity while simultaneously ensuring that it is profitable.

One of the major metrics with regard to sustaining the interest of viewers and the profitability of sponsorships is to continuously track and improve the League's competitive balance. Competitive balance determines the uncertainty of the outcome of individual encounters and overall championships within a league (Owen & King, 2013). The competition becomes more attractive when the results of games are harder to predict, which in turn reflects a higher level of competitive balance in the league (Rottenberg, 1956).

Up to the last edition of the EPL, Manchester United have won the title 13 times out of 28, with only five other teams ever winning the title. Having stated this, it is important to study the league's sustainability, by analyzing its competitive balance so that stakeholders in the league may improve the balance of the league in the near future.

Competitive balance has often been used among a very large sphere of researchers. Competition becomes more attractive when it is harder to

DOI: 10.4324/9781032640488-22

predict the result of the games due to a greater level of competitive balance (Rottenberg, 1956). Similarly, Forrest and Simmons (2002) have reiterated that a higher degree of competitive balance means greater unpredictability.

Following the above definitions and the studies that have previously been conducted, it is evident that competitive balance is directly related to the uncertainty principle (Sloane, 1971). Sloane distinguishes the multidimensionality of competitive balance into short-run and long-run uncertainty. Short-run uncertainty is the competitive balance between teams playing within one season, while long-run uncertainty is defined as competitive balance across seasons. Uncertainty is categorized into three kinds – match uncertainty, seasonal uncertainty and championship uncertainty (Szymanski, 2003). Match uncertainty is described as the uncertainty of the outcome of a match played between two teams, whereas seasonal and championship uncertainties are the uncertainty of outcomes across seasons and within a championship respectively.

Daly and Moore (1981) used Spearman's rank correlation to measure competitive balance in Major League baseball. Later the same metric was used by Maxcy and Mondello (2006) to measure competitive balance among North American professional team sports leagues. This can be one of the measures for determining seasonal uncertainty.

The technique of one-way analysis of variance (ANOVA) has been applied to the English Football League system to determine a statistically significant decline in competitive balance across all leagues (Ramchandani et al., 2018). This is a great measure for determining seasonal as well as championship uncertainty.

The Noll-Scully Index has been a consistently used measure in the study of competitive balance. The Noll-Scully ratio is identified as a measure of competitive balance that shows how far a particular league's distribution of wins deviates from a purely random outcome (i.e., equal paying strength). The Noll-Scully ratio is calculated as a ratio of the real standard deviation and the idealized standard deviation of the average wins (Noll, 1988; Scully, 1989). On a scale of 0 to 1, the higher the Noll-Scully ratio, the better the competitive balance.

Berri (2012) and Berri and Harris (2015) have used the Noll-Scully ratio to calculate competitive balance in the NBA and the WNBA, and found WNBA had a better competitive balance than the NBA.

After taking into consideration the strengths and weaknesses of the data available and the limitations of the measures, the following objectives have been chalked out as apt for the study:

1. to determine the intensity of the reordering of teams to ascertain seasonal imbalance in the EPL.
2. to check the real and idealized standard deviation of average wins in order to calculate the Noll-Scully ratio.

3. to find out whether there is any significant difference in the average points won across teams and seasons.
4. to find the proportion of points gained by the top 5 teams in each season to the total points gained by all teams.
5. to determine the total number of appearances in the top 5 positions for a team in all seasons.

For determining objective No. 3, as listed above, two hypotheses are created as follows:

- H_{0A}: There is no significant difference between teams based on average points scored.
- H_{0B}: There is no significant difference between seasons based on average points scored.

Methods

Data were collected from the outcomes of the 27 seasons between the inception of the EPL and its most recently finished league results. For comparison over teams and seasons, two kinds of uncertainty were taken into account: seasonal imbalance and the dominance of teams over seasons. Since both these uncertainties cannot be determined by a single measure, five different techniques were used to calculate the competitive balance and further validate each other through the consistency of results. Rank correlation and the Noll-Scully ratio were used to determine competitive balance specifically concentrating on seasonal uncertainty. A two-way ANOVA was conducted to ascertain any significant difference across seasons and teams at a 5% level of significance. To understand the dominance of teams across seasons in the league, a C5 index and K5 rankings across seasons were minted.

Results and Discussions

Rank correlation was used to determine the intensity of reordering. The rank correlation values vary between –1 and +1. A value of 1 determines that there is absolutely no reordering in the ranks compared to the previous season, while a value close to –1 represents complete reversal of the standings.

The results in Table 18.1 below show that the rank correlation values indicate an increasing trend from +0.673 to +0.808. This means that the competitive balance is far from good and has got worse in recent seasons, as compared to the first few seasons of the league. As observed in Table 18.1, the trend seems to be more constant with an average of 0.818, showing that team management needs to be more agile with regard to the selection of players to make the league more exciting and unpredictable in the future.

Table 18.1 Rank Correlation Values Calculated S-O-S

YEAR	RANK CORRELATION
1993–1994/1992–1993	0.67348
1994–1995/1993–1994	0.74816
1995–1996/1994–1995	0.60644
1996–1997/1995–1996	0.78063
1997–1998/1996–1997	0.76877
1998–1999/1997–1998	0.86364
1999–2000/1998–1999	0.91551
2000–2001/1999–2000	0.92836
2001–2002/2000–2001	0.76186
2002–2003/2001–2002	0.79743
2003–2004/2002–2003	0.73715
2004–2005/2003–2004	0.75939
2005–2006/2004–2005	0.8083
2006–2007/2005–2006	0.84634
2007–2008/2006–2007	0.84338
2008–2009/2007–2008	0.84783
2009–2010/2008–2009	0.86611
2010–2011/2009–2010	0.91749
2011–2012/2010–2011	0.91156
2012–2013/2011–2012	0.90613
2013–2014/2012–2013	0.82312
2014–2015/2013–2014	0.93083
2015–2016 / 2014–2015	0.82658
2016–2017/2015–2016	0.81126
2017–2018 / 2016–2017	0.80929
2018–2019 / 2017–2018	0.80829
2019–2020 / 2018–2019	0.80823
Average	0.818

Source: Authors' calculation

The results in Table 18.2 show that the Noll-Scully ratio calculated season-on-season (S-O-S) is increasing (moving farther from 1), and its highest value is during the 2018–2019 season, at 2.242. The lowest Noll-Scully value is 1.059 for the first season of the league, reflecting a good competitive balance at the start and decreasing competitive balance as the league progressed.

With reference to Table 18.3, ANOVA provides information about whether there is any significant difference between teams and between seasons, to find out the effect on competitive balance across teams and across seasons. The results depict that the values of p are not significant, and both the null hypotheses mentioned below are rejected.

- H_{0A}: There is no significant difference in average points between teams.
- H_{0B}: There is no significant difference in average points between seasons.

Table 18.2 Noll-Scully Ratio Value Calculated S-O-S

Season	Values
1992–1993	1.059457
1993–1994	1.406152
1994–1995	1.317179
1995–1996	1.64089
1996–1997	1.26096
1997–1998	1.3179
1998–1999	1.561305
1999–2000	1.731251
2000–2001	1.468977
2001–2002	1.767669
2002–2003	1.664357
2003–2004	1.614512
2004–2005	1.7708
2005–2006	1.991672
2006–2007	1.685854
2007–2008	2.091576
2008–2009	1.9573
2009–2010	1.915818
2010–2011	1.362335
2011–2012	1.823971
2012–2013	1.871199
2013–2014	2.045873
2014–2015	2.045873
2015–2016	1.71356
2016–2017	2.143081
2017–2018	1.972105
2018–2019	2.242254
2019–2020	1.98256

Source: Authors' calculation

Table 18.3 ANOVA Calculation

ANOVA

Source of Variation	SS	Df	MS	F	P-value	F crit
Between Teams	131114	19	6900.735	387.5829	8.8733E–290	1.606849
Between Seasons	9018.271	27	334.0101	18.75983	5.46206E–60	1.507536
Error	9133.729	513	17.80454			
Total	149266	559				

Source: Authors' calculation

As the hypotheses are rejected, it depicts a poor competitive balance and shows that point distribution is not close to idle probabilistic values as of now. This might show improvement as future seasons roll out, based on whether the actions of the team management support equal team strength in the future.

The C5 index has been calculated in Table 18.4 to show the ratio of the points gained by the top 5 teams in each season with respect to the total points shared by all teams in the respective season. The results can be predicted, as a C5 ratio closer to 1 suggests a poor competitive balance in a particular season, while a ratio farther from 1 shows positive improvement in the competitive balance in relation to earlier seasons. The results below show that C5 ratios have been almost stagnant at 0.350, with minor deviations on both sides. If we look into the C5 ratios for the 5 most recent seasons, we

Table 18.4 C5 Index Ratio

SEASONS	VALUES
1992	0.290
1993	0.317
1994	0.316
1995	0.343
1996	0.334
1997	0.327
1998	0.347
1999	0.348
2000	0.340
2001	0.367
2002	0.344
2003	0.349
2004	0.363
2005	0.365
2006	0.353
2007	0.381
2008	0.378
2009	0.370
2010	0.342
2011	0.365
2012	0.375
2013	0.379
2014	0.358
2015	0.343
2016	0.386
2017	0.387
2018	0.382
2019	0.365

Source: Authors' calculation

Table 18.5 K5 Rating Calculation

Teams	Appearances in Top5	Percentage of Appearances in Top 5	Cumulative Percentage
Arsenal	24	17%	17%
Manchester United	23	16%	34%
Liverpool	19	14%	47%
Chelsea	19	14%	61%
Manchester City	12	9%	69%
Tottenham Hotspur	11	8%	77%
Newcastle United	7	5%	82%
Leeds United	7	5%	87%
Everton	4	3%	90%
Aston Villa	3	2%	92%
Blackburn Rovers	3	2%	94%
Leicester City	2	1%	96%
Norwich City	1	1%	96%
Queens Park Rangers	1	1%	97%
Nottingham Forest	1	1%	98%
West Ham United	1	1%	99%
Ipswich Town	1	1%	99%
Sheffield United	1	1%	100%

Source: Authors' calculation

will see that they have moved closer to 0.4 which suggests poor competitive balance in the league in relation to the past.

K5 ratings (Goossens, 2006) have been used to determine the greatest number of appearances in the top 5 on the basis of points scored by teams across seasons. Table 18.5 below shows that Arsenal, Manchester United, Liverpool, Chelsea and Manchester City have appeared almost 70% of the time in the top 5 across seasons. This is an indication that the points table shows a high level of positive skew toward these five teams, and thus it is clear that these teams have a higher probability of winning when they encounter any other team in the league. Fort and Quirk (1995) suggests that competitive balance can only improve when the unpredictability of the outcome of the games increases, which has not been the case in the seasons conducted thus far, apart from some minor exceptions here and there.

Conclusion

Keeping in mind the above results, and on the basis of interpretation done in the wake of past studies on competitive balance, it is evident that the English

Premier League is not well balanced in terms of predictability of outcome for most of the encounters during a season. Even across seasons, competitive balance is not improving, as shown by the results derived in ANOVA, well supported by the K5 ratings, the Noll-Scully ratio, and the correlation matrix. The results depicted under C5 also support the claim that competitive balance is far from good in the league across seasons. When it comes to measuring competitive balance between teams it is found that only five to six teams rule the roost when it comes to points table standings every season. In fact, a recent Forbes study explains that the top ten teams in world football in terms of revenue include the top five teams according to the K5 rating of the EPL mentioned above (Forbes, 2019). Thus, the financial ability of the top few teams to acquire productive players, coaches, and team managers may be a reason for the non-improvement of competitive balance. This is consistent with conclusions drawn by Scarfe et al. (2020) that "the best players might be willing to play for the best teams", and therefore that inequality among teams arises within the league, as reflected in the results above.

Apart from the financial constraints, the difference in use of technology-based analytical tools in preparation for an encounter, including the lack of use of analysts, the quality of training infrastructure, and lean fan followings, can be considered as reasons that need to be objectively looked at before narrowing down actionable means of improving competitive balance.

In the current study, only a few apt measures have been considered when analyzing the status of competitive balance in the league. The study can be extended to other soccer and other sporting leagues, and additional variables – fan attendance, fan followings, and team financials – can be used to establish further cause-effect relationships which may lead to improvements in the sustainability of the league.

References

Berri, D. J. (2012). Did the players give up money to make the NBA better? Exploring the 2011 collective bargaining agreement in the national basketball association. *International Journal of Sport Finance*, 7(2), 158–175.

Daly, G., & Moore, W. (1981). Externalities, property rights, and the allocation of resources in Major League Baseball. *Economic Inquiry*, 29(1), 77–95.

Forbes (2019). The business of soccer – The list. https://www.forbes.com/soccer-valuations/list/#tab:overall

Forrest, D., & Simmons, R. (2002). Outcome uncertainty and attendance demand in sport: The case of English soccer. *Journal of the Royal Statistical Society, Series D (The Statistician)*, 51(2), 229–241.

Fort, R., & Quirk, J. (1995). Cross-subsidization, incentives, and outcomes in professional team sports leagues. *Journal of Economic Literature*, 33, 1265–1299.

Goossens, K. (2006). Competitive balance in European football: Comparison by adapting measures: National measures of seasonal imbalance and Top 3. *Rivista di Dirittoedeconomiadello Sport*, 2(2), 77–122.

Harris, J., & Berri, J. D. (2015). Predicting the WNBA draft: What matters most from college performance? *International Journal of Sport Finance*, *10*(4), 299–309.

Matchett, K. (2017). Ranking the most entertaining leagues in world football. Retrieved September 25, 2020 from Bleacher Report. https://bleacherreport.com/articles/2691880-ranking-the-most-entertaining-leagues-in-world-football

Maxcy, J., & Mondello, M. (2006). The impact of free agency on Competitive Balance in North American Professional Team Sports Leagues. *Journal of Sport Management*, *20*(3), 345–365.

Noll, R. G. (1988). Professional basketball. *Stanford University Studies in Industrial Economics*, Paper no. 144.

Owen, P. D., & King, N. (2013). *Competitive balance measures in sports leagues: The effects of variation in season length*. Federal Reserve Bank of St Louis.

Ramchandani, G., Plumley, D., & Wilson, R. (2018). Mind the gap: An analysis of Competitive Balance in the English Football League System. *International Journal of Sport Management and Marketing*, *18*(5), 357–375.

Rottenberg, S. (1956). The baseball players' labor market. *The Journal of Political Economy*, *64*(3), 242–258.

Scarfe, R., Singelton, C., & Telemo, P. (2020). Do High Wage Footballers play for high wage teams? The case of major league Soccer. *International Journal of Sport Finance*, *15*(4), 177–190.

Scully, G. W. (1989). *The business of Major League Baseball*. University of Chicago Press.

Sloane, P. J. (1971). The economics of professional football: The football club as a utility maximiser. *Scottish Journal of Political Economy*, *17*, 121–146.

Szymanski, S. (2003). The economic design of sporting contests. *Journal of Economic Literature*, *41*(4), 1137–1187.

Tansey, J. (2014). Statistically ranking the World's Top 10 Football Leagues. Retrieved September 25, 2020 from Bleacher Report. https://bleacherreport.com/articles/1922780-statistically-ranking-the-worlds-top-10-football-leagues

Chapter 19

Innovative Strategies in the Hospitality Industry
A Systematic Literature Review

Pratim Chatterjee and Smita Datta

Introduction

Innovation means any good, service, or idea that is considered as novel or new. An innovative hotel offers new services, products, processes, or marketing methods (Ottenbacher & Harrington, 2010; Pavia & Foričić, 2017; Salman et al., 2017). To impart higher value to the customer and to go beyond the requirements of their potential guests, a hotel needs to continuously answer the changing wants and needs of the customer through innovation (Grissemann et al., 2013; Nagy, 2014; Pena et al., 2016). As in the manufacturing industry, new product development has become a feature of the service industry which is essential for their survival and growth, and through consistent upgrades and innovation only can firms differentiate themselves from their competitors in this modern era (Orfila-Sintes & Mattsson, 2009; Line & Runyan, 2011; Backman et al., 2017). Different hotel categories are a means for hotels to differentiate themselves from other properties (Becerra et al., 2013). Hotels need to research and identify their distinctive personal tastes and preferences to come up with distinctive value-added and innovative products and services, along with their existing ones, to offer a memorable experience to the customers (Bharwani & Mathews, 2016).

For hospitality and tourism, organization innovation is a major strategy for product/service development, and is the sole way of transforming challenges into opportunities (Chen, 2011; Hillman & Kaliappen, 2015; Aladag et al., 2020). The impact of external factors like rising tourist demand, competition, and changes in tourism and hospitality increases the need for innovation. An innovative hotel offers new products, services, processes or ideas (Pavia & Foričić, 2017; Toivonen & Tuominen, 2009; Langvinieno & Daunoraviþinjto, 2015). Though the hospitality industry is considered to be among the most competitive industries in the world, it has experienced lower productivity compared to other industries, and a lack of innovation is responsible for this phenomenon (Martin-Rios & Ciobanu, 2019). Research around innovation and customer orientation in the hospitality industry is rising rapidly, yet our insights in both these areas remain vague

(Tajeddini & Trueman, 2012; Sandvik et al., 2014). Thus, the main objectives of this study can be considered as follows:

- to synthesize the existing literature on innovative strategies for the hospitality industry in a systematic manner;
- to identify the effective innovation strategies for survival and growth of the hospitality industry;
- to recognize the research gap and scope of future research in this study area.

Further, the paper is structured as follows:

- research methodology for the systematic literature review;
- theoretical background of different innovation strategy in hospitality industry;
- conclusion with future scope for research.

Methods

A Systematic Literature Review methodology was adopted in this study to review and analyze articles. All articles with the terms "Hotel Innovation", "Hospitality Innovation", "ServiceInnovation", or "Organizational Innovation" have been searched for in the Google Scholar search engine. This paper spans a time horizon of almost two decades (2000-2021) and the last search was conducted in July 2021. After considering only articles concerning innovation in the hospitality industry, a total of 51 articles were included for review.

Innovation Strategies in the Hospitality Industry

In this section the theoretical backgrounds of different types of innovation strategies in the hospitality industry are explained. What are the different types of innovation? Which innovation strategy is suitable for a hospitality firm? To answer this question, definitions of "innovation" have been taken from the third edition of the OECD Oslo Manual (2005, p. 46), in which four types of innovations are presented: (1) product innovations, (2) process innovations, (3) marketing innovations, and (4) organizational innovations (Hjalager, 2010; Nagy, 2014; Gomezelj, 2016) These four types of innovations are reviewed with respect to hospitality in the following sections.

Product Innovation

Product innovation is the launch of a goods and services that are totally new or significantly modified with reference to their features or intended applications. Guisado-González et al. (2013), in their studies, discusses the introduction of new technology to help implement product innovation in hotels. Similarly, product differentiation and new product development processes have been widely considered to be innovative techniques that hospitality firms can use to position themselves above their competitors, as they are directly seen and experienced by the end user. Hjalager (2010), Becerra et al. (2013), Hassanien & Eid (2007), and Ivankovič et al. (2010), suggest that hotels with a greater number of different innovative products are more successful in terms of revenue. Similarly, further studies (Lewis and Chambers, 2000; Laugen et al., 2005; Nagy, 2014) show notable relations between product innovation and the successful running of hospitality firms.

Process Innovation

Process innovation is the implementation of new or uncommonly developed production or service methods that improve the effectiveness and quality of the production or service delivery process. Earlier studies in this area have explained the influence of process innovation on the hospitality industry. Tajeddini and Trueman (2012) encourages the development of a proper service method that motivates hotel employees to put forward creative ideas. Zhou et al. (2005) and Chen et al. (2009) analyze the positive influence of innovation orientation and service delivery innovation on financial and market performance. Further, some significant studies (Ottenbacher & Gnoth, 2005; Rodgers, 2007; Martínez-Ros & Orfila-Sintes, 2009; Hjalager, 2010; Chen et al., 2011; López-Fernández, 2011; Vila et al., 2012; Grissemann et al., 2013; Hilman & Kaliappen, 2015) have considered process innovation in the hospitality industry.

Marketing Innovation

Marketing innovation is the practice of an innovative marketing method that aims to change the promotional channel of the product, service, or package, and that is new to the organization. There can be numerous reasons for marketing innovation. Hankinson (2004) points out that the internet can be an innovative promotion medium where the marketing cost can be strictly controlled. Hjalager (2010) and Backman et al. (2017) have also contributed by considering firm or location-centric innovation. Further notable contributions (Mortensen & Bloch, 2005, p. 49; Scaglione et al., 2009; Line & Runyan, 2012; Vila et al., 2012; Pappas, 2015) have been made in this area.

Organizational Innovation

Organizational innovation is the introduction of a new organizational method in the firm's business practices, one that is newly evolved in the firm and is a strategic innovation initiative by its management. The introduction of a new category of hotel as a part of strategic management decision, like the concepts of the medical hotel or meditel, the spa hotel, the wellness hotel, the train hotel, the boutique hotel, etc., has high potential, yet has gained little attention (Victorino et al., 2005; Han, 2013). This type of hotel offers physical convenience, value for money, and makes a memorable impression on the guest (Gan & Fredrick, 2011; Heung et al., 2010; Han et al., 2015; Han & Hwang, 2013). Further, some significant studies (Jacob et al., 2003; Pikkemaat, 2008; GHN, 2011; Sandvik et al., 2014; Han & Hyun, 2014; Kazemha & Dehkordi, 2017) have covered organizational innovation in the hospitality industry. All this – the establishment of new categories of hotel, collaboration with other industries, and learning and development – is the result of organizational innovation.

Conclusion

The objective of this paper was to explore innovative strategies in hospitality management through a systematic literature review. From the research it is quite evident that innovation in any form that suits the organization is mandatory for their survival and growth in this fiercely competitive market. Among the different innovation strategies, following the OECD Oslo Manual (2005, p.46), we find a significant number of studies on process innovation, whereas there is a scope for more research on product, marketing, and especially organizational innovation in the hospitality industry. Though hospitality has the highest potential in the service industry, it is still the least innovative segment, and a lack of interest among academia and among policy makers in this area is quite a matter of concern (Tajeddini & Trueman, 2012; Martin-Riosa & Ciobanu, 2019). More research on hospitality innovation needs to be developed, and there is a need for more valid empirical evidence (Gomezelj, 2016; Hjalager, 2010) This study has brought forward areas for future research, which are as follows:

First, future research can focus on the feasibility of innovation activities for the hotel industry based on different criteria such as size, star category, type of property, etc.

Second, further studies can be conducted on the effects of product, marketing, and organizational innovation on the hospitality industry.

Third, future research can be conducted by considering the viewpoints of stakeholders who are directly connected to innovation in the hospitality industry.

References

Aladag, O., Köseoglu, M., King, B., &Mehraliyev, F. (2020). Strategy implementation research in hospitality and tourism: Current status and future potential. *International Journal of Hospitality Management*, 88, 102556. https://doi.org/10.1016/j.ijhm.2020.102556

Backman, M., Klaesson, J., & O'ner, O. (2017). Innovation in the hospitality industry: Firm or location? *Tourism Economics*, 23(8), 1591–1614. https://doi.org/10.1177%2F1354816617715159

Becerra, M., Santaló, J., & Silva, R. (2013). Being better vs. being different: Differentiation, competition, and pricing strategies in the Spanish hotel industry. *Tourism Management*, 34, 71–79. http://doi.org/10.1016/j.tourman.2012.03.014

Bharwani, S., & Mathew, D. (2016). Customer service innovations in the Indian hospitality industry. *Worldwide Hospitality and Tourism Themes*, 8(4), 4. http://doi.org/10.1108/Whatt-04-2016-0020

Chen, J. (2011). Innovation in hotel services: Culture and personality. *International Journal of Hospitality Management*, 30(1), 64–72. https://doi.org/10.1016/j.ijhm.2010.07.006

Chen, J., & Tsou, H. (2009). Service delivery innovation antecedents and impact on firm performance. *Journal of Service Research*, 12(1), 36–55. https://doi.org/10.1177%2F1094670509338619

Gan, L. L., & Frederick, J. R. (2011). Medical tourism facilitators: Pattern of service differentiation. *Journal of Vacation Marketing*, 17(3), 165–183. https://doi.org/10.1177%2F1356766711409181

GHN. (2011). Global Healthcare Network. Retrieved November 8, 2011, from http://www.globalhealthcarenetwork.com/. Global Healthcare Network

Gomezel, D. (2016). A systematic review of research on innovation in hospitality and tourism. *International Journal of Contemporary Hospitality Management*, 28(3), 516–558. https://doi.org/10.1108/IJCHM-10-2014-0510

Grissemann, U., Plank, A., & Brunner-Sperdin, A. (2013). Enhancing business performance of hotels: The role of innovation and customer orientation. *International Journal of Hospitality Management*, 33, 347–356. http://doi.org/10.1016/j.ijhm.2012.10.005

Guisado-González, M., Guisado-Tato, M., & Sandoval-Pérez, A. (2013). Determinants of innovation performance in Spanish hospitality companies: Analysis of the coexistence of innovation strategies. *The Service Industries Journal*, 33(6), 580–593. https://doi.org/10.1080/02642069.2011.614343

Han, H. (2013). The healthcare hotel: Distinctive attributes for international medical travelers. *Tourism Management*, 36, 257–268. http://doi.org/10.1016/j.tourman.2012.11.016

Han, H., & Hwang, J. (2013). Multi-dimensions of the perceived benefits in a medical hotel and their roles in international travelers' decision-making process. *International Journal of Hospitality Management*, 35, 100–108. https://doi.org/10.1016/j.ijhm.2013.05.011

Han, H., & Hyun, S. S. (2014). Medical hotel in the growth of global medical tourism. *Journal of Travel and Tourism Marketing*, 31(3), 366–380. https://doi.org/10.1080/10548408.2013.876955

Han, H., Kim, Y., Kim, C., & Ham, S. (2015). Medical hotels in the growing healthcare business industry: Impact of international traveler's perceived outcome. *Journal of Business Research*, 68(9), 1869–1877. https://doi.org/10.1016/j.jbusres.2015.01.015

Hankinson, G. (2004). Relational network brands: Towards a conceptual model of place brands. *Journal of Vacation Marketing*, 10(2), 109–121. https://doi.org/10.1177%2F135676670401000202

Hassanien, A., & Eid, R. (2007). Developing new products in the hospitality industry: A case of Egypt. *Journal of Hospitality and Leisure Marketing, 15*(2), 33–53. https://doi.org/10.1300/J150v15n02_03

Heung, V. C. S., Kucukusta, D., & Song, H. (2010). A conceptual model of medical tourism: Implication for future research. *Journal of Travel and Tourism Marketing, 27*(3), 236–251.https://doi.org/10.1080/10548401003744677

Hilman, H., &Kaliappen, N. (2015). Innovation strategies and performance: Are they truly linked? *World Journal of Entrepreneurship, Management and Sustainable Development, 11*(1), 48–63.https://doi.org/10.1108/WJEMSD-04-2014-0010

Hjalager, A. M. (2010). A review of innovation research in tourism. *Tourism Management, 31*(1), 1–12. https://doi.org/10.1016/j.tourman.2009.08.012

Ivankovič,J., Jankovič, S., &Peršič, S. (2010). Framework for performance measurement in hospitality industry – Case study Slovenia. *Economic Research-Ekonomskaistraživanja, 23*(3), 12–23.https://doi.org/10.1080/1331677X.2010.11517420

Jacob, M., & Tintore, J.,´ Aguilo´, E., et al (2003). Innovation in the tourism sector: Results from a pilot study in the Balearic Islands. *Tourism Economics, 9*, 279–295. https://doi.org/10.1177%2F135481660300900303

Kazehma, A., & Dehkordi, K. (2017). The principles of designing hospital hotelwith the approach of health tourism in kish island. *Journal of History Culture and Art Research, 6*(1), 515–531.https://doi.org/10.7596/taksad.v6i1.758

Langvinienơ, N., & Daunoraviþinjtơ, I. (2015). Factors influencing the success of business model in the hospitality service industry. *Procedia - Social and Behavioral Sciences, 213*, 902–910.https://doi.org/10.1016/j.sbspro.2015.11.503

Laugen, B. T., Acur, N., Boer, H., & Frick, J. (2005). Best manufacturing practices: What do the best-performing companies do? *International Journal of Operations and Production, Management, 25*(2), 131–150. https://doi.org/10.1108/01443570510577001

Lewis, R., & Chambers, R. E. (2000). *Marketing leadership in hospitality* (3rd edn.). Van-Nostrand Reinhold.

Line, N. D., & Runyan, R. (2011). Hospitality marketing research: Recent trends and future directions. *International Journal of Hospitality Management, 31*(2), 477–488. https://doi.org/10.1016/j.ijhm.2011.07.006

Line, N. D., & Runyan, R. C. (2012). Hospitality marketing research: Recent trends and future directions. *International Journal of Hospitality Management, 31*(2), 477–488. https://doi.org/10.1016/j.ijhm.2011.07.006

López-Fernández, M., Serrano-Bedia, A., & Gómez-López, R. (2011). Factors encouraging innovation in Spanish hospitality firms. *Cornell Hospitality Quarterly, 52*(2), 144–152. https://doi.org/10.1177%2F1938965510393723

Martínez-Ros, E., & Orfila-Sintes, F. (2009). Innovation activity in the hotel industry. *Technovation, 29*(9), 632–641. https://doi.org/10.1016/j.technovation.2009.02.004

Martin-Rios, C., & Ciobanu, T. (2019). Hospitality innovation strategies: An analysis of success factors andchallenges. *Tourism Management, 70*, 218–229. https://doi.org/10.1016/j.tourman.2018.08.018

Mortensen, P. S., & Bloch, C. W. (2005). *Oslo manual-guidelines for collecting and interpreting innovation data: Proposed guidelines for collecting and interpreting innovation data*. Organization for Economic Corporation and Development.

Nagy, A. (2014). The orientation towards innovation of spa hotel management: The case of Romanian spa industry. *Procedia - Social and Behavioral Sciences, 124*, 425–431. https://doi.org/10.1016/j.sbspro.2014.02.504

Orfila-Sintes, F., & Mattsson, J. (2009). Innovation behavior in the hotel industry. *Omega, 37*(2), 380–394. https://doi.org/10.1016/j.omega.2007.04.002

Ottenbacher, M., & Gnoth, J. (2005). How to develop successful hospitality innovation. *Cornell Hotel and Restaurant Administration Quarterly, 46*(2), 205–222.https://doi.org/10.1177%2F0010880404271097

Ottenbacher, M., & Harrington, R. (2010). Strategies for achieving success for innovative versus incremental new services. Journal of Services Marketing, 24(1), 3–15.https://doi.org/10.1108/08876041011017853

Pappas, N. (2015). Marketing hospitality industry in an era of crisis. *Tourism Planning and Development, 12*(3), 333–349. https://doi.org/10.1080/21568316.2014.979226

Pavia, N., & Floričić, T. (2017). Innovative accommodative facilities in tourism and hospitality industry-integrated hotels. *Tourism in Southern and Eastern Europe, conference*, 437–450.

Pena, M., Núnez-Serrano, J., Turrion, J., & Velazquez, F. (2016). Are innovations relevant for consumers in the hospitality industry? A hedonic approach for Cubanhotels. *Tourism Management, 55*, 184–196. https://doi.org/10.1016/j.tourman.2016.02.009

Pikkemaat, B. (2008). Innovation in small and medium-sized tourism enterprises in Tyrol, Austria. *The International Journal of Entrepreneurship and Innovation, 9*(3), 187–197.https://doi.org/10.5367%2F000000008785096601

Rodgers, S. (2007). Innovation in food service technology and its strategic role. *International Journal of Hospitality Management, 26*(4), 899–912.https://doi.org/10.1016/j.ijhm.2006.10.001

Salman, D., Tawfik, Y., Samy, M., & Artal-Tur, A. (2017). A new marketing mix model to rescue the hospitality industry: Evidence from Egypt after the Arab Spring. *Future Business Journal, 3*(1), 47–69. https://doi.org/10.1016/j.fbj.2017.01.004

Sandvik, I., Duhan, D., & Sandvik, K. (2014). Innovativeness and profitability: An empirical investigation in the Norwegian hotel industry. *Cornell Hospitality Quarterly, 55*(2), 165–185. https://doi.org/10.1177%2F1938965514520963

Scaglione, M., Schegg, R., & Murphy, J. (2009). Website adoption and sales performance in Valais' hospitality industry. *Technovation, 29*(9), 625–631. https://doi.org/10.1016/j.technovation.2009.05.011

Tajeddini, K., & Trueman, M. (2012). Managing Swiss Hospitality: How cultural antecedents of innovation and customer-oriented value systems can influence performance in the hotel industry. *International Journal of Hospitality Management, 31*(4), 1119–1129. https://doi.org/10.1016/j.ijhm.2012.01.009

Toivonen, M., & Tuominen, T. (2009). Emergence of innovations in services. *The Service Industries Journal, 29*(7), 887–902. http://doi.org/10.1080/02642060902749492

Victorino, L., Verma, R., Plaschka, G., & Dev, C. (2005). Service innovation and customer choices in the hospitality industry. *Managing Service Quality, 15*(6), 555–576.https://doi.org/10.1108/09604520510634023

Vila, M., Enz, C., & Costa, G. (2012). Innovative practices in the Spanish hotel industry. *Cornell Hospitality Quarterly*, 53(1), 75–85.https://doi.org/10.1177%2F1938965511426562

Zhou, K. Z., Gerald, Y. G., Zhilin,Y., & Nan, Z. (2005). Developing strategic orientation in China: Antecedents and consequences of market and innovation orientations. *Journal of Business Research*, 58(8), 1049–1058.https://doi.org/10.1016/j.jbusres.2004.02.003

Chapter 20

Strategic Handling of the COVID-19 Crisis in the Christian Medical College, Vellore – A Case Study

Samuel NJ David, R. Raghunathan, Sonia Valas, Joy Mammen, AbiManesh S, Krupa George, Arun Bennet Samuel, and Prabakaran Ravindran

Introduction

Strategic management is a philosophy that is inseparable from leadership. It demands leaders who can inspire heroic behaviour in the face of seemingly overwhelming change. The complexity of healthcare makes it extremely difficult to make strategic decisions.

"For I dip into the future, far as human eye could see, Saw the Vision of the world, and all the wonder that would be". This quote by Alfred Lord Tennyson suggests that any healthcare organization that does not have a clear strategy today is fated to remain mediocre at best – and become a failure at worst – which would result in a poor quality of life for the community it serves.

The term "strategy" is derived from the Greek term *stratēgós*, meaning "a general", whose roots are "army" and "lead". The Greek verb *stratēgéo* means "to plan the destruction of one's enemies through effective use of resources". Due to its origins, the military was the first to use various terms related to strategy – objectives, mission, strengths, and weaknesses.

According to Mahoney and McCue (1999), the 50 strategic ideas examined by them fall into one of six categories: corporate strategy, resource allocation, cost and quality, financial engineering, business unit strategy, and employee motivation and evaluation. Of the 6six categories above, three are financial parameters, thereby illustrating the importance of financial strategies for every organization.

In the business environment, commonly used strategies have always included selecting the right business, understanding the driving forces behind success and efficiency, constantly innovating to renew business, and measuring success by creating superior shareowner value without forgetting the other stakeholders. After analyzing these strategic parameters, the next complication arises: getting results through people. This is often managed by the following steps (Ginter et al., 1997):

DOI: 10.4324/9781032640488-24

- describing an attractive and understandable overall mission for the business;
- getting good people and finding ways for them to "buy in" and find their role within the business;
- providing participants with freedom to act, free of stifling rules and bureaucracy;
- providing financial and psychic rewards for success;
- punishing recurrent failure';
- working resolutely to find and install people with leadership capabilities.

The Problem

The problem is the COVID-19 pandemic; it came as a surprise and took us like a storm, with the first wave, wherein the pandemic became a major health issue, hitting India in February 2020. After this, tackling COVID-19 became a routine and tedious task. The 2nd Wave of COVID-19 started in the month of March, 2021. The pandemic became a common ruthless enemy, which did not differentiate between corporate hospitals and NGOs, the public and private spheres, profit-based and non-profit-based issues, etc. The COVID-19 pandemic has led to a dramatic loss of human life worldwide and presents an unprecedented challenge to public health, food systems, and the world of work (Mammen, 2021). Isolation, contact restrictions, and economic shutdowns forced a sea change in the psychosocial environment of affected countries. As a result, anxiety, lack of peer contact and reduced opportunities for stress regulation became the primary concerns. Due to these contingencies in a crucial work environment like the healthcare setting, there arises the need for various training activities, including the following aspects:

1. equipping staff to work safely inside a COVID area;
2. enabling staff to work safely in regular clinical areas within the constraints of the pandemic;
3. focused expansion of services to handle critical case surges;
4. dissemination of relevant knowledge about COVID-19 management;
5. empowering staff to devise protocols and pathways for their own specialities;
6. addressing staff stress/fear/burnout;
7. impacting the local healthcare workers in the community, mission hospital network, and other hospitals.

In order to strategically plan to address needs and contingencies, PEST and SWOT analyses were carried out as shown in Table 20.1.

These analyses helped us develop the CMC management model for COVID-19 management from a strategic perspective, to allow us to handle

Table 20.1 PEST and SWOT Analyses of the COVID-19 Situation

Political	Economic	Social	Technological
Support from local and state government.	Monetary support from friends of Vellore, NGOs, NPOs, and other private organizations. Redeployment of staff.	Local community, national community, and global community all worked together against the pandemic.	Advancements in technology and the availability of resources (ex. the use of android devices and social media) facilitated in reaching the end-users.

Strengths
- Overall unity and team spirit of individuals and organizations belonging to various domains in working toward a common cause.
- Willingness of volunteers and organizations to participate and help during difficult times.
- Effective support and reassurance from CMC management.
- Support from friends of Vellore.
- Optimal use of HR.
- Togetherness of all systems, government and private, toward a common enemy.

Opportunities
- Opportunity to expand the service to other districts and states in collaboration with local and state governments respectively.
- Paved the path for reputed institutions working together and serving the community and society, thereby providing preparedness to handle similar crises in future, and also delivering a unique model of working together across various domains.

Weakness
- Technical difficulties in telecommunication.
- Limited to only Vellore and neighbouring districts.
- Issues with logistical inadequacies (lack of oxygen cylinders and bed management).
- Panic and fear.

Threats
- Death and dying.
- Business and system collapse.
- Joblessness.
- People were forced to stay inside.
- People were violating the rules.
- Fake medical products.
- Unethical opportunists.

Source: Author's analysis

present needs with an allowance for future variances/changes, particularly for any additional waves that might follow, as shown in Figure 20.1.

The CMC model, developed based on the previous analyses, would not have succeeded without the Grace of Almighty God. On receiving the initial bulletin about the SARS-Cov-1 virus variant, the hospital infection control committee (HICC) began their work immediately by conducting a review of existing and new literature and, using the information from the review, they created the initial set of protocols and our model for patient care and staff safety.

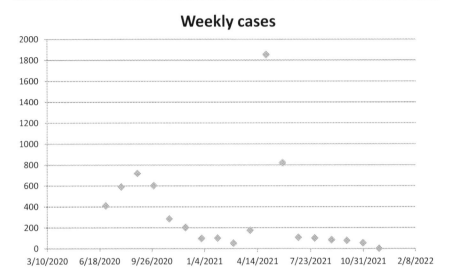

Figure 20.1 COVID 19 Management – The CMC Model.

Source: Author's analysis

Based on the model provided by the HICC, the administration created a core team comprised of leaders from various administrative sections and the Department of Hospital Management Studies and Staff Training and Development; this created a focus for policy development and operations streamlining to ensure non-duplication of efforts. Moreover, the office of the General Superintendent coordinated physical arrangements creating designated pathways for access to COVID wards with dedicated donning and doffing and shower facilities.

The HICC synchronized screening and treatment protocol development based on up-to-the-minute literature after discussions with clinical teams. It also commenced patient and contact tracing and created data management and reporting teams. Housekeeping staff were provided with appropriate cleaning and disinfection protocols as well as work schedules to help them execute their roles effectively. Security personnel were also provided with appropriate training for specific front-line roles around access control and personnel protection for healthcare teams.

With regard to bed management, as the volume of COVID-19 patients being admitted began to escalate from the latter part of March 2020 (a local resident who had recently travelled to the UK being admitted as the first patient), at the height of the pandemic, over 900 beds were set apart for COVID care. Beds were arranged based on care levels (lowest being Level 1 to highest being Level 3 ICU beds).

In HR, commensurate staffing was organized by the HR team; training manuals were developed and training programmes were conducted to develop the abilities of the staff being posted to the ICU and to critical care areas. The Nursing Superintendent's Office coordinated the nursing services with regard to patient care management, including training nurses on patient care and staff safety. In the initial juncture of the COVID pandemic, some communities were disquieted about healthcare workers residing in their localities; to address this issue, staff from such localities were provided with temporary accommodation in hostels within the hospital premises.

Telecommunication was also enhanced, with ICU and Level 2 ward patient visits being conducted through video calls, with a liaison social worker helping patients connect with their loved ones. Voluntary staffing, to contribute skills (technical, clinical, computers, etc.) to assist in care management, was done through the "I – Volunteer screening" which was facilitated by the Medical Superintendent's Office, where interested staff signed up to help. Patient appraisal, the tracing of patient contacts, and the expedition of patient admissions were collaboratively carried out by the HICC, the MS office and the nursing team.

In terms of preparedness, team planning activities began in March 2020. The training activities were divided into two broad categories:

- For staff posted in COVID-19 areas – the donning and doffing of PPE and anxiety management were taught.
- For staff posted in non-COVID-19 areas –basic knowledge of hygienic practices to be followed, among other things, was taught.

In order to cover the large numbers of staff and other personnel in a systematic manner, the training was broadly divided into two major phases.

PHASE 1: training was conducted as live sessions between trainees and trainers.

PHASE 2: training involved a mix of live sessions and online sessions.

Staff categorised for training:

- Doctors;
- Support staff;
- Phlebotomists and respiratory therapists.

The training focus was on nasal anatomy and swab technique, the use of PPE, and dealing with anxiety.

PHASE 1: COVID-19 TRAINING OF TRAINERS

Training was imparted to 10 selected trainers in English and also to 4 selected trainers in Tamil. Through these 14 trainers, over 700 doctors were trained across the main campus in different batches. A separate session for the training of trainers was conducted for peripheral campuses. Training videos developed by the Department of Hospital Management Studies, Staff Training & Development were used to expedite the training of staff through these trainers. These videos were developed with the assistance of staff of the HICC and the Infectious Disease Training and Research Centre (IDTRC), whose demonstrations of the various procedures were filmed. The Department of Hospital Management Studies, Staff Training & Development recorded the demonstrations and edited the recordings for easy understanding.

For the COVID-19 medical volunteers/staff working in COVID areas with live demonstrations, doctors and medical interns from various departments were trained by the faculty from Medical-ICU (clinicians) who covered various aspects of clinical management and general preparedness, including self-management of anxiety. These staff included:

- support personnel;
- hospital attendants;
- hospital housekeeping attendants;
- general service staff;
- clerical staff;
- outsourced staff (dietary, security, ambulance, IT, life operators).

These sessions were conducted by various personnel from the IDTRC and the HIC, focusing on COVID-19 and infection control basics (such as BMW handling, etc.). The sessions for this module were conducted for the staff of both the CMC Vellore-Town and the Kannigapuram campus. The sessions were conducted between 9 March 2020 and 6 October 2020. The statistics are as shown in Table 20.2.

For the COVID-19 preparedness programme for the peripheral centres of CMC Vellore, three training sessions were conducted in the RUHSA and

Table 20.2 Statistics of Training Conducted

Staff category	Number of sessions conducted	Total staff trained
Doctors	7	118
HA/HHKA	6	99
Kannigapuram (various categories)	6	126
General services staff	2	61
Respiratory technicians	3	40
Chaplains	1	14
Phlebotomists	1	14
Ambulance staff (outsourced)	3	51
Dietary staff (outsourced)	2	22
Security (outsourced)	2	20
RKH (outsourced)	1	26
Engineering staff	5	32

Source: Author's analysis

the Mental Health Centre. In the Mental Health Centre, 45 doctors and 22 MCTTs and pharmacists were trained. A total of 11 and 45 doctors respectively were trained. In the RUHSA, a total of 11 doctors, 18 nurses, and 31 general service staff of various categories were trained. In the Schell Eye unit, a single training session was conducted; a total of 19 optometrists and AHS interns as well as 2 MROs/secretaries were trained. These sessions were carried out between 7 March 2020 and 27 March 2020.

For nasopharyngeal swab training, the Department of Otolaryngology (ENT) took the initiative to participate in the COVID-19 preparedness training, wherein training sessions were conducted by expert clinical faculty from the ENT. The training comprised both classroom and practical aspects of learning. The classroom sessions covered the theory of nasopharyngeal sampling, demonstrations of sampling techniques by the faculty, and students practising the techniques on mannequins; and additional aspects covered the donning and doffing of PPE and general preparedness. The primary foci of this training programme were:

- understanding nose anatomy and swab technique with reference to a mannequin;
- PPE and addressing anxiety while working in COVID areas, via discussions;
- hands-on training.

Challenges Faced During Phase I:

1. COVID was relatively new – less reliable information was available;
2. significant fear among staff – novel disease – concerns about personal health;
3. preceded by stringent lockdowns – restricted health care access;
4. a significant number of hospital-acquired infections – no vaccine;
5. No effective therapy;
6. PPE training.

STRATEGIES: PHASE 2

COVID COMMAND CENTRE

One of the wings was the COVID Command Centre (CCC) which was created to oversee the management of all COVID related operations in the hospital. A clinical management handbook was written to cover general training for COVID and all COVID related queries. The queries were collected by Q&A sessions conducted in the Town Hall on Saturdays by staff who were posted in the COVID area. Based on the Town Hall sessions, the clinical management module was formulated with the help of the Distance Education Unit (DEDU).

NON-INVASIVE VENTILATOR TRAINING

Developments in the clinical management of COVID made it necessary for clinicians to be trained in the procedure of Non-Invasive Ventilation (NIV).

The trainees were required to practice on mannequins in the skills lab.

This module was covered in seven sessions for doctors of the mission network.

A total of 104 doctors attended this training. The sessions were conducted between 28 September 2020 and 7 October 2020.

The "CMC Handbook for Management of COVID-19" was another vital tool, wherein covered areas included common co-morbid illnesses, for which appropriate specialists in different departments were approached and chapters were added based on feedback, and this had multiple refined revisions.

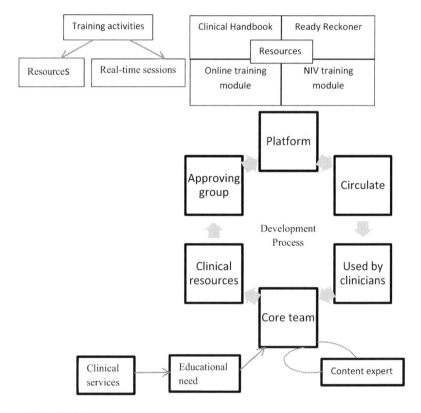

Figure 20.2 CMC Training Initiatives.

Source: Author's analysis

Online Training In Clinical Management

This included 3 pre-recorded lecture videos, of 1.5 hours each. Modules included the clinical management of COVID-19, infection control, the use of PPE, risks to health workers, and communication with patients and families. Core areas were identified and these were tailored into interactive, scenario-based learning with concise information and extra information links. Content development was done on the MOODLE platform followed by trial runs carried out by various department training coordinators. Zoom sessions were used to demonstrate these sessions. 231 staff members attended the course. An NIV training module was conducted as well, in which 153 participants underwent training and were certified accordingly. Online training were conducted in lecture and learning module.

Additionally, real-time sessions were conducted as well, which included the following:

- 10 Weekly Q&A sessions were conducted via Zoom, addressing common issues faced by doctors working in the COVID wards. These were attended by 450 members (all levels of doctors) and followed by a feedback session.
- The CMC Vellore COVID Public Lecture Series (COVID PULSE) was conducted weekly, and provided clinicians with up-to-date knowledge on integral aspects of COVID-19 management like drugs and other interventions, and simple, evidence-based ideas for further innovation. This interactive series of 11 lectures brought together 1773 doctors from diverse backgrounds, and helped clinicians design or refine protocols in the context of available resources. These sessions were shared on social media, and live-streamed on the YouTube platform.
- Project IMAI-A, a joint venture of the Indian Medical Association, Vellore, CMC Vellore, and VIT Alumnus Project. IMAI was one of its kind, a unique project started in Vellore during the second wave of the pandemic in May 2021 as a 24/7 helpline for the public of the Vellore, Ranipet, Arcot district. The aim of the helpline was to use volunteers to monitor the patients' in-home care and also to answer common queries from the public. As the project started, members from the VIT alumnus network joined the cause. With the help of Thryve Digital Healthcare, Chennai, we could get the help of Tevotel, an online portal that had inbuilt software to handle helplines. The technical team took up the responsibility of helping in the installation, guidance, and support of the software, which was quite a challenge and required their presence at all times. We had many glitches in the initial stages which were corrected ably in a matter of minutes by them. The volunteers were divided into 4-hour shifts, thereby covering the whole day, including during the night.
- The UDHAVI initiative was a free monitored telephonic advisory service offered by CMC in collaboration with IMAI, VIT alumni. The COVID

helpline was open on all days of the week and functions from 8.00 am to 8.00 pm. COVID patients and their caregivers were able to connect with healthcare professionals and felt more at ease with complying with guidelines. UDHAVI has four verticals:

1. General Information – this channel provided reliable information about the infection, testing, vaccination, and home isolation.
2. Medical Channel – offered medical advice to home-isolated patients and caretakers.
3. Counselling Channel – offered counselling over telephone to those who requested it.
4. Logistics Channel – assisted in routing calls to locate medication, oxygen, and essential services.

- These services were partnered with NGOs and civil society organizations. Volunteers of different ranks like doctors, nurses, medical technicians, and support staff from various departments were given training to help in the UDHAVI initiative. Weekly training sessions were conducted through Zoom meetings to train and address the issues faced by the volunteers. A total of 179 volunteers attended 9 different training sessions across the 4 channels. All the volunteers who were involved in UDHAVI initiative were given participation certificates appreciating their time and work during this pandemic. Including the IMAI, a total of 333 volunteers have been given certificates of appreciation.
- COVID Suraksha was a training programme for frontline community healthcare volunteers and the general public. This was a two-week online programme, in collaboration with the "distance education department of Christian Medical College, Vellore and AzimPremji Foundation". The curriculum consisted of basic knowledge about COVID-19, prevention, health education, and care for home isolation and pandemic-related psychosocial issues.

Training challenges of PHASE 2 (late phase)

- Due to a massive flow of patients, rapid training for a large staff population was crucial.
- Doctors needed to manage a wide spectrum of diseases.
- There was an exponential increase in the knowledge of the disease and its therapy – however promulgating it in a simple and easily understood form was a challenge.
- Multiple levels of care – primary, inpatient and critical care services – had to be catered to.
- For training our mission hospital network and other hospitals, novel strategies were the need of the hour.

Table 20.3 Strategic Lessons Learnt during Pandemic

a) Training is fundamental	b) Core group
• We have to equip people to respond appropriately. • We cannot rely on traditional methods. • We have to understand real-time needs.	• Central role should be of significance. • We have to identify needs/lacunae in knowledge of the organization. • We need to develop proper resources. • It is crucial to define skills/competencies. • Adaptability and timeliness are to be emphasized.
c) Technology	d) Feedback
• Good IT support is invaluable. • Multiple modalities are necessary to disseminate information. • Rapid dissemination is crucial.	• Feedback from end-users is necessary for modifying strategy as required. • Both formal & informal methods can be adopted. • It is important to critically evaluate training / resources.

Source: Author's analysis

Conclusion

In conclusion, strategic planning along with coordination and the cooperation of stakeholders involved in healthcare delivery, including appropriate HR strategies such as manpower planning, scheduling, training, and the efficient management of resources, helped CMC manage the pandemic effectively.

References

Ginter, P. M., Duncan, W. J., & Swayne, L. E. (1997). *The strategic management of health care organizations*. Blackwell Publishing. ISBN-13p. 978-1557869685.

Mahoney, R. J., & McCue, J. A. (1999). *Insights from business strategy and management- big ideas of the past three decades: Are they fads or enablers?* Center for the Study of American Business, Washington University.

Mammen, J. (2021). COVID-19 management- the CMC model. *Christian Manager*, *20*(4), 10–13.

Chapter 21

Determinants of Brand Loyalty and Purchase Intention for FMCG Products in the Days of COVID-19

Mrinal Kanti Das, Soumya Mukherjee, and Dipak Saha

Introduction

The First Moving Consumer Goods (FMCG) sector has been experiencing stiff competition, along with the curse of the pandemic, like other sectors. The producers and marketers of low-involvement products are finding it hard to establish themselves in the intensely competitive market. The outbreak of the coronavirus pandemic has created pandaemonium in our lives, and has thus brought drastic changes. Previously, marketers concentrated immensely on product quality and brand name. To gain a competitive edge today, however, marketers cannot restrict themselves only to these factors. To promote their brand appropriately, modern marketers need to be sceptical. They should focus on the best mode of promotion to persuade prospects to buy their brands. In this grim situation, marketers direly need to determine the proper matrix of promotion. To reap rich dividends in the market, marketers have to derive other factors that help prospects to get in touch with their brands, even when facing a financial crisis. The financial constraint can hardly be evolved as a barrier with respect to their choice. Moreover, it is of the utmost importance to avail their desired product in the days of the crisis within their vicinity. In our study, we have made a humble effort to shed light on those factors that help marketers not only to excel but to get an edge over their competitors.

Customers are often found to be loyal due to a sense of the hazards of switching. Even satisfaction with their existing brand evokes loyalty among customers (Fornell, 1992). Loyal customers are even eager to undertake the risk of paying a premium price to avoid the risk of change (Yoon & Kim, 2000). Loyalty has an integral relationship with various factors, but the user experience is regarded as the prime factor in evoking loyalty (Aaker & Keller, 1990). Undeviating positive correlations exist between customer satisfaction and repurchase intention in a wide variety of product and service studies. These studies point out that overall customer satisfaction plays a crucial role in persuading an individual to buy the product (Anderson & Sullivan, 1993; Bolton, 1998; Cronin & Taylor, 1992; Fornell, 1992; Oliver, 1980;

DOI: 10.4324/9781032640488-25

Patterson & Spreng, 1997; Rust & Zahorik, 1993; Selnes, 1998; Swan & Trawick, 1981; Taylor & Baker, 1994; Woodside et al., 1989). Hellier et al. (2003) propose a model where they elaborate on seven important factors (service quality, equity and value, customer satisfaction, past loyalty, expected switching cost, and brand preference) that have a significant contribution toward repeat purchasing behaviour. From their study, we come to know that perceived value, along with customer satisfaction, is the main influencing factor in brand preference. Khraim (2011) contributes to the observation that product quality plays a pivotal role in developing brand loyalty among customers. He also highlights certain factors (preferred brand name, product quality price, promotion, store environment, and service quality) which influence brand loyalty. Kohli & Thakor (1997) point out the significant contribution of brand loyalty toward purchase intention, and they also emphasize the fact that the establishment of a brand name is an expensive and time-consuming process that encourages repeat purchases. Product quality and price play a decisive role in enticing women customers toward a particular brand. The brand images also allure women prospects toward the brand (Sharma et al., 2013). Govender (2015) argued that point-of-purchase displays not only help create brand loyalty but also increase sale volumes without a price reduction.

The outbreak of COVID-19 hurts every sphere of life, and forces individuals to change their tastes and preferences. Even the FMCG segment is not spared from the curse of the pandemic. From the existing literature, it has already been proven that brand name and product quality are undoubtedly the determining factors in the purchase of FMCG products. To excel in the immensely competitive market, marketers have to pay heed to other influencing factors as well. In this grim situation, we have administered a pilot study to determine the other decisive factors persuading prospects toward FMCG products. From the pilot study, it has been revealed that advertisement & celebrity endorsement, pack size, retail & shop displays, and availability can also be determining factors in enticing potential customers. Based on these, we propose the following hypotheses:

H1: Advertisement & Celebrity Endorsement has an impact on brand loyalty.
H2: Advertisement & Celebrity Endorsement induce purchase intention.
H3: Pack Size helps to create brand loyalty.
H4: Pack Size improves the probability of purchase intention.
H5: Retail & Shop Display instigates brand loyalty.
H6: Retail & Shop Display influences purchase intention.
H7: Availability plays a significant role in brand loyalty.
H8: Availability induces purchase intention.
H9: Brand loyalty has a significant contribution toward purchase intention.

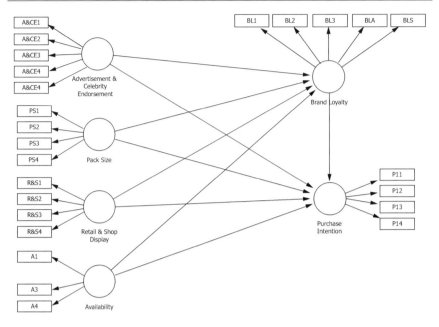

Figure 21.1 Proposed Conceptual Model.

Source: Author's analysis

Methods

Besides being exploratory, our study was descriptive as well as cross-sectional in nature. This study is significant in the current context owing to rapidly changing customer profiles, tough competition, erratic brand loyalty, and the rising expectations of customers. To explore the exclusive factors for the research, we resorted to an online survey using the non-probability purposive sampling method. We employed a pilot study to select 17 items in the questionnaire. A 7-point Likert Scale (strongly disagree to strongly agree) was used to understand the views and opinions of 292 respondents. To run structural equation modelling we used the Smart PLS Software 3.3.2 version, since it provides greater flexibility to the study. Moreover, it offers the option of the multivariate analytical method (Hair et al., 2017; Hair et al., 2019; Hair et al., 2020; Nitzl et al., 2016; Richter et al., 2016; Rigdon, 2016; Ringle et al., 2014). G* Power (Faul et al. 2007; 2009) was specifically administered to get an idea regarding the minimum sample size required for this study. It has been revealed that at 5% level of significance, 115 samples are enough to evaluate the output of the research.

Results & Discussions

Descriptive Analysis

The demographic statistics of the respondents for FMCG products are duly reflected in Table 21.1. The respondents were from a diverse group and

Table 21.1 Demographic Profile of Respondents

Demographic Variable	Item	Frequency	Percentage %
Age	Below 30 years	45	15.41
	31 - 40 years	97	33.21
	41 -50 years	82	28.08
	Above 50 years	68	23.28
Gender	Male	162	55.47
	Female	130	44.52
Family Income	Less than 50,000	115	39.38
	50,000 -100,000	97	33.21
	1,00,000 -200,000	58	19.86
	More than 200,000	22	7.53
Occupation	Unemployed	52	17.80
	Self-Employed	74	25.34
	Service Holder	138	47.26
	Retired	28	8.90

Source: Author's analysis

directly engaged in making buying decisions regarding FMCG products. The Table shows that 55.47% are male and 44.52% are female. Moreover, they are from varied occupations and different family incomes. These descriptive statistics would be enough to shed light on our research.

Measurement Model Assessment

The study paid heed to the outer model, specifically emphasizing internal reliability and convergent validity, in order to go ahead with this study. We administered a confirmatory study with the help of partial least square structural equation modelling (Schuberth et al., 2018; Nitzl et al., 2016). In reference to Yildirim and Correia (2015), Composite Analysis (CCA) was performed to investigate the impact of four factors on brand loyalty and purchase intention. To begin with, the score of latent variables was calculated. Cronbach's Alpha, Dijkstra and Henseler's rho, and Composite Reliability were considered to measure the internal reliability. The threshold value of both Cronbach's Alpha and rho is considered to be 0.70 in the social sciences (Hair et al., 2017; Hair et al., 2020). The values found in our study were well above 0.70 for both cases, except for availability. To establish Convergent Validity, we need to focus on Average Variance Extracted (AVE). AVE values over 0.50 are considered satisfactory to proceed with the study (Fornell & Larcker, 1981; Hair et al., 2019). In our study, the values found were more than 0.5 in each instance, thus proving convergent validity. Again, Composite Reliability is regarded as good to satisfactory if the value ranges from 0.7 to 0.9 (Diamantopoulos et al., 2008). Here in our study, the Composite Reliability of all constructs was more than 0.8 but less than 0.9. So we may rightly say that the evaluation of internal reliability and

208 Mrinal Kanti Das et al.

Table 21.2 Quality Criterion for Reflective Model Assessments and Composite Model

Construct	Items	Type	Loading/ Weights	Cronbach's Alpha	rho A	CR	AVE
Advertisement &Celebrity Endorsement	A&C 1	Reflective	0.787	0.792	0.797	0.859	0.551
	A&C 2		0.613				
	A&C 3		0.802				
	A&C 4		0.791				
	A&C 5		0.7				
Pack Size	PS1	Reflective	0.767	0.722	0.737	0.826	0.544
	PS2		0.764				
	PS3		0.767				
	PS4		0.644				
Retail & ShopDisplay	R&S1	Reflective	0.812	0.734	0.763	0.832	0.556
	R&S2		0.6				
	R&S3		0.754				
	R&S4		0.796				
Availability	A1	Reflective	0.811	0.683	0.685	0.826	0.612
	A2		0.797				
	A3		0.738				
Brand Loyalty	BL1	Reflective	0.641	0.798	0.798	0.862	0.556
	BL2		0.757				
	BL3		0.789				
	BL4		0.805				
	BL5		0.725				
Purchase Intention	PI1	Reflective	0.802	0.781	0.83	0.860	0.611
	PI2		0.698				
	PI3		0.642				
	PI4		0.949				

Source: Author's analysis

convergent validity were thus duly established as reflected in Table 21.2. Table 21.3 gives us a realistic picture of the uniqueness of each construct.

Besides using the traditional method of investigating discriminant validity, an innovative criterion, the Heterotrait-Monotrait ratio of correlations (HTMT), was used in this study. The HTMT inference method requires that all HTMT values should be less than 1. Henselar et al. (2015) suggest that the permissible value is 0.85, whereas Gold et al. (2001) accept any value within 0.9. In this study, the constructs of Availability and Retail & Shop Display exceeded the permissible value at 0.935. To liberally establish discriminant validity, we used the HTMT inference method, and all values were found to be within the permissible limit. The uniqueness of each construct was thus revealed and thereby reflected in Table 21.4 below.

Table 21.3 Discriminant Validity Assessments

Constructs	Purchase Intention	Brand Loyalty	Advertisement &Celebrity Endorsement	Availability	Pack Size	Retail &Shop Display
Purchase Intention	**0.742**					
Brand Loyalty	0.641	**0.783**				
Advertisement & Celebrity Endorsement	0.597	0.66	**0.746**			
Availability	0.531	0.631	0.54	**0.737**		
Pack Size	0.611	0.57	0.571	0.487	**0.782**	
Retail &Shop Display	0.543	0.631	0.582	0.685	0.552	**0.746**

Source: Author's analysis

Structural Model Assessment

The relationship between the constructs and predictive relevance is to be given due emphasis in structural model assessment (Hair et al., 2017). We have diligently employed a bootstrapping process, using the recommended 5000 bootstraps, to shed light on the p values, so as to test the hypotheses in the study (Hair et al., 2020). For formative measurement models, we need to compute each set of predictor constructs of the structural inner model (Cassel et al., 1999). Collinearity issues are the first to be addressed and for this purpose tolerance and inflation factor (VIF) were to be given due importance. Diamantopoulos et al. (2008) pointed out that the VIF value should be below 3.33, and here in this study, the values of VIF for both brand loyalty and purchase intention were 2.067, well below the threshold value. So no collinearity issue was further evoked in our study. The importance and significance of Path Coefficients need to be assessed after that. It is desirable that the coefficients should be within −1 and +1 when considering the bootstrapping process with 5000 subsamples in the PLS algorithm.Figure 21.2 shows Structural Model Assessments with Control Variables. The coefficient of determination (R^2) was also investigated for the endogenous constructs in our study. For each of the endogenous constructs, the variance is usually assessed by R^2 and the threshold value of R^2 is usually determined based on the context. We can even accept a low value of R^2 in PLS-SEM analysis (Raithel et al., 2012). The R^2 values for brand loyalty and purchase intention were 0.512 and 0.472 respectively. While considering the social sciences, we may suggest that the endogenous constructs in both cases are well accepted (Hair et al., 2017). So it can be concluded from our study that brand loyalty and purchase intention are significantly dependent on those four factors for FMCG products.

Table 21.4 HTMT Ratio of Correlations for Discriminant Validity Assessments

HTMT Criterion	Purchase Intention	Brand Loyalty	Advertisement & Celebrity Endorsement	Availability	Pack Size	Retail & Shop Display
Purchase Intention						
Brand Loyalty	0.870CI.900[0.753;0.973]					
Advertisement & Celebrity Endorsement	0.749CI.900[0.616;0.852]	0.886CI.900[0.799;0.964]				
Availability	0.687CI.900[0.551;0.807]	0.880CI.900[0.725;1.011]	0.697CI.900[0.56;0.818]			
Pack Size	0.747CI.900[0.635;0.85]	0.757CI.900[0.634;0.868]	0.709CI.900[0.592;0.812]	0.618CI.900[0.463;0.739]		
Retail & Shop Display	0.699CI.900[0.526;0.827]	0.871CI.900[0.729;1.008]	0.732CI.900[0.623;0.822]	**0.935CI.900[0.795;1.039]**	0.709CI.900[0.571;0.811]	

Source: Author's analysis

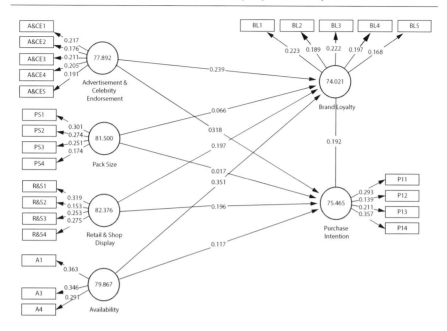

Figure 21.2 Structural Model Assessments with Control Variables
Source: Author's analysis

The Standardized root means square residual was implemented to measure the goodness of fit. The goodness of fit model depends significantly on the SRMR value (Hair et al., 2020). The threshold value of SRMR is 0.08 (Henseler et al., 2016; Hu & Bentler, 1999). In our study, the SRMR value was exactly 0.08. Besides the structural model, we may now consider hypothesis testing as well for the study.

Table 21.5 shows that four factors play a decisive role in creating brand loyalty and purchase intention. F^2 and Q^2 were also computed under this study to assess predictive importance and relevance. Cohen (1988) pointed out that the proposed limit for assessing the impact of exogenous constructs on endogenous constructs is 0.02 (small effect), 0.15 (moderate effect), and 0.35 (large effect). The f^2 value of Advertisement & Celebrity Endorsement for purchase intention is 0.096, and for brand loyalty it is 0.063, signifying that Advertisement & Celebrity Endorsement has a moderate effect on both purchase intention and brand loyalty. The f^2 values of Retail & Shop Display for purchase intention and brand loyalty are 0.029 and 0.034 respectively. These values once again prove that a moderate effect exists for Retail & Shop Display on purchase intention and brand loyalty. For the other two factors, Pack Size and Availability, it has been shown that these two factors have a small effect on purchase intention (as the f^2 values are less than .02) and hardly any effect on brand loyalty. Again, the f^2 value of brand loyalty on

Table 21.5 Structural Model Assessment

Hypothesis	Path Relationship	Original Sample (O)	Sample Mean (M)	2.50%	97.50%	SUPPORTED/NOT SUPPORTED
H1	Advertisement &Celebrity Endorsement -> Brand Loyalty	0.237	0.237	0.126	0.346	SUPPORTED
H2	Advertisement &Celebrity Endorsement ->Purchase Intention	0.312	0.32	0.185	0.454	SUPPORTED
H3	Pack Size ->Brand Loyalty	0.017	0.018	-0.102	0.143	NOT SUPPORTED
H4	Pack Size -> Purchase Intention	0.065	0.067	0.04	0.19	SUPPORTED
H5	Retail & Shop Display -> Brand Loyalty	0.19	0.191	0.081	0.306	SUPPORTED
H6	Retail & Shop Display ->Purchase Intention	0.187	0.181	0.034	0.317	SUPPORTED
H7	Availability -> Brand Loyalty	0.115	0.112	-0.021	0.242	NOT SUPPORTED
H8	Availability -> Purchase Intention	0.347	0.345	0.205	0.476	SUPPORTED
H9	Brand Loyalty ->Purchase Intention	0.191	0.192	0.078	0.299	SUPPORTED

Source: Author's analysis

purchase intention is 0.11, which signifies that brand loyalty has a positive effect on purchase intention. Richter et al. (2016) explains that any Q^2 value above 0.02 has definite predictive power. Stone-Geisser's Q^2 value for brand loyalty is 0.271 and that of purchase intention is 0.267, which is enough to conclude that both the independent factors play a significant role in the conceptual model of the study (Geisser, 1974; Stone, 1974).

Importance Performance Map Analysis

To make the results of the study more rational and realistic, we have employed priority map analysis, which is better regarded as Impact Performance Map or Importance Performance Matrix analysis (Ringle & Sarstedt, 2016). The main reason behind the application of IMPA is to find out the exact degree of impact of four factors on brand loyalty and purchase intention for FMCG products (Fornell et al., 1996).

In Table 21.6 we computed the total effects of Advertisement & Celebrity Endorsement, Availability, Pack Size, Retail & Shop Display and Brand Loyalty on Purchase Intention. The performance of purchase intention is computed as 75.465.

In Figure 21.3 if we increase one unit of Advertisement & Celebrity Endorsement from 77.892 to 78.892, the purchase intention would increase to 75.829 with a total effect of 0.364. Similarly, with a rise of one unit of Availability from 79.867 to 80.867, the purchase intention would increase to 75.650 with a total effect of 0.185. Again with the increase of one unit of Pack Size from 81.500 to 82.500, the purchase intention would increase to 75.495 with a total effect of 0.03. Next with the addition of one unit of Retail & Shop Display from 82.376 to 83.376, the purchase intention would rise to 75.699 with a total effect of 0.234. Lastly, with a rise of one unit of Brand Loyalty from 74.021 to 75.021, the purchase intention would increase to 75.657 with a total effect of 0.192. Thus purchase intention depends on all the above-mentioned factors for FMCG products, and thus marketers have no option but to pay heed judiciously to all the factors if they wish to yield a fruitful outcome in the immensely competitive market.

Table 21.6 Importance – Performance Map (Construct Wise Unstandardized Effects)

Construct	Importance	Performances
Advertisement & Celebrity Endorsement	0.364	77.892
Pack Size	0.030	81.500
Retail & Shop Display	0.234	82.376
Availability	0.185	79.867
Brand Loyalty	0.192	74.021

Source: Author's analysis

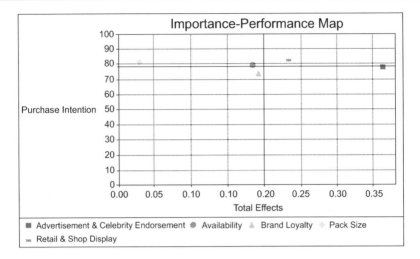

Figure 21.3 Adjusted Importance Performance Matrix for Purchase Intention.
Source: Author's analysis

Conclusion

The study significantly determines that all the factors play a decisive role in increasing purchase intention for FMCG products among prospects. To be more precise, this research emphasizes the fact that Advertisement & Celebrity Endorsement and Retail & Shop Display have a major contribution with respect to persuading potential customers to buy certain FMCG products. This study also revealed that Pack Size and Availability do not have such a considerable effect in terms of brand loyalty. The degree of impact is, thus, truly shown in IMPA. Marketers have to diligently give emphasis to Advertisement & Celebrity Endorsement and Retail & Shop Display, and frame their strategies accordingly, to excel in the competitive market.

References

Aaker, D. A., & Keller, K. L. (1990). Consumer evaluations of brand extensions. *Journal of Marketing*, 54(1), 27–41.
Anderson, E. W., & Sullivan, M. W. (1993). The antecedents and consequences of customer satisfaction for firms. *Marketing Science*, 12(2), 125–143.
Bolton, R. N. (1998). A dynamic model of the duration of the customer's relationship with a continuous service provider: The role of satisfaction. *Marketing Science*, 17(1), 45–65.
Cassel, C., Hackl, P., & Westlund, A. H. (1999). Robustness of partial least-squares method for estimating latent variable quality structures. *Journal of Applied Statistics*, 26(4), 435–446.

Cohen, J. (1988). *Statistical power analysis for The behavioral sciences* (2nd ed.). Lawrence Erlbaum Associates.

Cronin, J. J. Jr., & Taylor, S. A. (1992). Measuring service quality: A reexamination and extension. *Journal of Marketing, 56*(3), 55–68.

Diamantopoulos, A. (2008). Formative indicators: Introduction to the special issue. *Journal of Business Research, 61*(12), 1201–1202.

Faul, F., Erdfelder, E., Buchner, A., & Lang, A. G. (2009). Statistical Power Analyses Using G*Power 3.1: Tests for correlation and regression analyses. *Behavior Research Methods, 41*(4), 1149–1160.

Faul, F., Erdfelder, E., Lang, A. G., & Buchner, A. (2007). G*Power 3: A flexible statistical power analysis program for the social, behavioral, and biomedical sciences. *Behavior Research Methods, 39*(2), 175–191.

Fornell, C. (1992). A national customer satisfaction barometer: The Swedish experience. *Journal of Marketing, 56*(1), 6–21.

Fornell, C. G., Johnson, M. D., Anderson, E. W., Cha, J., & Bryant, B. E. (1996). The American customer satisfaction index: Nature, purpose, and findings. *Journal of Marketing, 60*(4), 7–18.

Fornell, C. G., & Larcker, D. F. (1981). Evaluating structural equation models with unobservable variables and measurement error. *Journal of Marketing Research, 18*(1), 39–50.

Geisser, S. (1974). A predictive approach to the random effect model. *Biometrika, 61*(1), 101–107.

Gold, A. H., Malhotra, A., &Segars, A. H. (2001). Knowledge management: An organizational capabilities perspective. *Journal of Management Information Systems, 18*(1), 185–214.

Govender, J. P. (2015). Point-of-purchase displays in the FMCG sector: A retailer perspective. *Journal of Governance and Regulation, 4*(4), 51–459.

Hair, J. F., Howard, M., & Christian, N. (2020). Assessing measurement model quality in PLS-SEM using confirmatory composite analysis. *Journal of Business Research, 109*, 101–110.

Hair, J. F., Hult, G. T. M., Ringle, C., & Sarstedt, M. (2017). *A primer on partial least squares structural equation modeling (PLS-SEM)* (2nd ed.). SAGE Publications.

Hair, J. F., Sarstedt, M., & Ringle, C. M. (2019). Rethinking some of the rethinking of partial least squares. *European Journal of Marketing, 53*(4), 566–584.

Hellier, P. K., Geursen, G. M., Carr, R., & Rickard, J. A. (2003). Customer repurchase intention: A general structural equation model. *European Journal of Marketing, 37*(11), 1762–1800.

Henseler, J., Hubona, G. S., & Ray, P. A. (2016). Using PLS path modeling in new technology research: Updated guidelines. *Industrial Management and Data Systems, 116*(1), 1–19.

Henseler, J., Ringle, C. M., & Sarstedt, M. (2015). A new criterion for assessing discriminant validity in variance-based structural equation modeling. *Journal of the Academy of Marketing Science, 43*(1), 115–135.

Hu, L. T., & Bentler, P. M. (1999). Cutoff criteria for fit indexes in covariance structure analysis: Conventional criteria versus new alternatives. *Structural Equation Modeling: A Multidisciplinary Journal, 6*(1), 1–55.

Khraim, H. S. (2011). The influence of brand loyalty on cosmetics buying behavior of UAE female Consumers. *International Journal of Marketing Studies*, *3*(2), 123–133.

Kohli, C., & Thakor, M. (1997). Branding consumer goods: Insights from theory and practice. *Journal of Consumer Marketing*, *14*(3), 206–219.

Misra, S. K., Mehra, P., & Kaur, B. (2019). Factors influencing consumer choice of celebrity endorsements and their consequent effect on purchase decision. *International Journal on Emerging Technologies*, *10*(2), 392–397.

Mukherjee, S., & Das, M. K. (2018). Exploring driving forces for the prospects of FMCG brands. *International Journal of Advance and Innovative Research*, *5*(4-XVIII), 81–87.

Nitzl, C., Roldan, J. L., & Cepeda, G. (2016). Mediation analysis in partial least squares path modeling: Helping researchers discuss more sophisticated models. *Industrial Management and Data Systems*, *116*(9), 1849–1864.

Oliver, R. L. (1980). A cognitive model of the antecedents and consequences of satisfaction decisions. *Journal of Marketing Research*, *17*(4), 460–469.

Patterson, P. G., & Spreng, R. A. (1997). Modelling the relationship between perceived value, satisfaction and repurchase intentions in A business-to-business, services context: An empirical examination. *International Journal of Service Industry Management*, *8*(5), 414–434.

Raithel, S., Sarstedt, M., Scharf, S., & Schwaiger, M. (2012). On the value relevance of customer satisfaction. Multiple drivers and multiple markets. *Journal of the Academy of Marketing Science*, *40*(4), 1–17.

Richter, N. F., CepedaCarrión, G., Roldán, J. L. & Ringle, C. M. (2016). European management research using partial least squares structural equation modeling (PLS-SEM) [Editorial]. *European Management Journal*, *34*(6), 589–597.

Rigdon, E. E. (2016). Choosing PLS path modeling as analytical method in European management research: A realist perspective. *European Management Journal*, *34*, 598–605.

Ringle, C. M., & Sarstedt, M. (2016). Gain more insight from your PLS-SEM results: The importance-performance map analysis. *Industrial Management and Data Systems*, *116*(9), 1865–1886.

Ringle, C. M., Sarstedt, M., & Schlittgen, R. (2014). Genetic algorithm segmentation in partial least squares structural equation modeling. *OR Spectrum*, *36*(1), 251–276.

Rust, R. T.,& Zahorik, A. J. (1993). Customer satisfaction, customer retention and market share. *Journal of Retailing*, *69*(2), 193–215.

Schuberth, F., Henseler, J., & Dijkstra, T. K. (2018). Confirmatory composite analysis. *Frontiers in Psychology*, *9*, 1–14.

Selnes, F. (1998). Antecedents and consequences of trust and satisfaction in buyer-seller relationships. *European Journal of Marketing*, *32*(3/4), 305–322.

Sharma, A., Bhola, S., Malyan, S., & Patni, N. (2013). Consumer brand loyalty: A study on FMCGs-personal care products in rural and urban areas of India. *Global Journal of Management and Business Studies*, *3*(7), 817–824.

Stone, M. (1974). Cross-validatory choice and assessment of statistical predictions. *Journal of the Royal Statistical Society*, *36*(2), 111–147.

Swan, J. E., & Trawick, I. F. (1981). Disconfirmation of expectations and satisfaction with a retail service. *Journal of Retailing*, *57*(3), 49–67.

Taylor, S. A., & Baker, T. L. (1994). An assessment of the relationship between service quality and customer satisfaction in the formation of consumers' purchase intentions. *Journal of Retailing*, *70*(2), 163–178.

Woodside, A. G., Frey, L. L., & Daly, R. T. (1989). Linking service quality, customer satisfaction, AndBehavioral intention. *Journal of Health Care Marketing*, *9*(4), 5–17.

Yildirim, C., & Correia, A. P. (2015). Exploring the dimensions of nomophobia: Development and validation of A self-reported questionnaire. *Computers in Human Behavior*, *49*, 130–137.

Yoon, S. J., & Kim, J. H. (2000). An empirical validation of a loyalty model based on expectation and disconfirmation. *Journal of Consumer Marketing*, *17*(2), 120–136.

Table 21A.1 Measurement Scales Used

Construct I: Advertisement & Celebrity Endorsement (first three items adapted from Mukherjee & Das, 2018 from last two items adapted from Misra et al., 2019)

A&C 1	Advertisement helps to make choices among the available brands.	7 point Likert 1=Totally Disagree 7= Totally Agree
A&C 2	Advertisement helps to identify hidden needs with the available brands	
A&C 3	Advertisement helps to develop a strong attachment with the FMCG brands.	
A&C 4	Brands explicitly advertised by celebrities are of good quality.	
A&C 5	The credibility of a celebrity affects me while making a purchase decision	

Construct II: Pack Size (first two items adapted from Mukherjee & Das, 2018)

PS 1	Pack sizes of the FMCG brand increase the affordability of customers	7 point Likert 1=Totally Disagree 7= Totally Agree
PS 2	FMCG companies have come up with reduced pack sizes to boost the consumption of consumers	
PS 3	Reduced pack sizes help to increase regular consumption	
PS 4	Small packs have a big market in cities and rural areas	

Construct III: Retail & Shop Display (first two items adapted from Mukherjee & Das, 2018)

R&S 1	Shop display affects consumers' buying decision	7 point Likert 1=Totally Disagree 7= Totally Agree
R&S 2	Visibility of FMCG brand in self influence prospective customers	
R&S 3	Visual merchandising helps customers to select their preferred brands from available brands	
R&S 4	Positive display adds to products value	

Construct IV: Availability (first two items adapted from Mukherjee & Das, 2018)

A 1	Most FMCG brands are available in your locality	7 point Likert 1=Totally Disagree 7= Totally Agree
A 2	FMCG Brands offer a wide variety of products	
A 3	FMCG Brands fulfil the demand for regular consumption.	

Construct V: Brand loyalty (first two items adapted from Mukherjee & Das, 2018)

BL 1	Advertisement evokes brand loyalty	7 point Likert 1=Totally Disagree 7= Totally Agree
BL 2	The credibility of a celebrity increases brand loyalty	
BL 3	Retail and Shop Display instigates prospects to be brand loyal	
BL 4	Small pack size creates an opportunity to use the preferred band and be brand loyal	
BL 5	Availability increases accessibility and being brand loyal	

Construct V: Purchase Intention

PI 1	Advertisement and celebrity endorsement persuades the prospects more toward FMCG brands	7 point Likert 1=Totally Disagree 7= Totally Agree
PI 2	Retail and shop display entices prospective customers toward preferred FMCG brands	
PI 3	Reduced pack size allures prospects to afford available FMCG brands	
PI 4	Brand loyalty increases purchase intention	

Chapter 22

Customers' Attitudes to Using Artificial Intelligence-Enabled Applications for Internet-Based Home Services in their Daily Lives

Pritha Ghosh and Rabin Mazumder

Introduction

We are witnessing a broad implementation of AI technology in industries like medicine, e-commerce, education, law, and manufacturing (Verma et al., 2021). Artificial Intelligence (hereafter AI) is rapidly finding a place in people's daily lives, personally and professionally (Makridakis, 2017). The current research gap relates to the fact that people are still ill-informed and uncertain of the concept and application of the various AI-enabled internet services like Urban Company, BookMyShow, and MakeMyTrip, which slows the potential development of AI systems in business. Most research focuses on the advantages and disadvantages, operating activities, specifications, and various fields of specialization in AI (Suresh & Rani, 2020). There is considerable potential for research on people's and organizations' acceptance of or attitudes toward AI (Pillai & Sivathanu, 2020) and people's awareness of and preference for AI-enabled applications (Suresh & Rani, 2020). The general attitude toward AI plays a role in its acceptance (Schepman & Rodway, 2020). Businesses are keen to understand their customers' understanding of AI technology to improve customer experience and engagement.

Customer experience forms the foundation of digital transformation, helping to improve regular activities for users. Research on the current topic is inadequate for policymakers and managers planning to invest in AI within their business models. AI can transform how we live and work concerning our daily repetitive tasks and customize services based on people's preferences. The application of AI is still in the nascent stage, and its future development is uncertain (Haenlein et al., 2019; Haenlein & Kaplan, 2019; Jarek & Mazurek, 2019) and the awareness and technological capability of the people (Davenport et al., 2020), especially in a developing country like India. India lacks expertise and attention to AI's potential application and use (Chakraborty, 2021). Research should seek to understand to what extent people are prepared to adopt AI and how their perceptions and attitudes toward AI will help businesses adopt appropriate business models (Vasiljeva et al., 2021). Prior research has been done on quantitatively exploring customers' attitudes toward internet-based services like online food delivery ordering (Jun et al., 2022)and OTT (over-the-top) platforms like Netflix (Cebeci et al., 2019). Wankhede et al. (2021) conducted a qualitative study to understand the outlook of millennials toward the various current and future applications of AI in different industries like the automotive, healthcare, insurance, education, manufacturing, and retail sectors. In a similar line of research, a qualitative study focusing on customers' attitudes toward internet-based home services will help understand the gaps existing in the present meeting of customers' needs. To the authors' best knowledge, no prior qualitative study exists on this topic. Therefore, to address this research gap, firstly, the study will aim to demonstrate a conceptual model. Secondly, it will document customers' attitudes toward AI-enabled applications for internet-based home services in their daily lives. The present study qualitatively explores customers in Kolkata using the classical grounded theory (hereafter GT) approach.

GT is a widely used (Bitsch, 2005), well-described methodology (Oliver, 2012) that denotes a systematic inductive approach implemented through a process of constant comparison and reduction; using this approach, researchers can develop a tight and integrated theory of well-defined concepts from empirical research in comprehending complex social processes (Glaser, 1978; Wimpenny & Gass, 2000). The present study adopted GT because it is valuable when the topic of interest is not widely studied and will bring structure and rigor to the analysis of qualitative data (Foley &Timonen, 2015) to build up a theory from the interpretation to create meaning from inter-subjective experiences (Suddaby, 2006).

Methods

Design and Participants

The method presents an illustrative description of applying the qualitative coding procedure in which codes categorize the data (Charmaz, 2006). The inclusion criteria for participants could be anyone who has used internet-based home services – purposive sampling finds the participants in Kolkata. To avoid biases and obtain in-depth data, we selected participants from different socio-economic strata of varying age ranges, education levels, professions, and income groups.

Data Collection

We conducted a semi-structured questionnaire and individual face-to-face interviews to gain direct and maximal information by exploring customers' experiences (Glaser, 1978; Charmaz, 2006). The interviews were flexible and open-ended (Glaser, 1999). We organized the discussions in the places suggested by the participants in close vicinity, mostly in small coffee shops, where unnecessary crowds were absent, owing to safety concerns, and audio-recorded with permission from the participants. We decided on the time to conduct each interview at the participant's convenience and consent, lasting between 30 and 35 minutes.

The questionnaire has three parts. The interviews commenced with participants revealing their emotional well-being. The ice-breaking question was, "How did you learn about internet-based home services?". For readers to get an insight into the actual use of internet-based home services, the second part included questions to determine the frequency of use, the names of the applications, and the types of services used by the customers. To deeply understand the phenomenon, which encompassed a variety of experiences, we made the questions open-ended. The participants articulated the advantages and challenges they faced while digitally booking the services, dealing with the professionals on the job, and the customer service response when encountering an unseen issue. Although the participants were free to reminisce about experiences, digging below the surface required much probing. A few examples of such probing questions were: Why do you do so? Why not? Is that the only reason? Was it good? Then what happened? The last part was an in-depth discussion in which we interrogated the participants about their future use and their recommendations for the services to their friends and family. Sampling and data collection continued until we reached theoretical saturation.

Data Analysis

Data collection and analysis are firmly connected and carried out in constant alteration. Interpretations of the audio recordings of the interviews were based on numerous listenings to every recording to isolate the holistic representation of the participants' stories, followed by a part-by-part explanation of critical opinions in hand-written text. Two coders coded each interview. The data were analyzed using open and axial coding, following the procedure defined by Corbin and Strauss (1990). The initial codes were identified in the data, followed by evaluating the degree of similarity among these codes. For data coding procedures, in each case, interpretations of parts (whether pieces of recording or entire recording) were incessantly compared to each other and the whole, known as the constant comparison method. We used phrases and sentences as open codes in the study. Two coders coded separately and compared the findings, directly comparing their codes, agreements, and disagreements. Consistent with GT guidelines, we cannot decide on the prior sample size. The progression of theory development dictated the number of interviews, a process known as theoretical sampling. This technique allows for theory to emerge from the analysis of the data from the initial participants, which, in turn, guides the selection of appropriate subsequent interviews. Concepts and categories develop from the raw data. We assume that participants' descriptions of their experiences would yield rich data adequate for generating a theory.

Inter-rater reliability

Inter-rater reliability is concerned with the degree to which various raters or coders appraise the same information (events, features, phrases, and behaviors) similarly (Van den Hoonaard, 2008). Upon completing the independent class, we computed a tabulation of agreement, disagreements, and inter-rater reliability using Cohen's Kappa ($\kappa = 0.62$)through SPSS 22.00 software. We tailed the agreements and disagreements amid coders for each survey participant by directly comparing the codes applied to the same (or similar) excerpts. As each coder might not have incorporated a similar context in their coding, authors considered phrases, mainly the matching section and the exact code, to be an agreement between coders. Cohen's kappa coefficient measures the level of agreement beyond chance agreement (Tang et al., 2015).

Kappa

To measure reliability is to calculate the percentage of agreement between raters. It involves simply adding up the number of cases coded the same way by the two raters and dividing the total number of cases. However, raters are expected to agree a certain percentage of the time simply based on chance (Cohen, 1960). Cohen's kappa calculates reliability, which approaches '1' as the coding is perfectly reliable and '0' if we expect no agreement by chance. Kappa is:

$$K = (PA-PC) / (1-PC)$$

Where the PA= proportion of units in which raters agree
PC= proportion of units for which agreement by chance is expected

Two coders coded separately and compared the findings, followed by a direct comparison of the codes, and then we compiled the agreements and disagreements. The initial codes were identified in the data, followed by evaluating the degree of similarity among these codes. Cohen's kappa coefficient measures the level of agreement beyond chance agreement (Cohen, 1960). Based on guidelines provided by Altman (1999) and adapted from Landis & Koch (1977), Cohen's kappa (κ) of ($p<.0005$) was evaluated as 0.62, which represents a substantial agreement.

We derive the percent agreement calculation by summing the values in the diagonals (i.e., the proportion of the time the two raters agreed)to findthe proportion of agreement over and above chance agreement.Based on the guidelines from Altman (1999) and adapted from Landis & Koch (1977), a Cohen's kappa (κ) of 0.62 ($p<.0005$) represents a substantial agreement.

Results and Discussions

Table 22.1 presents the demographic features of the twenty participants.

Table 22.1 Demographic Profile of the Total Sample

Demographic Profile	Description	Frequency
Gender	Male	9
	Female	11
Age (in years)	25–40	18
	41–55	2
	56–70	0
Educational Qualification	Undergraduate	0
	Graduate	3
	Postgraduate	17
	PhD	0
Monthly Household income (in rupees)	<25,000	1
	>26,000–40,000	4
	41,000–60,000	5
	>61,000	10

Source: The authors

After data analysis, we categorize the themes and subthemes in Table 22.2. Figure 22.1 presents the conceptual model.

Due to inductive/qualitative analyses and interpretation, there are limitations to this study that need to be empirically validated. The implementation of one-on-one interviewing provided detailed data, but it also risks the interviewee's influence. The research was conducted in Kolkata, which may compromise the study's validity as other cities in India or other countries might not share the same opinions, exposures, and experiences. GT's purposive sampling technique limits the findings. The study depends on retrospective interpretations of past personal experiences. We assumed that the participants narrated all the significant aspects of previous experiences and that they would repeat them. Both assumptions may not be accurate. Further studies can extend this by validating theory studies or theoretical expansion studies. Additional research can explore the extent to which the value indicators are interrelated.

Conclusion

The application of AI can improve the quality of our lifestyles, as well as human productivity. AI has helped industries find innovative and intelligent ways to do business that can help attain and leverage an enormous amount of information to anticipate the user's next move. It is beneficial because customers can access internet-based home services anytime and from anywhere, including on holidays, 24/7. Chatbots within the applications assist customers with customization and efficiency. AI enriches the experience, as customers can gain benefits like online or offline bill payment transactions and ensure privacy and

Table 22.2 Categorization of Themes and Subtheme

Serial No.	Themes	Subthemes	Codes
1	Usefulness	Benefit factors	1. Directly cater to the needs of a customer 2. It can specify the exact trouble and appliance for repair 3. Transparency in prices before the service 4. Hassle free experience with rare cases of negligence 5. Does the job at the click of a button 6. 24/7 availability with time slots at the user's convenience 7. Reduces transportation costs 8. Easy way of getting things done 9. Helps with time management 10. Flexible, as not limited to booked services only 11. Customer-friendly 12. Rates are comparable to the market
2	Ease of use	Facilitating conditions	1. Available in the Google Play Store and App Store 2. Simple user interface 3. Convenient/easy/efficient/straightforward/fast/smooth download and booking service 4. Hygiene for safety amid the pandemic 5. Professional behavior and well-trained with polite mannerisms and punctuality 6. Causes no disturbance to other family members during the service 7. Neat/creates no mess during and after service 8. No calls or visits to places to book the service 9. All services are available under one roof, i.e., in one application
3	Uncertainty	Risk factors	1. Professionals suggest unnecessary replacements or additional services to increase their money 2. The process of resolving problems can take time 3. On an order basis, service quality can differ according to the varied professionalisms and expertise of the professionals assigned 4. It can be expensive sometimes. 5. It can be challenging as it needs tech skills and can be especially hard for elderly customers. Non availability in tier 2 and tier 3 cities 6. I am an offline person and rarely use online services 7. Recurrence of the issue anytime soon can mount up expenses later 8. Possibility of unavoidable technical glitches

(Continued)

Table 22.2 (Continued)

Serial No.	Themes	Subthemes	Codes
			9. Navigation problems can lead to too many calls by the professional
			10. The customer care number is difficult to get sometimes, owing to engagement with other calls
			11. Professionals share personal numbers and ask customers to contact them directly for a discounted price
			12. Professionals push customers to give them a five-star rating, even if the job is not up to the mark
			13. Error in transactions can happen
4	Social media marketing	Social influence	1. I got to know about it through advertisements on televisions, print media, and primarily through social media like Instagram, Youtube, Facebook, links sent on Whatsapp groups
			2. Pop-up advertisements on social media
			3. I got to know about it during lockdown
			4. Social networks
			5. Suggestions from family and friends/know someone working in such a company
5	Convenience	Enjoyment	1. Haircut for the kid at home
			2. Party decoration at home
			3. Salon services for women in the comforts of their homes amid the pandemic
			4. It saves money for conveyance to salons, and the benefits are more economical
			5. The friendly staff of the salon services makes it a worthwhile experience
6	Dependability	Trust	1. A definite alternative is the offline resolution, but it may not be available easily
			2. Advanced technical knowledge and skills
			3. Party decorations precisely as I wanted
			4. Need not reach out repeatedly to customer care service for the same problem
			5. It is a good resolution for older citizens who are less mobile
			6. Refund on cancellation of pre-paid bookings without difficulty
			7. Refund nonavailability of professionals at the scheduled slot
			8. Customer care service is always good

Source: The authors

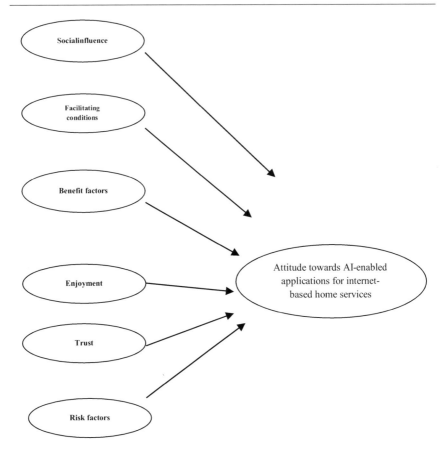

Figure 22.1 Conceptual model.
Source: The authors

security. The survey suggests that the customers believe that internet-based home services make life easy by solving the day-to-day problems of maintaining their homes, offices, and vehicles. Many participants expressed that they preferred AI-enabled personal assistants over humans and were ready to pay more for AI-enabled services. Through their experience, participants pointed out that AI has advantages such as high efficiency and low cost compared to traditional human assistance, but also, on the flip side, some expressed concern about inflexibility, rigidness, and lack of care or emotion, as well as the privacy of their data. Participants also believe that the government must encourage AI to improve applications in the health, education, and other sectors, and overall, people are ready to accept AI technology, with tremendous growth potential.

References

Altman, D. G. (1999). *Practical statistics for medical research*. CRC Press.
Bitsch, V. (2005). Qualitative research: A grounded theory example and evaluation criteria. *Journal of Agrobusiness*, 23(1), 75–91. https://doi.org/10.22004/ag.econ.59612
Cebeci, U., Ince, O., &Turkcan, H. (2019). Understanding the intention to use Netflix: An extended technology acceptance model approach. *International Review of Management and Marketing*, 9(6), 152–157. https://doi.org/10.32479/irmm.8771
Chakraborty, M. (2021, January 6). Artificial intelligence: Growth and development in India. *Artificial Intelligent Latest News*. https://www.analyticsinsight.net
Charmaz, K. (2006). *Constructing grounded theory: A practical guide through qualitative analysis*. SAGE Publications.
Cohen, J. (1960). A coefficient of agreement for nominal scales. *Education and Psychological Measurement*, 20(1), 37–46. https://doi.org/10.1177/001316446002000104
Corbin, J. M., &Strauss, A. (1990). A grounded theory research: Procedures, cannons and evaluation criteria. *Qualitative Sociology*, 13(1), 3–21. https://doi.org/10.1007/BF00988593
Davenport, T., Guha, A., Grewal, D., &Timna, B. (2020). How artificial intelligence will change the future of marketing. *Journal of the Academy of Marketing Science*, 48(1), 24–42. https://doi.org/10.1007/s11747-019-00696-0
Foley, G., &Timonen, V. (2015). Using grounded theory method to capture and analyse health care experiences. *Health Services Research*, 50(4), 1195–1210. https://doi.org/10.1111/1475-6773.12275
Glaser, B. G. (1978). *Theoretical sensitivity: Advances in the methodology of grounded theory*. Sociology Press.
Glaser, B. G. (1999). The future of grounded theory. *Qualitative Health Research*, 9(6), 836–845. https://doi.org/10.1177/104973299129122199
Haenlein, M., &Kaplan, A. (2019). A brief history of artificial intelligence: On the past, present, and future of artificial intelligence. *California Management Review*, 61(4), 5–14. https://doi.org/10.1177/0008125619864925
Haenlein, M., Kaplan, A., Tan, C.-W.,&Zhang, P. (2019). Artificial intelligence & management analytics. *Journal of Management Analytics*, 6(4), 341–343. https://doi.org/10.1080/23270012.2019.1699876Zhang
Jarek, K., &Mazurek, G. (2019). Marketing and artificial intelligence. *Central European Business Review*, 8(2), 46–55. https://doi.org/10.18267/j.cebr.213
Jun, K., Yoon, B., Lee, S., &Lee, D.-S. (2022). Factors influencing customer decisions to use online food delivery service during the COVID-19 pandemic. *Foods*, 11(64), 1–15. https://doi.org/10.3390/ foods11010064
Landis, J. R., &Koch, G. G. (1977). The measurement of observer agreement for categorical data. *Biometrics*, 1(33), 159–174. https://doi.org/10.2307/2529310
Makridakis, P. S. (2017). The forthcoming artificial intelligence (AI) revolution: its impact on society and firms. *Futures*, 90, 46–60. https://doi.org/10.1016/j.futures.2017.03.006
Oliver, C. (2012). Critical realist grounded theory: A new approach for social work research. *The British Journal of Social Work*, 42(2), 371–387. https://doi.org/10.1093/bjsw/bcr064

Pillai, R., &Sivathanu, B. (2020). Adoption of artificial intelligence for talent acquisition in IT/ITeSorganizations.*Benchmarking: An International Journal.* https://doi.org/10.1108/BIJ-04-2020-0186

Schepman, A., &Rodway, P. (2020). Initial validation of the general attitudes towards artificial intelligence scale. *Computers in Human Behavior Reports, 1,* 1–13. https://doi.org/10.1016/j.chbr.2020.100014

Suddaby, R. (2006). From the editors: What grounded theory is not. *The Academy of Management Journal, 49*(4), 633–642. https://doi.org/10.5465/AMJ.2006.22083020

Suresh, A., &Rani, J. (2020). Consumer perception towards artificial intelligence in e-commerce with reference to Chennai city, India. *Journal of IT and Economic Development, 11*(1), 1–14.

Tang, W., Hu, J., Zhang, H., Wu, P., &He, H. (2015). Kappa coefficient: A popular measure of rater agreement. *Shanghai Archives of Psychiatry, 27*(1), 62–67. https://doi.org/10.11919/j.issn.1002-0829.215010

Van den Hoonard, W. C. (2008). Re-imagining the "subject": Conceptual and ethical considerations on the participant in qualitative research. *CienciaandSaudecoletiva, 13*(2), 371–379. https://doi.org/10.1590/S1413-81232008000200012

Vasiljeva, T., Kreituss, I., &Lulle, I. (2021). Artificial intelligence: The attitudes of the public and representatives of various industries. *Journal of Risk and Financial Management, 14*(33), 1–17. https://doi.org/10.3390/jrfm14080339

Verma, S., Sharma, R., Deb, S., &Maitra, D. (2021). Artificial intelligence in marketing: Systematic review and future research direction. *International Journal of Information Management Data Insights, 1*(1), 1–8. https://doi.org/10.1016/j.jjimei.2020.100002

Wankhede, A., Rajvaidya, R., &Bagi, S. (2021). Applications of artificial intelligence and the millennial expectations and outlook towards artificial intelligence. *Academy of Marketing Studies Journal, 25*(4).

Wimpenny, P., &Gass, J. (2000). Interviewing in phenomenology and grounded theory: Is there a difference?*Journal of Advanced Nursing, 31*(6), 1485–1492. https://doi.org/10.1046/j.1365-2648.2000.01431.x

Index

AbiManesh, S. 193–203
Adamo, Susana 50n1
advertisement and celebrity endorsement 204–214
Agrawal, A. 113
agricultural sector 6, 99, 105; *see also* sustainable agriculture
agro-waste management 143, 145, *145*
Ahad, M. 31
Ahuja, R. 155
Ajmi, A.N. 11
Altman, D.G. 222
American Psychological Association (APA) 27
Ansaril, Md.A. 166
Arivalagan, K. 155
Arora, S. 32
Artificial Intelligence (AI) 7, 166, **169**, **224–225**, 226; data analysis 221; data collection 220–221; demographic features 222, *223*; design and participants 220; grounded theory (GT) 223; inter-rater reliability 222; kappa 222
artisans 111–116
Aslan, A. 11
Atal Mission for Rejuvenation and Urban Transformation (AMRUT) 49
Atasoy, B.S. 11

Babuna, P. 132
Backman, M. 187
Baek, J. 11
Banik, S. 112
Baragash, R.S. 78
Bashir, I. 79
Becerra, M. 187
Below Poverty Line (BPL) families 23, 156

Bergmann, Jonas 50n1
Berri, D.J. 177
Berri, J.D. 177
Bhat, R. 154
biodiversity protection 44, 45, 142, 143
biogas 44, 147, 150
blended learning: Bartlett's Test of Sphericity 79, **80**; classification 80, **82**; data collection 79; difference-in-difference method 78; evolution 78–79; face-to-face (F2F) learning mode 78; Hosmer–Lemeshow Goodness of Fit Test 80, **82**; interaction value 77; Kaiser-Meyer-Olkin Measure of Sampling Adequacy (KMO) 79, **80**; Krakow University students 78; learning engagement 77; principal components analysis (PCA) 79; regression analysis 77–78; rotated component matrix 80, **82**; semester-long experiment 78; student satisfaction 78; total variance 80, **81**
blockchain technology 165, 171, 172
bottom of the pyramid (BOP) 19, 20, 23–25, 100
brand loyalty 7, 204–214
business as usual (BAU) practices 42, 43

Campbell, C. 112
capital-intensive operational hazards 2
carbon dioxide emissions 4, 11, 12, 14, 15, **15**, 22, 45, 141
cashless transaction 156
cause-related marketing (CRM) 25, 36
Central Drugs Standard Control Organization (CDSCO) 104
Central Government Health Scheme (CGHS) 155–158

Index

Chandra, B. 112
Chaturvedi, S. 53
Chauhan, Ashish 49
Chen, J. 187
Chinese Central Bank 42
Chowdhury, F.N. 20
Christian Medical College (CMC), Vellore: CMC Vellore COVID Public Lecture Series (COVID PULSE) 201; commensurate staffing 196–197; COVID Command Centre (CCC) 199; COVID Suraksha 202; hospital infection control committee (HICC) 195–196; management 195, *196*; Non-Invasive Ventilation (NIV) 200, *200*; PEST and SWOT analyses 194, **195**; Project IMAI-A 201; telecommunication 197; training challenges 202, **203**; training of trainers 194, 197–199, **198**; UDHAVI initiative 201–202
Churchill, Winston 165
Cipla 104
Clean Cooking Alliance 22, 23
Clement, Viviane 50n1
climate change 22, 42–49, **46**, *46*, **48**, 139–141, 146, 147
Cohen, J. 211
collaboration 24, 78, 158, 188, 201, 202
communication 72, 73, 78–79, 100, 112, 167, 201
community involvement 36
Congregado, E. 11
Continuous Innovation (CI) 24
Corbin, J.M. 221
corporate philanthropy 36
corporate social responsibility (CSR) 4, 19; benefits 39; cause-related marketing (CRM) 36; classification 36, **37**; community involvement 36; corporate philanthropy 36; definition 35; distribution 37, **37**, 38, **38**; environmental and social obligations 39; environmental sustainability 36; ethical marketing 36; European Commission 39; global economy 39; in India 36, **37**; institutional environments and pressure 36; integration 39; large firms standards 40; practitioners, NGOs, and international agencies 39; social entrepreneurship 36; social marketing 36; stakeholders expectations 36; sustainability and competitiveness 40; "Triple Bottom Line" perspectives 35
Correia, A.P. 207
Covaxine, Bharat Biotech 104
cover crops 145–146
COVID-19 pandemic 3, 5, 6; blended learning 77–82, **80–82**; Christian Medical College (CMC), Vellore 193–203; climate change 42–49, **46**, *46*, **48**; FMCG products 204–214; Indian economy 97–107, *98–101*, 106; insurance companies, share prices 129–136, *130*, *131*, **133–135**; online learning 70–74, *73*; psychological distress, employment *vs.* unemployment 27–32, **30**, **31**, *31*, *32*; Reliance Industries Limited (RIL) 165–172; reverse migration 62–67, **66**, **67**; social entrepreneurship 19–26
COVID Vaccine Intelligence Network (Co-WIN) 105
Covishield, Serum Institute 104
crop rotation 145
Crunchbase 21
customer attitudes 219–226

Daly, G. 177
Dasgupta, A. 112
Debnath, J. 65
Deepa, L.R. 42
Demirer, V. 78
demonetization 98
depression 27, 32, 71
de Sherbinin, Alex 50n1
Design and Development (DD) Cell 115, 116, *116*
Diamantopoulos, A. 209
digitalization 20, 21, 132, 166, 172
Dutta, B. 113
Dziuban, C. 77, 78

e-commerce 111
economic empowerment of women (EEW) 54–55, **56**
economic growth 4, 5, 12–16, 36, 37, 105–107, *106*
economic insecurity 31–32
Economic Times 21
education 3, 13, 14, 19–20, 29, 53, 63, 65, 70–75, 77–83, 102–103, 114, 120–127, 220, 223, 226

Eid, R. 187
eKutir 20
Elliott, G. 14
Employees State Insurance Scheme (ESIS) 155–157, **158**
employment 12, 27–32, **30**, **31**, *31*, *32*, 36, 38, 53, 98, 100, 101, 107, 150
English Premier League (EPL) 6; analysis of variance (ANOVA) 177–179, **180**, 181; C5 index **181**, 181–182; competitive balance 176–177; K5 rating 182, **182**; Noll-Scully ratio 177–179, **180**; objectives 177–178; Spearman's rank correlation 177, 178, **179**; uncertainty 177, 178
environmental degradation 4, 12–16
Environmental Kuznets Curve (EKC) hypothesis 4; Dickey Fuller Generalized Least Squares (DF-GLS) unit root 14, **15**; economic growth 12; environmental degradation 12; Ordinary Least Squares (OLS) technique 14–15, **15**; policy implications 15–16; quality growth (qg) index 12–14, *13*, **14**
environmental protection 2, 35
environmental quality 4, 11, 12
Ernst 114
ethical marketing 24, 36
European Commission 39

Filippidi, A. 78
financial crisis 3, 97–99, 105, 129, 120
financial empowerment of women (FEW) 54–55, **57**, 59
financial literacy 5; Bartlett's Test 123, **123**; classification table 126, **126**; framed questionnaire 121, 122; government programmes and access 121; Hosmer and Lemeshow Test 125–126, **126**; improvement 121; Kaiser-Meyer-Olkin Measure of Sampling Adequacy (KMO) 123, **123**; Omnibus Tests of model coefficients 125, **126**; reliability statistics 123, **123**; restrictions 121; rotated component matrix 125, **125**; social security scheme 121; total variance 123, **124**, 125; variables 126–127, **127**
fiscal policy 43, 106
FMCG products 6–7, *206*, **218**; customer satisfaction 205; descriptive analysis 206–207, **207**; Importance Performance Matrix analysis (IMPA) **213**, 213–214, *214*; measurement model assessment 207–208, **208–210**; structural model assessment 209, *211*, 211–213, **212**
Forgia, G. 155
Forrest, D. 177
Fort, R. 182
Frost, E. 22
Future Generali India Insurance Company Limited 132

Ghanaian insurance market 132
Ghaziabad Nagar Nigam 48–49
Ghosh, A. 131
Ghouse, S.M. 111
global economy 40, 129, 132
Global Hunger Index 2019 139
Gold, A.H. 208
Google 167
Govender, J.P. 205
Grabinski 78
Grameen Bank, Bangladesh 20–21
green bonds 4, 44–49, **46**, *46*
green buildings 44, 45
green finance: business as usual (BAU) practices 43; definition 45; financial investments 43–44; Ghaziabad Nagar Nigam 48–49; government of India 44; green bond issuance 45–47, **46**, *46*; International Capital Market Association (ICMA) 45; Lucknow Municipal Corporation 49; market-oriented mechanisms and financial products 44; municipal bonds 47–48, **48**; Paris Agreement 44; Securities and Exchange Board of India (SEBI) 45; stock markets 44
greenhouse gas (GHG) emissions 11, 14, 16, 21, 22, 42–44, 139, 146
Greenway Appliances: *chulhas* 21–22; Continuous Innovation (CI) 24; empathy 24; framework 22, 23, *23*; funding 23; investment opportunities 25; low cost, eco-friendly, and technology-led solutions 23–25; partnering with organizations 25; social impact 22; solid biomass fuels 22; in Vadodara, Gujarat 22; World Bank (WB) 25
Gross Domestic Product (GDP) 98, *98*, 153
Grossman, G.M. 11

grounded theory (GT) 223
GST 98, 160
Guisado-González, M. 187

Handbook of Statistics on Indian Economy (2020–21), RBI 100
handicraft sector 5; craft consumers 112–113; enablers 114, *115*; intermediaries 113; low education levels 114; operational model 115, 116, *116*; raw materials 113; schemes 114
Hankinson, G. 187
Harris, J. 177
Harris, T.F. 132
Hassanien, A. 187
health insurance 6, 129; challenges 158, 160; community based schemes 157; definition 153; domestic health expenditure 153–154, *154*; equity, affordability, and quality 155; ESIS, CGHS, and RSBY schemes 155; evolution 156; government schemes 157; Gross Domestic Product (GDP) 153; market-based systems 157; non-communicable diseases 154; policy recommendations 160; population coverage 157, **158**, *159*; strategic purchasing 158; subsidies for premiums 155; tax exemptions 155
Hellier, P.K. 205
Henselar 208
Heuser, Silke 50n1
Hjalager, A.M. 187
Hooda, S.K. 154
hospitality industry 6; external factors 185; marketing innovation 187; organizational innovation 187–188; process innovation 187; product innovation 186–187
household insurance 132
Hub and Distribution (HD) Cell 115, 116, *116*

Indian economy: Asian Development Bank 98–99; demand and supply 98, *98*; development measures 105; economic sustainability 105–107, *106*; GVA by Agriculture, Forestry Fishing 99, *99*; health and communication sector 100; IMF report 97–98; industrial sector performance 99–100, *100*; life insurance market 129–136, *130*, *131*, **133–135**; overall employment 100–101; policy recommendations 105–106; public health burden 103–105; rate of growth of GVA 99, *99*; service sector 100, *101*; societal impact 102–103; tourism and construction 100; trade loss 98
industrial pollution control 44, 85
inequality 2, 12, 20, 55, 59, 183
Infectious Disease Training and Research Centre (IDTRC) 198
information technology (IT) sector 4, 29–33, **30**, **31**, *31*, *32*
innovation 25, 39, 43, 44, 166, 185, 201; marketing 187; organizational 187–188; process 187; product 186–187
Insurance Regulatory and Development Authority (IRDA) Act 156
integrated farming 146
Intel Award for Green innovation in 2012 22
International Capital Market Association (ICMA) 45
internet 71, 72, 102, 112–113, 171, 187
internet-based services 7, 219–226
IoT technologies 171
isolation 70, 194, 202
Ivankovič, J. 187

Janssen COVID-19 single-dose vaccine 104
Ji, X. 12, 15
JioMart 169
John, S. 20
Jones, Bryan 50n1
Jou, M. 78
Juneja, Neha 22
Jutting, J. 155

Kamble, S.S. 113
Khraim, H.S. 205
knowledge 5, 6, 12, 44, 78, 112, 114, 122, 125, **127**, 128, 142, 194, 201, 202
Koch, G.G. 222
Kohli, C. 205
Krueger, A.B. 11
Kumar, D. 111, 112
Kumar, N.G. 113

Kumar, S.S. 155
Kuri, P.K. 54
Kwak, D.W. 78

Laha, A. 54
Landis, J.R. 222
Lavanya, V.L. 53
life insurance companies 5–6; China's insurance market 132; claim–settlement ratio 130–131; death claims 130; exploratory study on Ethiopia 132; Ghanaian insurance market 132; growth in 131; HDFC Life 133, **133**, **134**, 135–136; ICICI PRU 133, **135**, 135–136; impact analysis 132–133; new business premiums 131, *131*; percentage growth in premiums 130, *131*; purchasing decisions 132; SBI Life 133, **134**, 135–136; US policies 132
Life Insurance Corporation (LIC) 132
lifelong learning (LLL) 70–74, **73**
Lim, D.H. 77
Long, X. 12, 15
Lopez-Perez, M.V. 78
Lucknow Municipal Corporation 49

machine learning (ML) **169**, 171
macro-prudential policy 106
Mahara, T. 111, 113
Mahatma Gandhi National Rural Employment Guarantee Act (MGNREGA) scheme 4–5; economic empowerment of women (EEW) 54–55, **56**; factors 52–53; financial empowerment of women (FEW) 54–55, **57**, 59; issues and challenges 53; job card holders 54; social empowerment of women (SEW) 55, **58**, 59
Mahima, S. 53
Mahoney, R.J. 193
Major League baseball 176, **179**
Mantravadi, P. 166
Manwaring, K.C. 78
Mari, G. 53
Martinez, M.M. 16n2
Martinez-Caro, E. 78
Martynova, M. 166
Mathur, Ankit 22
Maxcy, J. 177
McCue, J. 193

McCusker, Brent 50n1
media 25, 105, 121, 132, 201
"Mediclaim" policy 156
Menon, V. 112
mental health 28, 32
mergers and acquisitions (M&A) 166–168, 172
Micro, Small and Medium Enterprises (MSMEs) 20, 25, 35, **37**, **38**
Midgley, Amelia 50n1
migrants 5, 62–65, 101
Ministry of Housing and Urban Affairs (MOHUA) 49
Mlachila, M.M. 12, 13, 16nn2–4, 7
machine learning (ML) **169**, 171
Mondello, M. 177
monetary policy 105, 106
Moore, W. 177
Moskal, P. 78
municipal bonds 47–49, **48**
Mustafa, M. 166

Nagpal, S. 155
National Expert Group on Vaccine Administration for COVID-19 (NEGVAC) 104
National Mission for Sustainable Agriculture (NMSA) 146–147
National Solar Mission 48
National Start Up Awards 19
negative externalities 5, 85; first-order condition (FOC) of optimization 88–89; isoquant of firm 87, *88*; marginal rate of technical substitution 87; Pareto optimal 92, *93*; Pigouvian production tax 90–91, *91*, *92*; production function of firm 86–87; second-order condition of optimization 89
NetMeds 169
news agencies 105
Nguyen, V.A. 78
non-governmental organizations (NGOs) 23, 25, 39, 105, 114, 115, 194, 202
non-pesticide management 142–143

Ober, Kayly 50n1
Ongan, S. 11–12
online learning 5, 102; asynchronous learning 71; content delivery 71; difficulties in understanding

instructions 72; lack of communication 72; perceptions of students 72–73; psychological stability 71–74, **73**; "student lives" 72; synchronous learning 71; technical problems 72; vulnerabilities 70
organic farming 24–25, 143
Oza, M.S. 111

Pandit, V. 24
Pankaj, L. 21
Pareto, Vilfredo 86
Parvin, N. 42
Pathak, R. 113
Perumal, R. 155
physical health 28, 72, 97
Pigou, A.C. 86
Pigouvian production tax 5, 90–91, *91*, *92*
poverty 12, 19, 20, 22, 25, 28, 156
Preda, A. 132
private health insurance 6, 155, 157, 158
psychological distress: data analysis 30; data collection 29; ethical considerations 30; Kessler Psychological Distress scale (K10) 29–30; levels of **30**, 30–32, **31**, *31*, *32*
psychological stability 71–75
public health burden 52, 194: endogenous ventilators 103; HIV, TB, and malaria programmes 103; lack of medical oxygen 103–104; maternal health services 103; vaccination 104–105

quality growth index (QGI) 4, 16n7; aggregation process 13, *13*; definition 12, **14**; development index 14; policy implications 15–16; regression results 14–15, **15**; unit root results 14, **15**; variables 13, **14**
Quirk, J. 182

Rajalakshmi, V. 53
Rajeev, P.V. 111, 112
Ramamoorthy, R. 155
Ramasamy, D. 132
Rao, S. 154
Rashtriya Swasthaya Bima Yojana (RSBY) programme 155, 156

Raut, R.D. 113
Ravenstein, E.G. 62
Ravinder 53
Rawat, P.S. 111
Reddy, A.V. 166
Reliance Industries Limited (RIL) 6; communication technology 167; digital segment 170–171, *171*; Fourth Industrial Revolution (4IR) 168, **169**; global investment 167, *168*; mergers and acquisitions 166–167; partnership with Microsoft 167; refining segment *171*, 171–172, *173*, **174**; retail segment 169, **170**, *170*; technological upgrading and innovation 166; voting rights in companies 167
renewable energy 24, 44, 45, 146
Renneboog, L. 166
Research and Development (R&D) 105, 168, 172, *173*
reverse migration 5; abundance of labour 64; convenience sampling technique 64–65; correlation matrix 66, **66**; descriptive statistics 66, **66**; discontinuation of income 63–64; internal migrants 63; perceptions 65; regression model 65, **66**, 67, **67**; structured questionnaire 64; wage discrimination 63
Richter, N.F. 213
Rigaud, Kumari 50n1
RIL Jio 170–171, *171*
Rupasingha, A. 11

Saha, S. 154
Saito, S. 28
Satar, M.S. 20
Scarfe, R. 183
Schewe, Jacob 50n1
Scott, S. 17n7
Securities and Exchange Board of India (SEBI) 45, 47
Seetharaman, P. 21
Sengupta, T. 20
Serraglio, A. 29
Sharif, M. 43
Simmons, R. 177
Sinha, N. 28
skilled labour 6, 63, 150
Sloane, P.J. 177
Small and Medium Enterprises (SMEs) 4, 35–40, **37**, **38**

Smart Cities Mission 48
social costs 85, 92, *93*
social distancing 97, 98, 102, 132
social empowerment of women (SEW) 55, **58**, 59
social enterprises (SEs): eKutir 20; government support 20; Grameen Bank 20–21; Greenway Appliances 21–25, *23*; individual factors 20; IT and digital transformation 21; organizational factors 20
social entrepreneurship 19–20, 36
social equity 142, *142*
social marketing 36
social welfare 5, 15–16, 38, 86, 90, 94
solar power 44, 45, 146
Soytas, U. 11
Sputnik V, Russian vaccine 104
Srivasatava, A.R. 111, 112
Srivastav, G. 111
Stand Up India 19, 25
Start Up India 25
Strauss, A. 221
stress 28, 32, 83, 105, 194
students 5, 199; blended learning 77–82, **80–82**; financial literacy 120–127, **123–127**; impact on 102–103; online learning 70–74, **73**
sustainable agriculture 6; climate change 141; deforestation 141; economy *142*, 142–146, **144**, *145*; environmental health 141, *142*; loan repayment 141; mono-cropping 140; monoculture 140; National Mission for Sustainable Agriculture (NMSA) 146–147; principles 142; social equity 142, *142*; soil erosion 141; tilling soil 140; use of chemicals 140–141; Uttar Pradesh Bio-Energy Development Board 147, **148–149**, 150
Swachh Bharat Mission 48

Tajeddini, K. 187
tax relief 106
Tennyson, Alfred Lord 193
Tevie, J. 11
Thakor, M. 205
Tiwari, A. 113
tourism 185–188
trap crops 143, **144**

Ujjwala Yojana programme 23

unemployment 12, 20, 29–32, **30**, **31**, *31*, *32*, 101, 105
United Nations Human Development Index 14
United States Department of Agriculture (USDA) 143
Universal Health Coverage (UHC) 153–160
Universal Health Insurance Scheme (UHIS) 156
Universal Immunization Program (UIP) 105
USAID Global Market Assessment for Handicrafts report (2006) 111
Uttar Pradesh Bio-Energy Development Board 147, **148–149**, 150

vaccines 27, 104–105, 202
Vats, N. 111
Venkataramanaiah, S. 113
Vijay, K. 43
volatile, uncertain, complex, ambiguous (VUCA) 1
Vyas, S. 32

wage discrimination 63, 65, **66**, 67
Wang, Y. 132
Wankhede, A. 220
waste management 36, 44, 45, *145*
Whatsapp 167, 169
wind power 44
women 2, 22, 23, 52–53, 141, 205; economic empowerment 54–55, **56**; financial empowerment 54–55, **57**, 59; social empowerment 55, **58**, 59
Worku, A. 132
World Bank 14, 25, 42, 54, 155, 156
World Development Indicators (2020) database 14
World Health Organization (WHO) 27, 103, 132, 153, 155, 156

Xavier, G. 53

Yadav, R. 111, 113
Yildirim, C. 207
Young 114

Zhang, L. 42
Zhou, K.Z. 187
ZyCoV-D, Cadila Healthcare 104

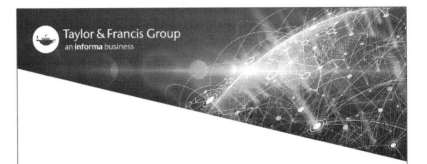

Printed in the United States
by Baker & Taylor Publisher Services